# TERRY FARRELL

# TERRY FARRELL

## URBAN DESIGN

**A.D.** ACADEMY EDITIONS · **E&S** ERNST & SOHN

*Front cover*: Charing Cross
*Page 2*: Alban Gate

Edited, designed and produced by
ANDREAS PAPADAKIS LTD.

First published in Great Britain in 1993 by
ACADEMY EDITIONS
An imprint of the Academy Group Ltd
42 Leinster Gardens London W2 3AN
and
ERNST & SOHN
Hohenzollerndamm 170, 1000 Berlin 31
Members of the VCH Publishing Group

ISBN 1 85490 125 7

Distributed to the trade in the United States of America by
ST MARTIN'S PRESS
175 Fifth Avenue, New York, NY 10010

Printed and bound in Singapore

# CONTENTS

INTRODUCTION 6
Ken Powell

*CHAPTER ONE*
THE CITY/CHEAPSIDE 12
Mansion House and Poultry 18
City of London 1984-1987
Paternoster Area, St. Paul's 24
City of London 1989-1992

*CHAPTER TWO*
THE CITY/LONDON WALL 34
Alban Gate 40
City of London 1986-1992
Moor House 50
City of London 1986-1991

*CHAPTER THREE*
THE RIVER THAMES 54
Vauxhall Cross 60
London Borough of Lambeth 1982-1992
East Greenwich 72
London Borough of Greenwich 1988
Brentford Dock 76
London Borough of Hounslow 1988
Hungerford Bridge 80
City of Westminster and London Borough of Lambeth

*CHAPTER FOUR*
MARKET HALLS 84
Tobacco Dock 92
London Borough of Tower Hamlets 1985-1990
Spitalfields Market 100
London Borough of Tower Hamlets 1991

*CHAPTER FIVE*
RAILWAY STATIONS AND RAILWAY LAND 106
Charing Cross 112
City of Westminster 1985-1990
King's Cross Railway Lands 126
London Boroughs of Camden and Islington 1987

*CHAPTER SIX*
LARGE INSTITUTIONS 134
South Bank Arts Centre 140
London Borough of Lambeth 1984-1992
Bloomsbury Hospitals 148
City of Westminster and London Borough of Camden 1988

*CHAPTER SEVEN*
GREEN LONDON: PARKS, SQUARES, GARDENS 154
Comyn Ching Triangle 160
London Borough of Camden 1978-1985
St John's Gardens 168
City of Westminster 1991-1992

*CHAPTER EIGHT*
THE PRIVATE WORLD 174
Crafts Council Gallery 178
City of Westminster 1980-1981
Lloyds Bank, Pall Mall 182
City of Westminster 1989-1991
Carlton Gardens 190
City of Westminster 1988
Lombard Street 196
City of London 1991-1992

*CHAPTER NINE*
OUTER VILLAGES 204
Wimbledon Town Centre 210
London Borough of Merton 1987-1988
Chiswick Park 214
London Borough of Hounslow 1989-1992

*CHAPTER TEN*
LEARNING FROM LONDON 224
Masterplan and New Conference/Exhibition Centre 244
Lothian Road, Edinburgh 1989-1992
Masterplan for Mixed Uses 256
Brindleyplace, Birmingham 1990-1992
Mixed Use Renovation and Redevelopment Scheme 266
Grey Street, Newcastle 1991-1992
Masterplan for Mixed Uses 270
Quayside, Newcastle 1991-1992
Airport Staff and Administration Centre 274
Frankfurt Airport, Germany 1989
Masterplan for Mixed Uses 278
Quarry Hill, Leeds 1989-1992
Consulate and British Council Offices 288
Hong Kong 1992-

LIST OF BUILDINGS AND PROJECTS 298

ACKNOWLEDGMENTS 300

# INTRODUCTION
## KEN POWELL

Unrepentant radical, ceaseless iconoclast and defiant nonconformist though he is, Terry Farrell has somehow managed to become one of the most successful British architects of the last decade without drifting into the ranks of the architectural establishment. He has completed a remarkable series of major projects in London and is now at work in other leading British cities. He is increasingly busy on the international scene. Yet he retains the uncompromising individuality which first marked him out as a force to be reckoned with in British architectural circles. He fits into no school and bows to no dogmatic credo. Yet there is a consistent theme running through all his work since 1980: it is that of city and of urban architecture.

Farrell was amongst the first high-profile architects to identify with the popular revolt against old-style modernism which began in earnest during the 1970s. He risked (and duly encountered) criticism, and even ostracism, from the defenders of orthodoxy. Yet the foundations of his philosophy of architecture and urban design - the defence of 'historic' buildings and of old buildings in general as a resource, the belief in the enduring qualities of the traditional city and a distrust of 'clean sweep' approaches to town planning and, more broadly, a defence of the pragmatic and the *ad hoc* against the grand gesture - have all become commonplaces of the current architectural scene. What was once - and not so long ago - eccentric if not outrageous has now become, if not uncontroversial, a defensible (and indeed popular) point of view.

For Farrell, however, the battle has hardly started. Half a century of modernist planning has left major European cities, including London (where so many of his past campaigns have been fought), mutilated and disabled, as he sees it, by the mistaken policies of the recent past and robbed of many of the qualities which made them places fit for people. A huge programme of repair, of urban 'mending' is needed, Farrell believes, to restore their humanity. But Terry Farrell is an optimist: our towns and cities (he believes) are full of rich opportunities for positive planning. It is the task of the architect and urbanist, working with politicians and developers, to allow the real identity of places to re-emerge. 'Trust the past to understand and plot the present', he urges - and all will be well. Building on the lessons of history: a truly Renaissance credo and an apt one for a Europe which is being reshaped in tandem with a striking urban revival.

The urbanistic concerns which are the centre of Farrell's approach to architecture derive in the first instance (ironically enough) from his post-graduate training in the United States, at the University of Pennsylvania. His dissertation at Pennsylvania (at a time when many of his contemporaries were obsessed with technology) was a study of public spaces and pedestrian movement. His response to such leading lights on the American scene as Louis Kahn and Buckminster Fuller was very different from that of, say, Sir Norman Foster or Sir Richard Rogers. It was as a philosopher of architecture and public space, rather than as a pioneer of 'high tech', that Farrell revered Fuller. Lewis Mumford's ambitious attempts to merge architectural and social history influenced Farrell and taught him to look at the forces which shape cities. Jane Jacobs' *The Death and Life of Great American Cities* (published in the USA in 1961) was a revelation for Farrell, though only gradually were its lessons accepted by most architects and planners. In due course, he warmed to the message of Robert Venturi's *Complexity and Contradiction* (1966) - Farrell has consistently admired Venturi as architect and didacticist. Rowe and Koetter's *Collage City* (1977) underlined the conclusions to which Farrell had come independently about the character and care of cities.

Vauxhall Cross

The American influence on Farrell's thinking has been more important than that of European critics of modernism such as Rob and Leon Krier. In consequence, Farrell's urbanism has a democratic, radical, non-hierarchic flavour which accords with his rejection of more literal traditionalism. Farrell has never considered himself anything but a modern architect in the sense that he designs modern buildings for modern needs. Only recently, with the Paternoster Square project in the City of London, has he been drawn into a (tense but mutually rewarding) alliance with 'canonic' Classicism and with architects to whom style *per se* is far more crucial an issue than it is for Farrell.

In the strictly demarcated circles of British architecture, Farrell is often described as simply a Post-Modernist. He considers the term fairly meaningless. 'I'm more anti-modern than post-modern', he says, insisting that his concerns are not primarily stylistic but about space in and around buildings. Farrell's rejection of modernism began with a conviction that the 'clean sweep' approach just did not work. In the mid seventies, he worked on a number of projects aimed at revitalising old - but neglected and undervalued - quarters of London, most significant amongst them the Comyn Ching triangle site in Covent Garden. It was the kind of area which could easily have been swept away in the 1950s and 1960s without anybody really caring and most of it was in a very poor condition. Farrell's scheme, which took some years to accomplish, included both careful refurbishment and the insertion of some new buildings. At its core, physically and conceptually, is a new public space - or rather a *semi*-public space of the sort which is typical of London. (It does not announce its presence - you have to find the way in.) The scheme was of great significance for Covent Garden, an area saved from total clearance but under enormous pressure from developers. Working to a frighteningly tight budget, Farrell managed to secure a healthy mix of uses (offices, shops and housing) which has since been echoed in several other projects in the area. Comyn Ching was nothing less than a blow struck for London and against the 'mono-cultural' approach to development which had been seen as the only way forward for the capital. It remains one of Terry Farrell's finest achievements and continues to inspire other architects and developers.

Comyn Ching made Farrell a hero to the conservation movement, which had grown immensely in influence during the seventies as the public turned to history in reaction to the horrors of modernity. His stock grew further when he lined up with the conservation lobby against Mr Peter (now Lord) Palumbo and his Mansion House Square project. Farrell's objection was not to the architecture proposed - he has admired the work of Mies van der Rohe since he saw Mies's buildings in the USA in the 1960s - but to the destruction of an historic area which has a future as well as a past. He was not happy when the battle rejoined, with the late Sir James Stirling (whose work has influenced his own approach on occasions) as architect for the redevelopment, but he did not waver in his views. He based his case not on the merits or defects of Stirling's scheme but on the common sense viability of a refurbishment scheme. The fact that, with Stirling himself dead, the redevelopment scheme is in limbo, gives further credibility to Farrell's arguments. His love of historic buildings is passionate, and he has been closely involved with the pressure group SAVE and with English Heritage.

Farrell has stated a 'strong belief that the *ad hoc* and pragmatic can achieve a particular kind of harmony. London is a web of virtuoso bits, which add up to create a unique and wonderfully livable city without grand gestures'. The Mansion House site could be seen as one of those 'virtuoso bits' (as could Comyn Ching, Tobacco Dock, Spitalfields and Charing Cross) but there are areas of London where the historic pattern has vanished.

London Wall, devastated in World War II, is one of them. It is the most radical piece of Corbusian planning in central London, a true 'city of towers'. The 'public domain' is at first floor level, with London Wall itself almost an urban motorway. The City of London has been slow to recognise the folly of this approach to planning and the upper-level circulation system has not, even now, been totally

Alban Gate

abandoned. Farrell had to strive to humanise an inherently inhuman place in his projects for Lee House and Moor House, two of the undistinguished sixties office towers there. The Alban Gate development, which has replaced Lee House, serves as a 'gateway' between the City core and the residential and cultural heart of the Barbican. Farrell has created a bold bridge across the traffic - which he could not remove. Significantly, the completion of this new link has led to more civilised conditions at street level. (In this, Farrell's new residential square has played an important role.) Moor House, still awaiting construction, will cement this 'bridging' process. Farrell is not in favour of destroying sound buildings merely because they are 'outdated'. The Barbican, he argues, could be transformed by eliminating the walkways and putting the people at ground level. How strange it is, he points out, that there are gardens and peaceful spaces which the public looks down into from above, an historic church which is a dead monument in a modernist landscape. Perhaps one day, the City will take his advice.

Paternoster Square, next to St Paul's, had inspired some bold proposals from a series of leading architects before the final acceptance of a broadly 'classical' masterplan for its rebuilding. Farrell was dismayed by the rigidity and sheer inappropriateness of most of them. He felt that the urban grain was still there, and could be reinstated, and that to ignore it was simply perverse. The approved scheme will, he believes, create a really enjoyable City neighbourhood. If there are tensions within the proposals, they are not so much stylistic as more broadly urban - the deletion of a possible residential element will make this a working (rather than a 'twenty-four hour') part of London.

Farrell sympathises with the idealists who would have it otherwise. Yet he rejects idealism in favour of a broad acceptance of the world as it is. He stands in a British pragmatic tradition - the tradition which created Georgian London, that product of speculative building and high art, of commercial instincts enlightened by occasional flashes of genius. He especially admires John Nash, the brilliant pragmatist who created so much of the framework of the West End and gave London Regent's Park. Farrell has not yet had opportunities on this scale, yet his campaign to give London more and better open spaces has not been in vain. All his major developments have produced spin-offs in terms of new public spaces.

For an architect who has worked extensively in the commercial field - helping to break the iron grip of the old 'commercial' practices - Terry Farrell is, to the surprise of some, quite likely to break ranks and fight the development machine when he feels it is acting against the public interest. He fought major schemes for the centres of Hammersmith and Wimbledon, neither of them amongst the more glamorous parts of London, defended the Langham Hotel in Nash's Portland Place, when others dismissed it as valueless, and argued for an accretive, conservationist approach to the development of the much-contested Spitalfields area (the scene of proposals by, *inter alia*, Leon Krier, Quinlan Terry, Richard MacCormac and Sir Norman Foster). In none of these cases did he gain a commission as a result - and probably did not expect to do so. Yet his ideas for all of them have been incorporated into the built solutions for Hammersmith, Wimbledon and the Langham, while the current plans for Spitalfields (masterplanned by Benjamin Thompson) are in tune with his prescription.

Farrell was the first to point out that a joint public/commercial partnership could facilitate the development of London's Royal Opera House - a solution taken up by Jeremy Dixon in his scheme. It is not the fault of Farrell (or Dixon) that the problems of the market have undermined the public and private sectors. How much more pleasant, he says, to step out of a West End theatre into a real street, with pubs and restaurants nearby, than on to the concrete deck of the South Bank arts centre, a bleak cultural ghetto. The critics of his proposals for the South Bank who accuse him of 'commercialising' the area miss the point - Farrell believes the area is a failure, as it stands, because it is mono-cultural. No traditional city consists of just one use - as Leon Krier has pointed out, that is as unhealthy as a human diet which consists solely of water, or of bread, or of meat. The key to health - urban as well as bodily - lies in a healthy balance. Many architects look at a typical high street and see visual confusion and aesthetic chaos. Farrell looks at it and sees something basically satisfactory, needing improvement, maybe, but a better place than most of the comprehensive redevelopments planned by architects. Farrell is a popular - and to some degree a populist - architect, who believes that 'ordinary' people have something to contribute to the design process. (He had discovered 'community' architecture long before the Prince of Wales took up the cause.)

Until very recently, Farrell seemed destined, like John Nash, to be an architect whose greatest achievements were in London. But he is still in his early fifties and is moving far beyond London and far beyond Britain. In Birmingham, a city badly mauled by post-war planning blunders, he has developed a masterplan for Brindleyplace, an area of mixed uses which should provide a vivid contrast to the rather arid cultural quarter around the new Centenary Square. In Edinburgh, his Conference Centre (itself suggesting new themes in his architecture) forms part of an area critical for the future of the city, a link between Old and New Towns. The site of the latter, disused railway yards, recalls London's King's Cross, the scene of one of Farrell's less well known but most interesting planning exercises. In sharp contrast to Sir Norman Foster, who was eventually chosen to develop a plan for the area, Farrell eschewed grand gestures and striking effects in favour of a less spectacular, but more accretive approach, in which the reuse of existing historic buildings was a vital element.

Terry Farrell's urban design shares the same concerns as his architecture. Cities consist of a vast number of spaces, large and small, outside and within, public and private. His beloved Nash understood the art of overlapping the two: Nash's Royal Opera Arcade is neither entirely internal nor external; it is a private place, open to the public. Farrell wants to get public spaces into his buildings - Embankment Place, basically a large office building, includes an invaluable pedestrian link between Hungerford Bridge (which Farrell hopes one day to transform) and the Strand. The South Bank project is a complex exercise in interlocking public and private domains. Farrell even carves public space out of his Vauxhall Cross, which has become the high security headquarters of MI6.

On the verge of a new phase in his career, Terry Farrell remains a controversial but towering presence on the British architectural scene. As an urbanist, he is pre-eminent in Britain in the development of a post modern way of building cities. He has changed the look of Britain - for the better.

Charing Cross

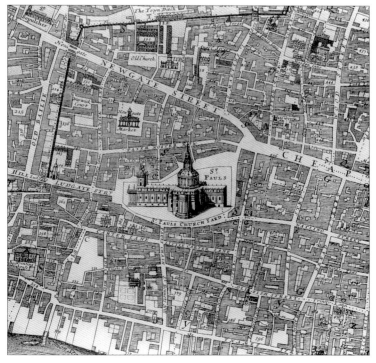

# THE CITY/CHEAPSIDE

Terry Farrell's approach to urban design 'relies upon a working method which begins with revealing, through research, the underlying nature of a place's true identity and then reinforcing this through the adopted architectural programme'. For Farrell urban design should be based upon a number of principles: a notion of continuum with the history and traditions of a specific area, a priority given to the pedestrian and the experience of the street, and a desire to create new places with an identity to encourage the return of the diversity of traditional urban life. Underlying his approach is a pragmatism that utilizes all a context has to offer.

The traditional urban grain of the City of London provides the architect and urban planner with a varied and rich context with which to work. The key pattern and qualities of the City are derived from the long linear form of the walled Roman city, delineated by the parallel boundaries of the River Thames and, to the north, the wall itself. This long northern boundary acted as both defence and, through the gates within the wall, as point of entry for produce from the countryside beyond. To the east and west were guarding points that protected each end of this enclosed linear settlement. The compact size of the Roman City, an area that can be crossed on foot in twenty minutes, generated a tight efficiency of space and movement that has been the basis of the success of the commercial City of London to the present day. This dense, compressed, urban form dictated the patterns of movement, the street network and space, and uses within it, in contrast with the sprawling nature of the rest of London, formed from a number of scattered villages beyond the walls.

Through the middle of this compacted urban form runs Cheapside, its role as the City's market place or High Street dating back to Norman times, when the street developed as the City's central food market. The linearity of this important thoroughfare dictated the gridiron pattern of the streets that run south to the river, and north to the gates within the boundary wall. At each end of Cheapside the streets radiate out, connecting to the various gates at the eastern and western edges of the City. It is these patterns of movement that have generated the unique characteristics of these two end sites, Mansion House and Paternoster Square, focal

*Opposite from above left to right*: Historical photographs of St Paul's Cathedral and Mansion House; Coronation procession of King Edward VI, Cheapside 1547; Historical maps of Cheapside and Newgate Market; *Left*: View of St Paul's Cathedral

MANSION HOUSE & POULTRY

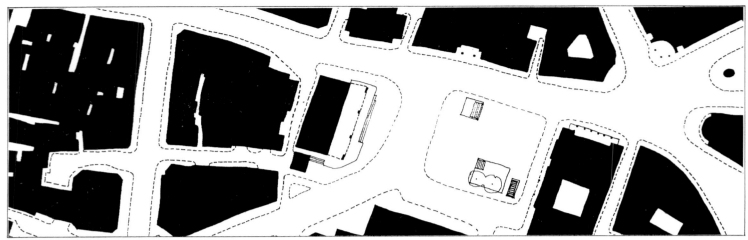

MIES VAN DE ROHE 1960s

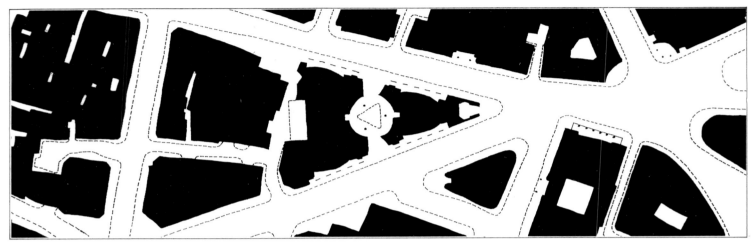

STIRLING 1985

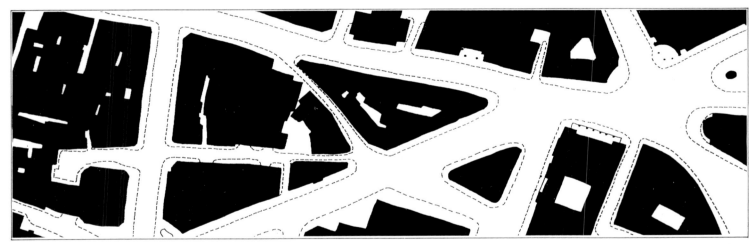

EXISTING 1992

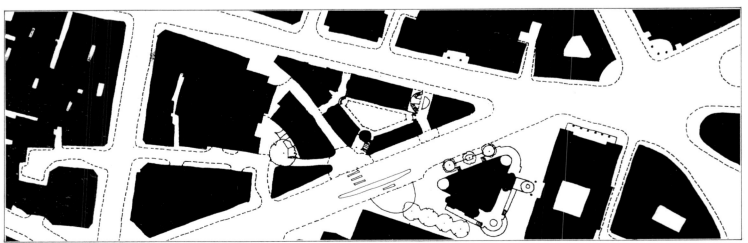

FARRELL 1984-85

points where the converging streets create a number of triangular sites, with an intensity of activity and interest.

Farrell's involvement with the Mansion House site began in 1984 when he was asked, by Save Britain's Heritage, to prepare a counter-proposal to Peter Palumbo's Mansion House scheme, based on a Mies van der Rohe design dating from 1968. Palumbo proposed to destroy all existing buildings on the site and the traditional street pattern, and to replace them with Mies van der Rohe's modernist composition consisting of a 25-storey glass tower facing a formal rectangular plaza. Designed for another location, Mies's design showed only indifference and disregard for the historical traditions and urban qualities of the City.

By contrast, Farrell's proposal was grounded upon the defence of the site's specific urban features: the traditional street pattern, the dynamic diagonal movement generated by the triangular forms of the building plots, and the presence of the only remaining coherent group of street architecture and flat irons built in a short period of thirty years after the construction of Queen Victoria Street in 1870. He viewed Mies's scheme as anti-urban and alien - one single-use building with one front door replacing the enormous number of front doors and variety of building uses, sizes and styles; and a single rectilinear plaza replacing the multitude of small spaces on the site.

Farrell characterized the existing buildings as examples of good street architecture and his proposal sought to emphasize their basic urban qualities inherent in the tripartite vertical organization of the plan, reflected in the elevation. These features were: use of ground floor for shops, thus increasing activity and interest at street level; the main body of accommodation for offices, reflected by restrained and repetitive middle storeys ; a modelled and eventful roofline to be viewed at longer distances across London. This was contrasted to Mies's building with floors of identical use and with shopping placed underground beneath the raised podium of the plaza, which also severed the flow of ground-level pedestrian routes. For Farrell, Mies's proposal exemplified modernism's failure to produce a workable approach to urbanism, particularly when dealing with existing cities.

At Paternoster Square, a similar battle was fought, but at this site the modernist vision had become reality. The urban characteristics of this area were its pattern of streets, generated by pedestrian routes from Cheapside to St Paul's Cathedral, that were crossed by diagonal routes connecting Cheapside to Ludgate Hill. This pattern was retained, even after the area was devastated by the Great Fire of 1666. Sir Christopher Wren was one of a number who seized the opportunity to submit masterplans for the rebuilding of London. But, due to pressures from commerce

*Left*: Mansion House; *Above*: Midland Bank, Fenchurch Street and Allied Irish Bank, Queen Street

PATERNOSTER SQUARE AREA, ST PAUL'S

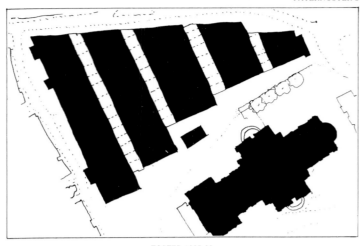

FOSTER 1987-88

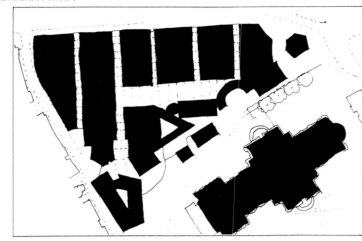

ISOSAKI 1987-88

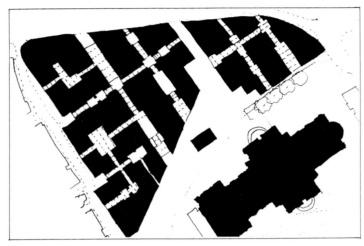

ROGERS 1987-88

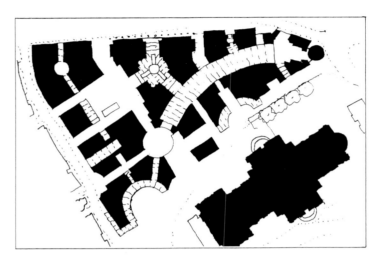

ARUP 1987-88

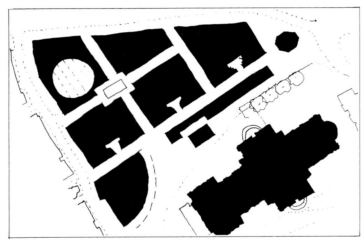

STIRLING 1987-88

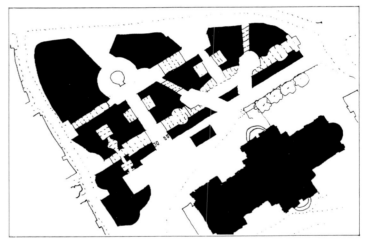

MacCORMAC 1987-88

SOM 1987-88

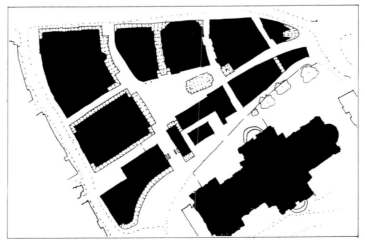

SIMPSON, BEEBY, FARRELL 1992

and the urgent need for housing, rebuilding began immediately, based on existing foundations and property boundaries. The development of the area was closely connected with that of St Paul's, and activities were dominated by industries, such as printing, that serviced the cathedral, the name Paternoster deriving from the makers of rosary beads, or paternosters, who lived near the cathedral from the thirteenth century.

Farrell's task, as masterplanner for Paternoster Associates, was the recreation of a piece of urban fabric that contained the features of good urbanity. These features had been destroyed by the existing modernist scheme based on the 1956 masterplan of the architect and planner, William (later Lord) Holford. With Holford's belief that 'there is more to be gained by contrast in design . . . than from attempts at harmony of scale or character or spacing', the network of traditional streets generated by patterns of pedestrian movements, was replaced by an arbitrary geometry, generated on the drawing board, with buildings and spaces placed at 90 degrees to St Paul's Cathedral. This destroyed the relationship between this public building and the surrounding built fabric. St Paul's became another large urban form set with others in an ordered rectilinear pattern. Traditional routes were broken by Holford's raised podium, which created a barrier to pedestrian circulation and left routes undefined and street activity at a minimum. Pre-war photographs of the site showed the area's variety of street architecture, and the activity generated by the number of shops and public entrances at ground-floor level. The street pattern, existing from medieval times, was the basis for Farrell's masterplan and re-established ground level as the public domain and recreated the variety of streetscape by the use of different architects, and by the difference in building plot size and shape.

Mansion House and Paternoster Square demonstrate Farrell's urban design process of using history and tradition, not for reasons of nostalgia, but to identify and build upon the qualities of urbanity inherent in the existing fabric. These two important sites also reveal the contrasting fates of two opposing school of thought on urban design - at one end the battle to replace good street architecture with Mies's tower, at the other end a 1960s' vision of urbanity being demolished to make way for traditional architecture.

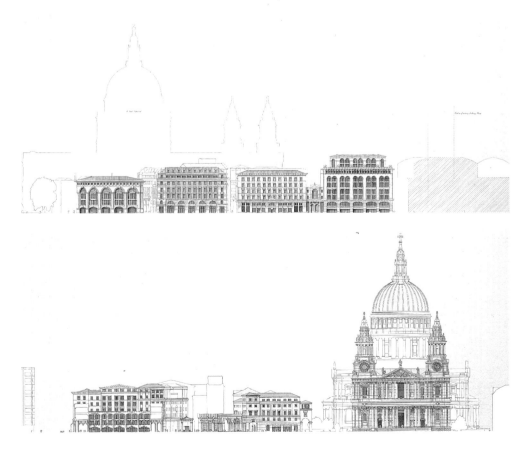

*Left*: Paternoster Square

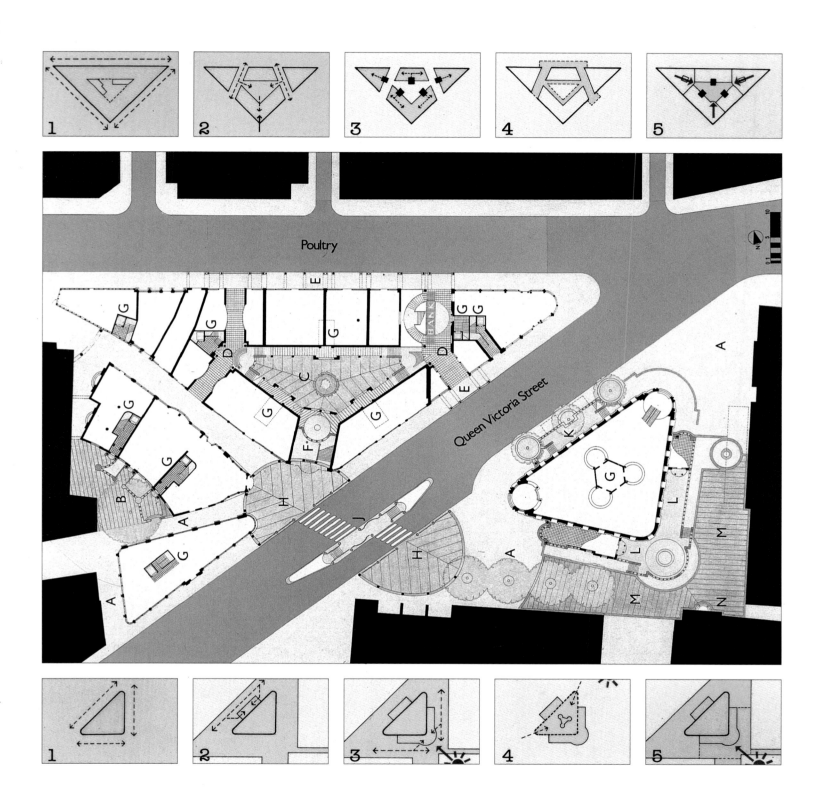

Poultry

Queen Victoria Street

BANK

THE MASTERPLAN AND CONCEPT STUDIES

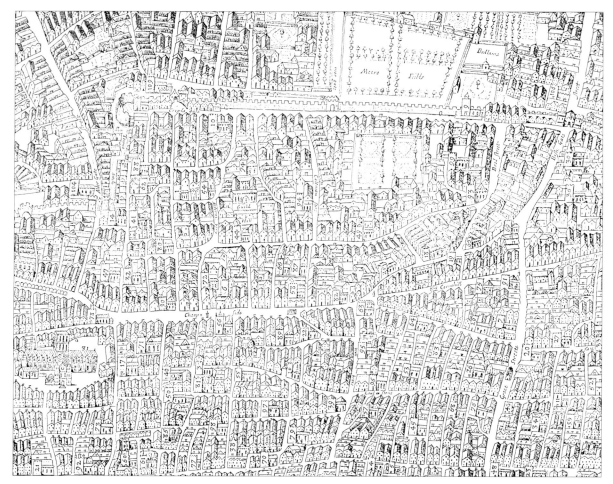

# MANSION HOUSE AND POULTRY

*CITY OF LONDON 1984-1987*

Farrell's Mansion House proposal set out to define, clarify and then enhance the very specific urban features of this unique City site, not just to create a continuity with history, but to defend them by reinforcing their importance as examples of good urbanity. The scheme was called The Triangles, in reference to the traditional triangular street pattern, to give the area an identity and emphasize its sense of place. The scheme, as an act of persuasion, was presented as an exercise in 'compare and contrast', and as an act of planning comprising a series of low-key modifications.

Farrell's argument centred on the conviction that the street was the public domain, reversing the modernist pro-traffic bias in favour of the pedestrian in a number of ways: the pedestrianization of five streets on the site; the narrowing of Queen Victoria Street to three lanes to create a central pedestrian island; the addition of covered diagonal arcades and canopies over shops and the Underground entrance to improve protection from wind, rain and noise pollution. The intricate and enclosed nature of public spaces in the City was taken as the model for two new courtyards - one at the rear of Bucklersbury and on St Pancras Lane, and one semi-private courtyard office precinct, 'Triangle Chambers'. The quality of three existing spaces, used by office workers at lunchtime, was enhanced by semi-enclosure, landscaping and street closure - one on either side of the Bucklersbury pedestrian crossing, and the area just north of St Stephen's Walbrook.

These interventions improved the environment at street level and enhanced circulation within and beyond the site.

The existing buildings adhered to Farrell's tripartite code of good street architecture, but these features were emphasized and improved. By a rationalization of internal planning and circulation, additional ground floor space was freed for retail provision to be created to supplement existing provision in the area. These facilities, such as those gathered around Poultry/Bucklersbury, provide a valuable contribution to the working life of the City and increase interest at street level. Office accommodation was upgraded with new servicing and circulation, and where possible rooflines were remodelled, creating additional space for rooftop boardrooms or plantrooms, and adding to the existing eventful skyline. The creation of eleven new office chambers, ranging from 4,000 to 12,000 sq.ft, improved the financial viability of the scheme.

The role of Farrell's scheme was to counter not only Mies but the modernist faction that supported Palumbo at the public enquiry. If Mies's scheme was the exemplar of modernist urbanism - rational, universal, self-referential, then Farrell's proposal embodied all the arguments that modernism rejected. The building of Mies's glass tower was considered essential for the future prosperity of the City, the irony being that today so many examples of the modernist visions that were built are now redundant, their inflexibility of design rendering them useless and expensive liabilities to their owners.

19

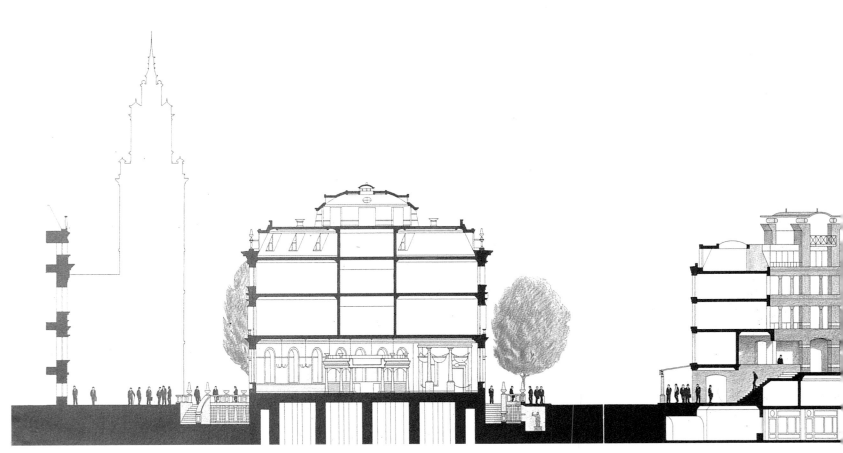

ELEVATION TO POULTRY

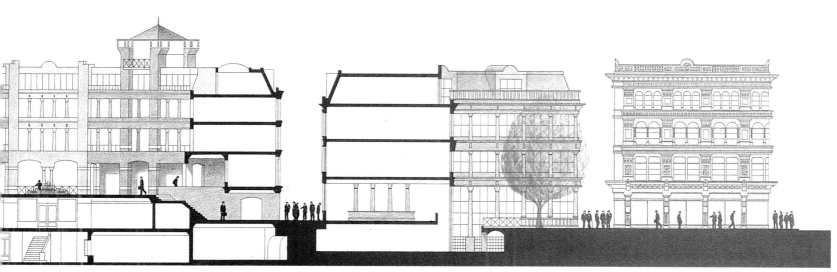

AND CROSS SECTION

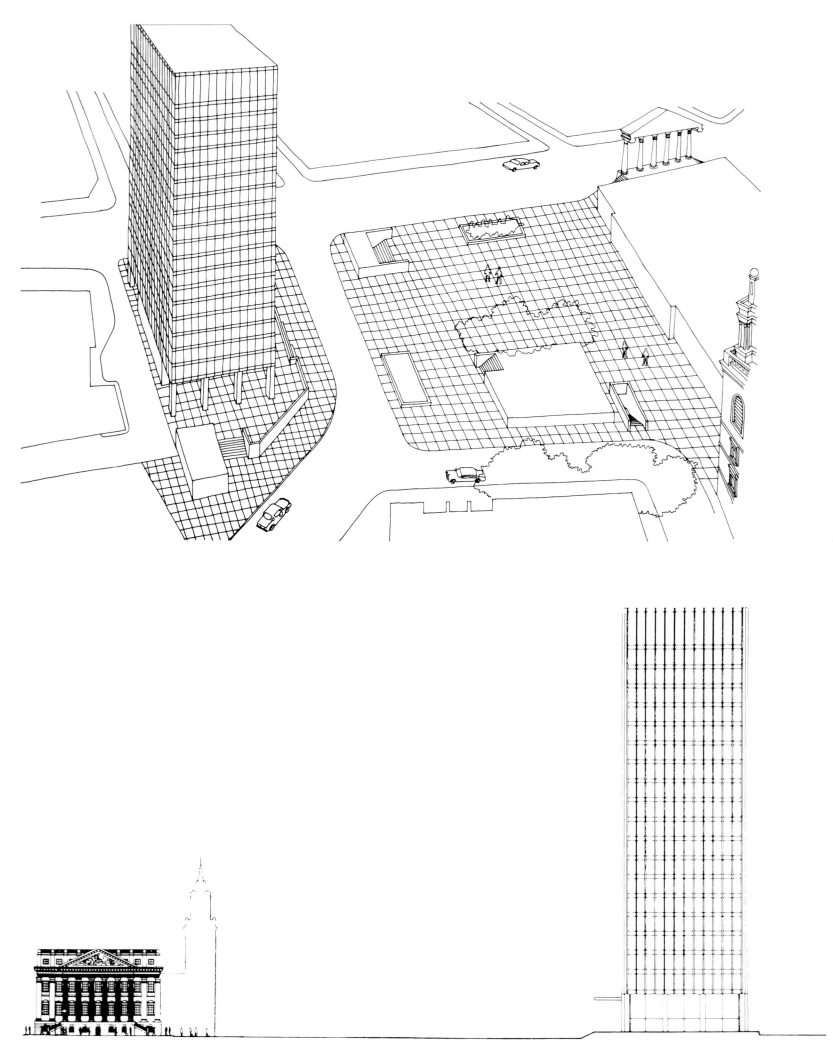

PROPOSALS BY MIES VAN DER ROHE

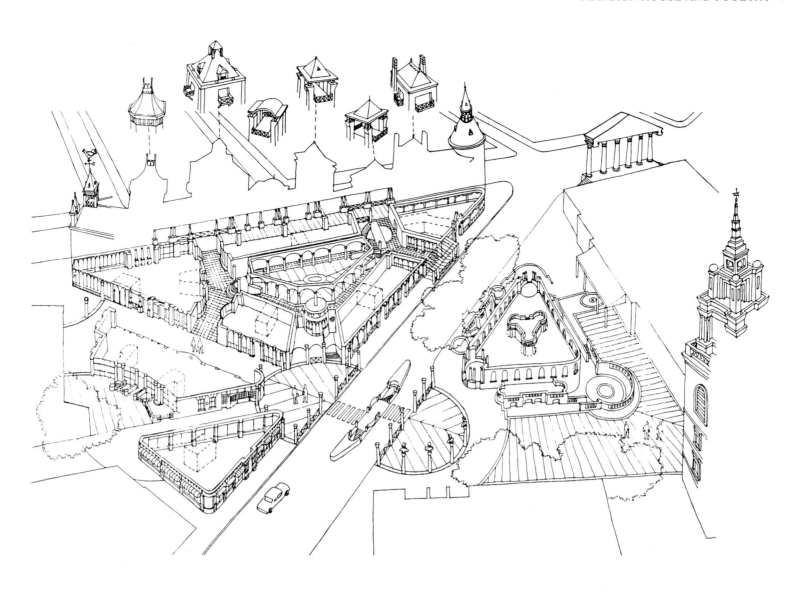

TERRY FARRELL'S PROPOSALS FOR 'SAVE'

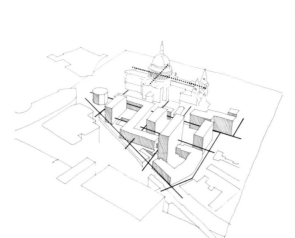

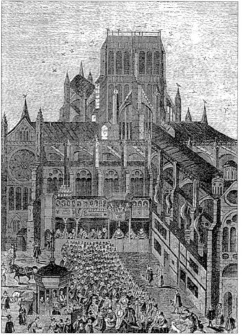

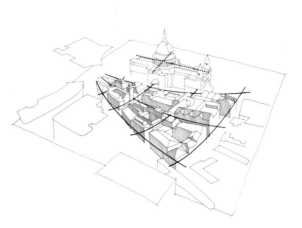

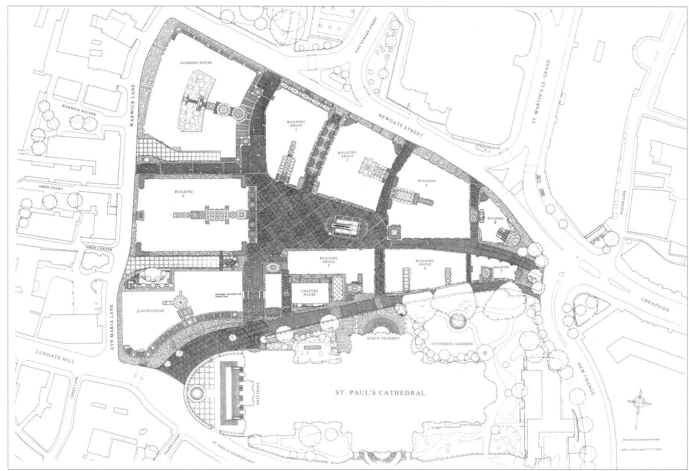

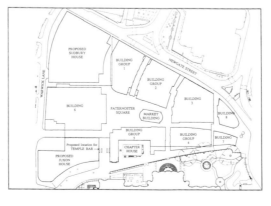

Building Group 1: Terry Farrell & Company
Sidell Gibson Partnership

Building Group 2: Terry Farrell & Company
Winchester Design Ltd

Building 3: Demetri Porphyrios Associates

Building Group 4: Allan Greenberg Architects

Building Group 5: John Simpson & Partners

Building 6: Hammond, Beeby & Babka

Building 7: Erith & Terry Architects

Building 8: Hammond, Beeby & Babka

Market Building: John Simpson & Partners

Sudbury House: Rolfe Judd

Juxon House: Whitfield Partners

# PATERNOSTER AREA, ST PAUL' S
## CITY OF LONDON 1989-1992

This scheme was the result of the collaboration of three masterplanners: John Simpson who initiated the proposals with a classical scheme, Tom Beeby and Terry Farrell. Additionally Farrell was the coordinating masterplanner and designed two of the buildings. At Paternoster Square, the modernist vision of the city exists, and since its announced demise the area has been the focus of debate about urban design in London and the site for a number of earlier urban design schemes by architects including Sir Richard Rogers and Sir Norman Foster. A number of theses schemes took their geometries from the cathedral, as Holford did, or established a rigid planning grid. The masterplanners, instead, identified the traditional street pattern of the site, and re-established a modified version with curved alleys that once again responded to pedestrian routes within the site and beyond, to St Paul's and Cheapside. The traditional alignment of St Paul's Church Yard was reinstated to improve the pedestrian flow from Cheapside to Ludgate Hill, and restore a defined built edge between the City and the public space of the cathedral gardens.

From this edge of the site the buildings rise in an even slope from the scale of the Chapter House to the grander commercial scale of Newgate Street, creating a continuity of built form across the site and beyond. The buildings adhere to St Paul's Heights, providing lost views of the cathedral and reinforcing the hierarchy between the great public building and the mass of ordinary buildings that lie in its shadow.

The reinstated urban form of Paternoster Square has been located in the centre of the site, and is surrounded by a number of buildings designed to respond to the geometry of the street pattern and the context each addresses. The new buildings, of various size and shape, have been designed by different architects, Demetri Porphyrios Associates, Allan Greenberg, John Simpson & Partners, Quinlan Terry, Hammond, Beeby & Babka, and Terry Farrell & Company, to create a natural variety of expression, this variety being tempered by the decision to develop a classical language for the whole site, considered appropriate because of the strong tradition of commercial classical buildings found in the City. The style also corresponds to the tripartite division of use, and accordingly all the buildings contain retail space of various designs for shops, banks and restaurants at ground level, a variety of office accommodation articulated by a repetitive piano nobile , and articulated roofline.

The street level has been re-established as the public domain with the creation of a traffic-free public space and pedestrianized alleys, with street-level activity generated by the numerous shops and front doors that line the streets. Paternoster Row, the main shopping street on the site, links the Square with Cheapside, building on existing shopping patterns in the City. A connection between the new square and St Paul's Underground Station in made via a lower-level shopping arcade.

For the detailed design of buildings 1 and 2, Farrell collaborated with Paul Gibson and Robert Adam.

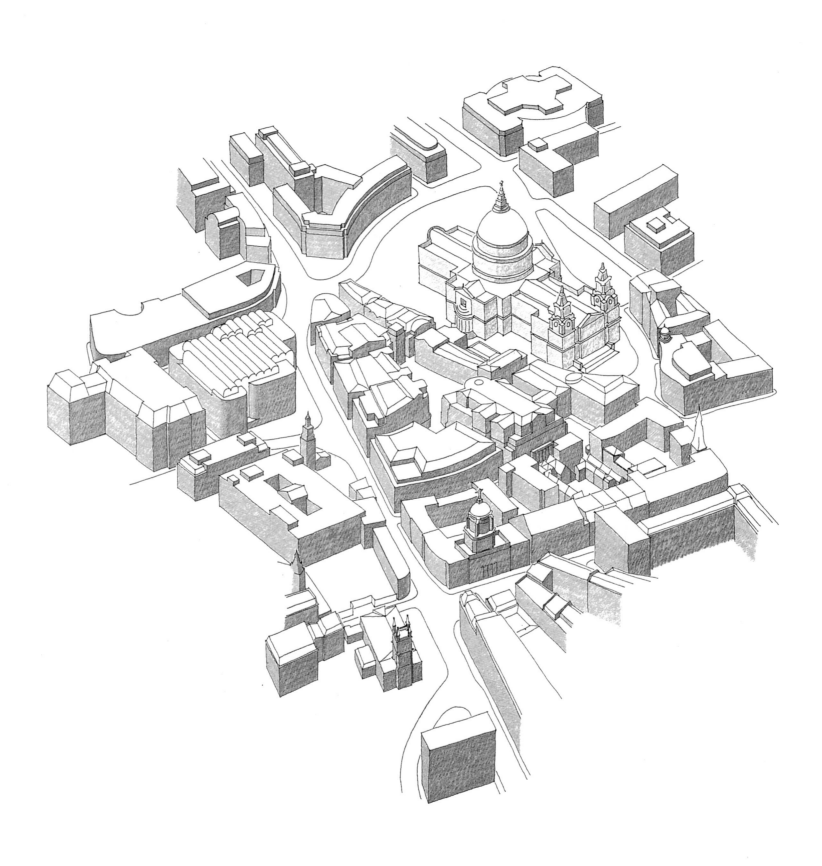

MASSING STUDY

PRE-WAR, POST-WAR AND 1960S' AERIAL VIEWS

RESTORING THE EDGE TO THE CATHEDRAL

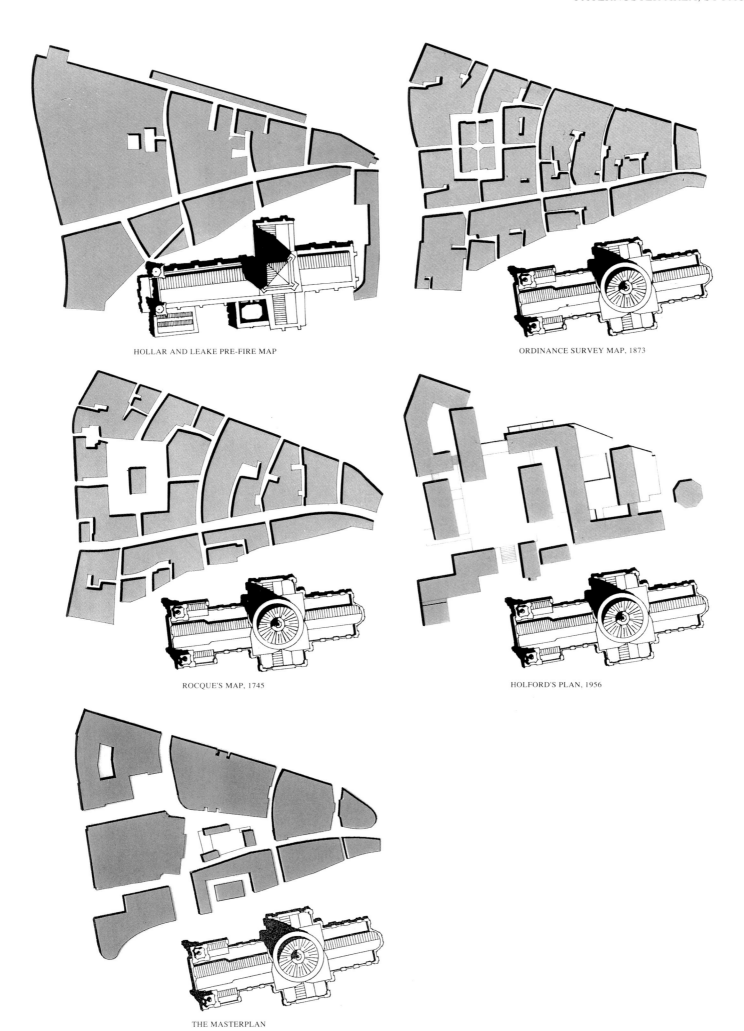

HOLLAR AND LEAKE PRE-FIRE MAP

ORDINANCE SURVEY MAP, 1873

ROCQUE'S MAP, 1745

HOLFORD'S PLAN, 1956

THE MASTERPLAN

FIGURE GROUND STUDIES

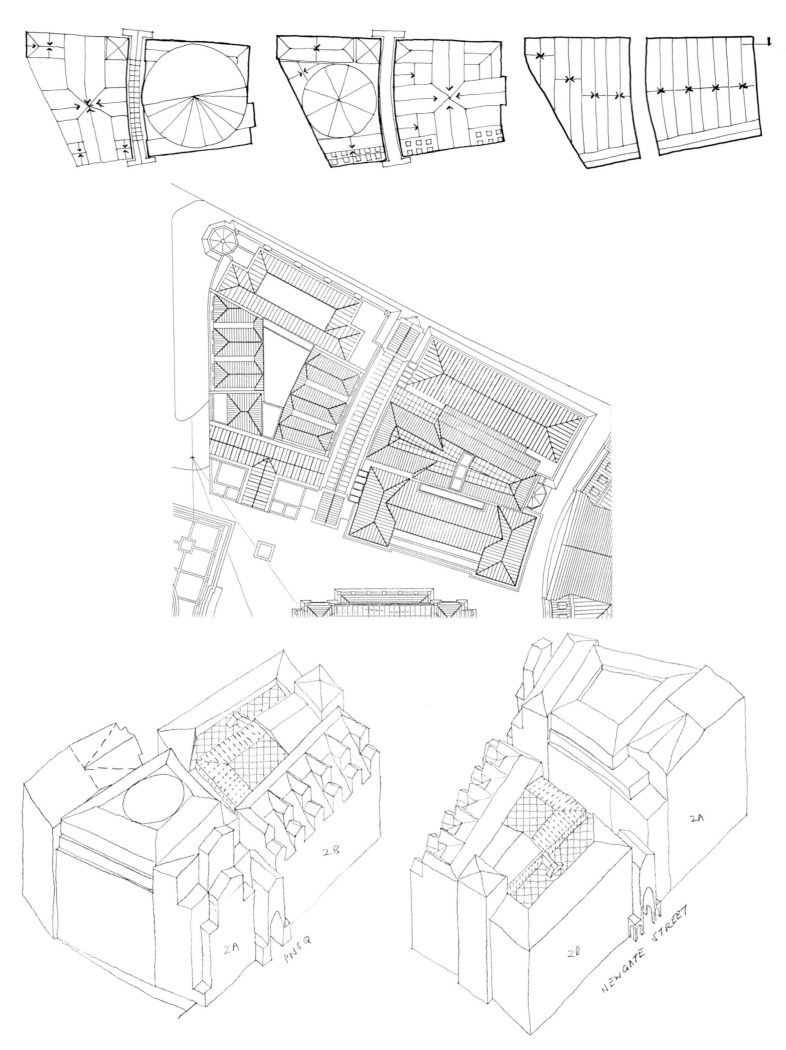

ROOF AND MASSING STUDIES, AND BUILDING GROUPS 1 AND 2

FARRELL'S ELEVATIONS TO BUILDING GROUPS 1 AND 2

The classical Lowther Arcade, the Strand, 1829–1902.

The Gothick Conservatory, Carlton House, London, by Thomas Hopper, 1807.

A classical detail of the Newgate Street Arcade entrance.

The Gothick window terminating the Arcade.

Classical detail of the Paternoster Square Arcade entrance.

A Gothick shopfront in the Arcade.

Location of Ivy Lane Arcade

A Gothick Arcade from Batty Langley's Gothick Architecture, improved by Rules...' (1742); a Gothick equivalent of classical forms.

Hawksmoor's classical Hall inside his Gothick design for All Souls College, Oxford, completed 1734.

Hawksmoor's project for a Gothick street front, All Souls College, Oxford, 1772.

IVY LANE ARCADE

*Between Building Group 1 & 2*

*ABOVE AND OPPOSITE*: FARRELL'S DESIGN FOR IVY LANE ARCADE

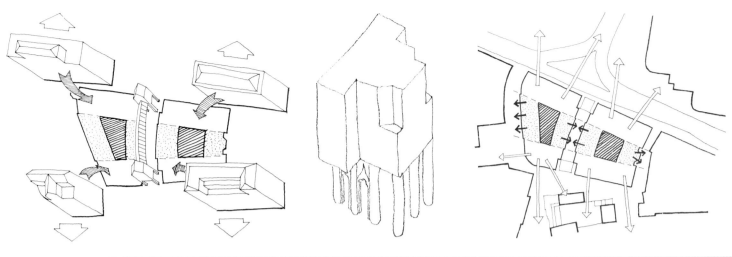

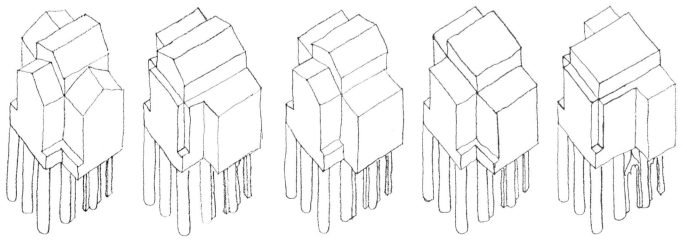

# THE CITY/LONDON WALL

The urban characteristics of this area that fascinated Farrell were the patterns of use which evolved from the presence of the Roman wall and its gates, and the nature and drama of this edge condition.

This area of London is one of the oldest known settled parts of the city, and lies at the north-east corner of the original Roman fort. The land on which the Barbican development now lies was originally called Moorfields, an area of marshland, used for recreation, just to the north of the fortifications. The London Wall lies upon the line of the long northern boundary of the original Roman wall which divided the enclosed protected area from the wild landscape of Britain beyond. A boundary where two worlds met: the civilized, ordered, protected world within the City, and the unordered, untamed world on the outside. This pattern of division continued through the Middle Ages, the walls protecting civilization from disorder, the gates of Moorgate and Cripplegate straddling this divide. The walls and gates were demolished in 1762, but the City did not spread outwards; instead the area beyond the walls developed as an industrial and warehousing zone. This traditional differentiation of uses continued after the second world war, during which the area was completely devastated by bombing.

The comprehensive development of the site occurred in the 1960s, with Sir Leslie Martin and Sir Hubert Bennett's 1959 plan for commercial development to the south of the new London Wall, and Chamberlin Powell and Bon's cultural and residential Barbican scheme to the north. To the south the business world of tower blocks, to the north the sixties' vision of city living in slab blocks and towers, the resident separated from the vehicle, given a new public domain of decks and walkways at podium level.

For Farrell the interest of the site lay in the problems specific to this notion of boundary and division, and the buildings along its edge. The post-war redevelopment recast this line of division as a mini-motorway, which acted as divisively upon its surroundings as the old wall had. The seven office blocks that lined London Wall established an edge to the City, but the decision to place these blocks

*Opposite*: Alban Gate; *Left*: Historical photograph of Wood Street and historical map showing Moorgate

1740s

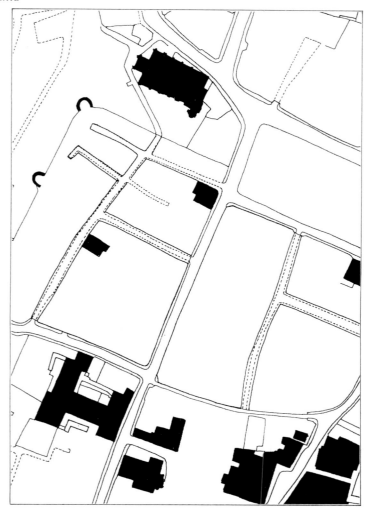

1954

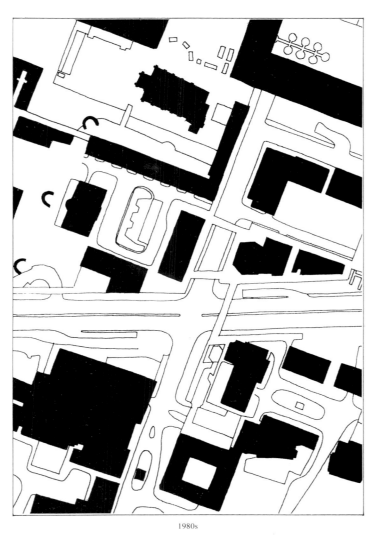

1980s

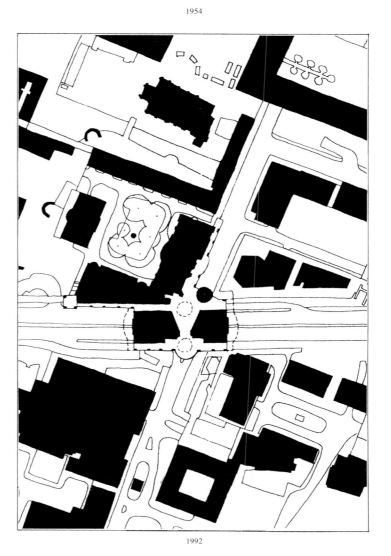

1992

on both sides of the road meant that those on the north side brought the intrusion of vehicles and office life into the quieter residential area, to the detriment of spaces such as Monkwell Square which became little more than a service yard.

These office blocks have proved to be inflexible and poor containers for modern business and since London Wall was declared an expansion zone in 1986, a number of schemes have been developed for the replacement of these redundant buildings. Farrell's involvement in the redevelopment of this area began at Lee House, situated half way along London Wall, then later at Moor House which sits on the site of Moorgate, at the eastern end of London Wall and at Fore Street, on the Post Office/Telephone Exchange site. Other schemes designed for this area include Sir Richard Rogers's Diawa Europe House, and Sir Norman Foster's Number One London Wall, both translucent structures that confront their street corners with glazed curved facades.

The Lee House site lies at the midpoint of London Wall, on the corner of Wood Street and London Wall, the only junction in this stretch of the road. This point is the site of the old Cripplegate, that once defined a boundary and also served as a point of entry and access. The City of London had given the owner of Lee House permission to double the size of his building, but proposals to double its height, to that of the Nat West tower, met with great opposition. Farrell's suggestion was to expand laterally onto the non-site over London Wall, producing a twin building to the existing that would straddle the road, just as Cripplegate had. The client commissioned Farrell to begin the design of the new building, Alban Gate, with twin elements, a gate building on the point of transition, historically between town and country, now between the different urban forms of the City and the Barbican. Within the scheme Farrell sought to address a number of problems identified in the Barbican development. It suffered, as did many modernist urban schemes, from agoraphobia, containing vast areas of concrete with no defined use and empty windswept pavements, generating barren areas with little activity or ground-level occupation. Farrell's great concern was to identify a major entrance to the Barbican, which would counter the scheme's lack of orientation and access for the pedestrian, and also to form a connection between the City street pattern and the Barbican circulation network at podium level.

The site of Moor House was one of the first of the London Wall plots to be sold, and was originally developed by Sir Charles Clore. The building sits on the junction of London Wall and Moorgate, and marks the point where the London Wall development meets the traditional urban fabric of the Moorgate area. At Moor House, Farrell again identified opportunities to restore connections and

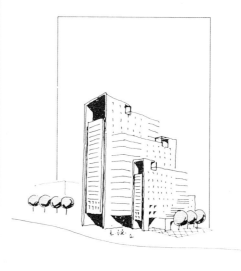

*Left*: Existing Lee House and Alban Gate;
*Above*: Moor House

View from St Albans tower

links, using the building, as at Alban Gate, as a gateway, but this time at ground level. A new route to connect the Barbican, across Fore Street, through the building to the Moorgate area of the City, could be created, which would also connect along the vista through Cripplegate with the church tower in the distance. The announcement of the proposals for the Cross London Rail Link added another dimension to the building's role as gateway, serving as a point of transport interchange that would link the area to counties on either side of London.

In the Fore Street redevelopment the existing buildings sat more comfortably within the surrounding context in a quiet area to the north of the boundary of London Wall. As a result the new building played a less prominent role than the major civic roles created for Alban Gate and Moor House, and its influence upon its context was more discreet. From the site there were no direct access points onto the podium level circulation network that dominated the area, to the detriment of the routes both in and through the site. Within the scheme Farrell designed a number of new pedestrian routes at podium level that connected with and improved the existing circulation system at this level.

All of these schemes share similarities in the urban roles Farrell has designated for them - to repair the urban fabric of their immediate surroundings. The integration of the buildings into their context is developed in the ground plan but also in the massing of the built forms. At Alban Gate and Moor House, Farrell was particularly interested in the problem of how to assimilate the scale of new large office blocks with that of the old buildings to provide some continuity. He approached the gradation of scale differently in each scheme. The form of Lee House consists of a number of components and blocks, arranged as set pieces in the context, which relate to a gradation from the scale of the Victorian street. Moor House was more of an investigation of collage, with the building composed of four main building elements of different scales assembled together, the composition forming a connection between the varied scales of the buildings to which it relates.

Both of these schemes emphasize the ground plan and the pedestrian domain, and create continuity with the historical and existing patterns of movement in the area. They also form a continuity with the historical associations and the effect of the wall and its gates, which dictated the characteristics and patterns of use in the area. This is a boundary site, a point of transition, with the Barbican on one side and the City on the other.

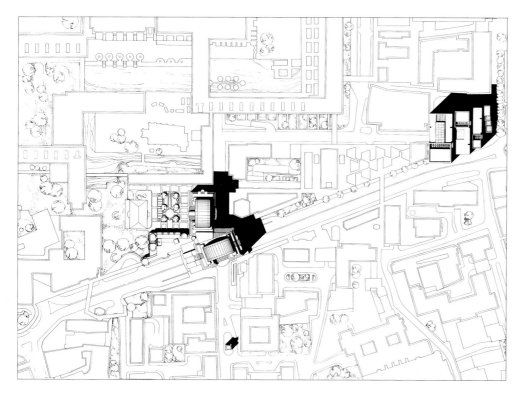

*Opposite*: Alban Gate; *Left*: Location plan showing Alban Gate and Moor House

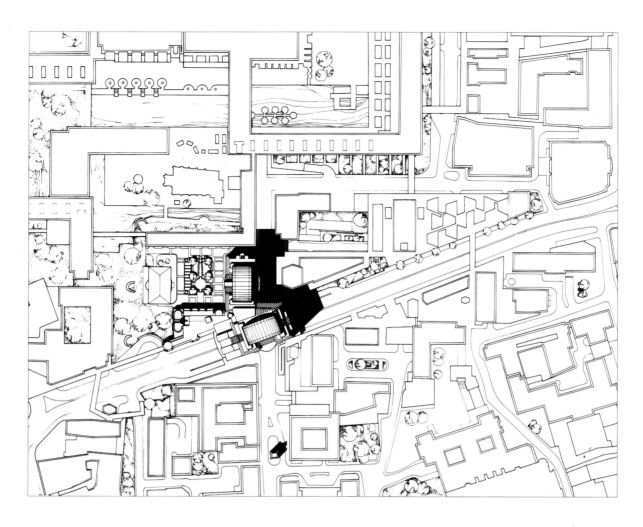

## ALBAN GATE
### *CITY OF LONDON 1986-1992*

*As well as providing modern flexible office space, Farrell sees Alban Gate as playing an important civic role as a gateway, repairing ruptured connections and fragmented spaces, acting as mediator between different urban forms and uses. The twin towers draw their geometry from the existing street pattern, which sets them at a 60/30 degree angle to each other, and each plays a different role.*

*The air-rights building, the more exuberant of the pair, serves as a four-way gateway with traffic flowing through at ground level while pedestrians cross at podium level, which connects the City to the network of circulation decks in the Barbican complex. By straddling the chasm of London Wall the building acquires a front door in the City, thereby reinforcing the traditional division of use along this edge, as well as offering a prospective increase in rental value. The pedestrian route that crosses London Wall is defined by a dramatic concourse, bounded on both sides by glazed curtain walls, and articulated by diagonal structural steelwork, seating and planting. There is provision for this route to be inhabited by retail units and cafes. The building also serves as a new formal gateway to the cultural centre at the Barbican. This role is expressed within the elevation by the spectacular grand arched portico of the transfer structure at the base of the building. Above this, the internal planning and elevation draws from the features of the inhabited gatehouse form of*
*Cripplegate, with large central rooms and public spacestheabove the gate entrance, flanked by secondary rooms to side. Alban Gate has a series of glazed atria and conservatories in the centre of the facades, providing areas for informal meetings and social occasions, with more defined use spaces forming granite-clad solid corner towers to either side. The significance of the civic role of the new building is expressed by the dramatic glazed vaults which top the towers and announce Alban Gate on the skyline of London.*

*The quieter twin makes its contribution by repairing and relating to the urban design of its immediate surroundings. The elevation of this block reads as a sparsely detailed tower rising from a heavily modelled six-storey base, which relates to the neighbouring buildings and new residential flanking block. This block, faced in brick and given a distinct identity, runs westward along London Wall and encloses the south side of Monkwell Square. With the removal of the old Lee House entrance and pub, Monkwell Square is established, once again, as a purely residential area. The centre of the space is enhanced with landscaping, trees and seating and the removal of the intrusive car park ramp. Farrell has also designed a link between Monkwell Square and London Wall to encourage pedestrian activity along the major road, to transform it into more of an urban road than a motorway.*

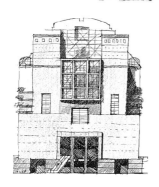

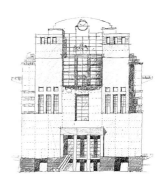

*ABOVE*: THE PRIMARY GATEWAY FACADE FACES THE CITY AND ST. PAUL'S
*OPPOSITE*: CITY GATEWAY FACADE WITH WREN'S ST. ALBAN'S CHURCH TOWER

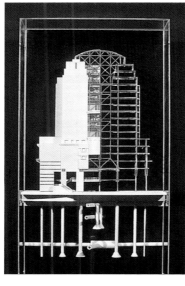

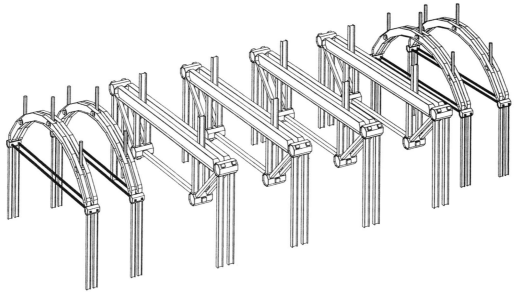

*ABOVE*: INSIDE THE BRIDGE SCALE ENGINEERING OF THE TRANSFER STRUCTURE IS THE PUBLIC CONCOURSE WITH SHOPS AND RESTAURANTS
*OPPOSITE*: VIEW FROM UNDER THE ARCH STRUCTURE OVER LONDON WALL

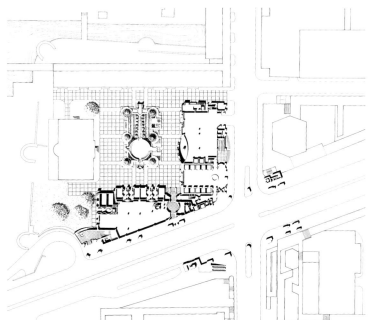
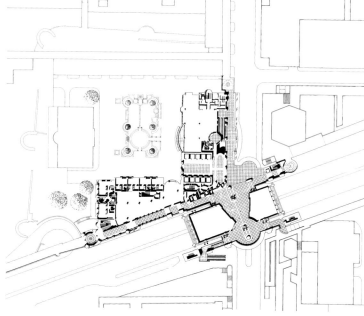

*ABOVE*: THE NEW MONKWELL SQUARE REINTEGRATES EXISTING AND NEW BUILDINGS
*OPPOSITE*: NEW RESIDENTIAL ACCOMMODATION BESIDE MONKWELL SQUARE

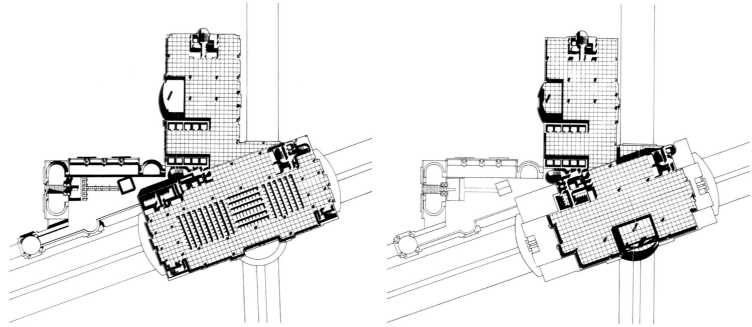

PLANS AND ENTRANCE AREAS TO OFFICES

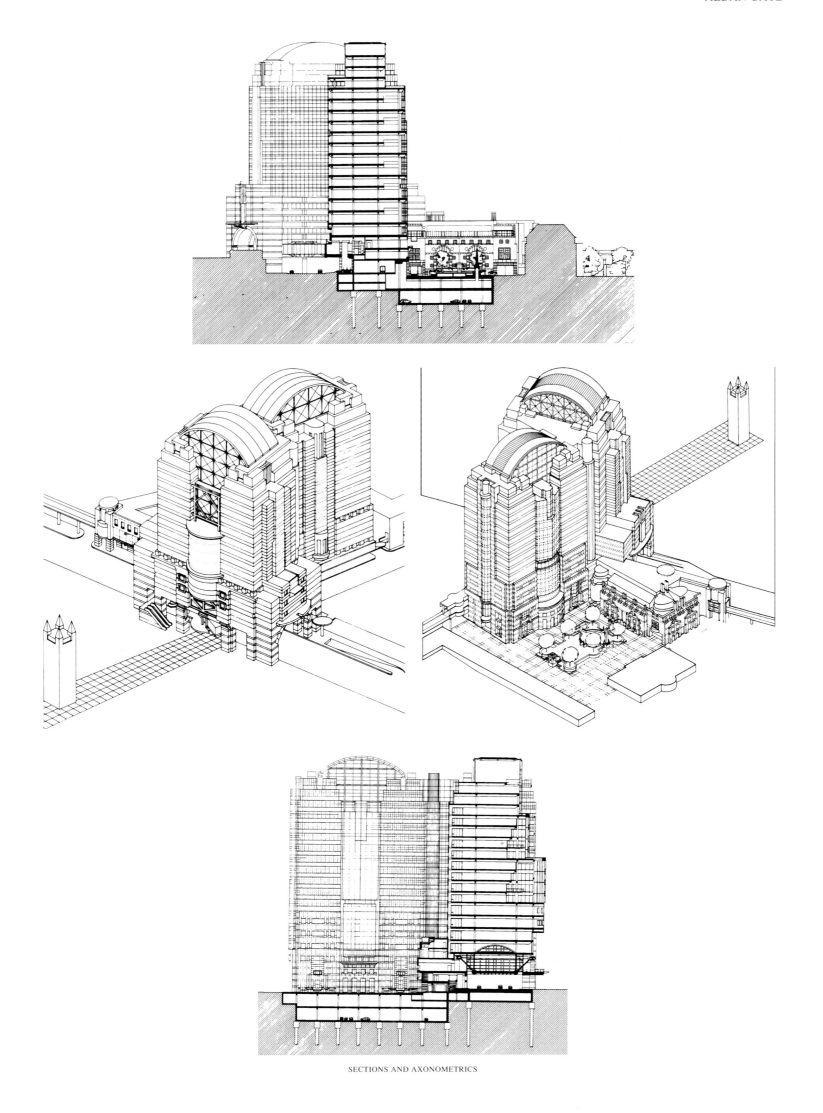

SECTIONS AND AXONOMETRICS

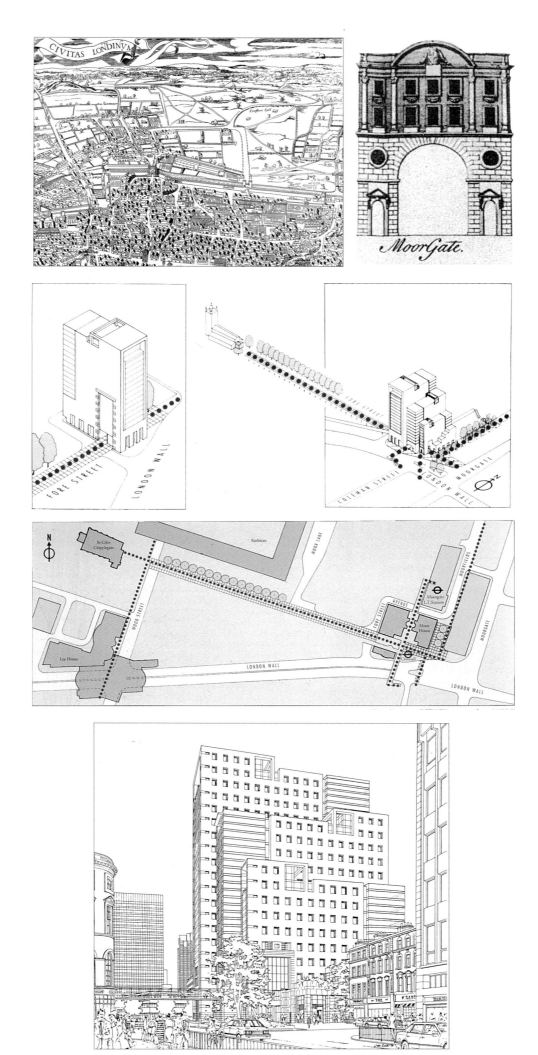

HISTORICAL DRAWINGS, VIEWS AND SITE PLAN

# MOOR HOUSE
## *CITY OF LONDON 1986-1991*

*Farrell's proposal for Moor House contains a number of similarities to Alban Gate. The scheme involves the replacement of a 1960s' office block with a new building that responds to the requirements and patterns of the surrounding context, and relates to the urban characteristics of boundary and gateway.*

*Once again, concerns for the public domain dictated the design of the ground floor of Moor House, with routes delineated by the building itself acting as a gatehouse and point of connection. Building upon the traditional patterns of circulation around and through the site, a new public concourse was established at ground level. Aligned with the existing east-west axis of Fore Street and St Giles Cripplegate, this route forms the principal entrance to the building and connects the Crossrail and Moorgate Underground transport interchange to the cultural facilities at the Barbican. A new enclosed bridge links the podium level concourse with St Alphage High Walk, across London Wall to the Guildhall and the City.*

*Within Moor House, at the junction of these routes, Farrell has designed new public spaces which provide a variety of civic amenities. Comprising a ground-level and podium-level concourse, connected by stairs, escalators and a lift, these new spaces provide retail and restaurant facilities for office workers and visitors. These new spaces create a sheltered and dramatic environment to work,* *meet and shop beneath the vast atrium located in the centre of the building, enhancing the quality of street life in the area.*

*The integration of the building with its context is further addressed by the formal massing of the building as a series of connected mini-blocks, which rise from a two-storey elevation on Moorgate, relating the intimate scale of the 19th-century buildings to a 20-storey façade adjacent to London Wall. The mass of the building is further broken down by the use of two contrasting types of cladding: banded glazing and stone. The elevation of Moor House articulates the tripartite division found in good street architecture. Interest at the base in generated by a variety of glazed openings and doorways which provide a high level of visual transparency, and highlight the building's ground-level permeability to its surroundings and its role as gateway and point of connection and interchange. The repetitive middle floors are crowned at the top with deep shaded loggias, which provide visual drama to the skyline and enhance the buildings three-dimensional qualities.*

*Moor House is less exuberant than its Big Bang neighbour - a consequence of its less pivotal role as gateway between the Barbican and the City, and also Farrell's desire to produce a more refined interpretation of the modern office building type.*

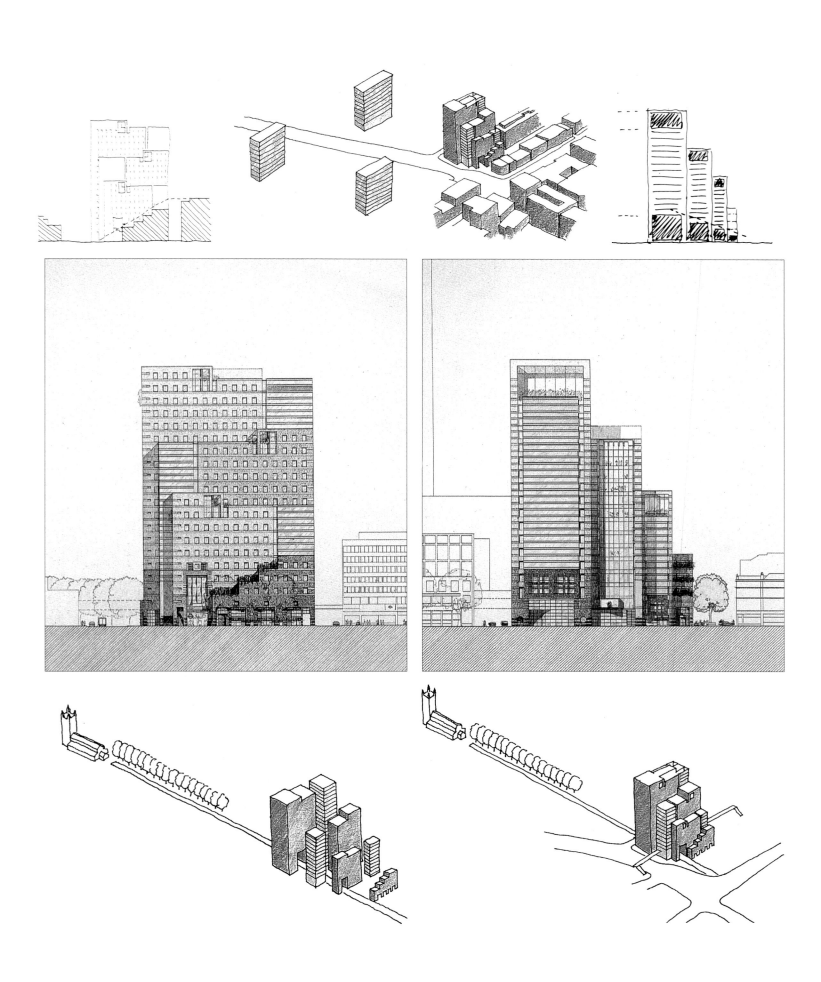

CONCEPT SKETCHES AND ELEVATIONS

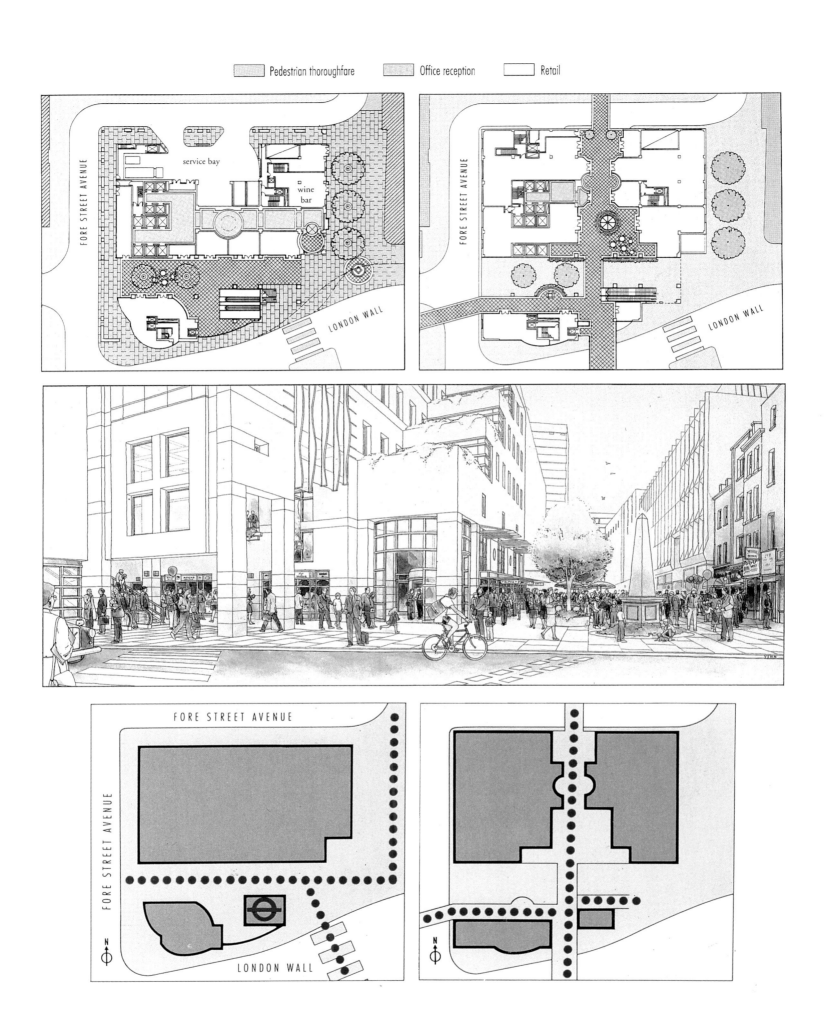

Pedestrian thoroughfare    Office reception    Retail

GROUND LEVEL AND PODIUM LEVEL PLAN; VIEW AND PUBLIC CIRCULATION AT GROUND AND PODIUM LEVEL

# THE RIVER THAMES

Today the River Thames lies in a state of redundancy. Bereft of function, it stands as an underused and isolated resource. For Farrell the importance of the river lies in the opportunity to realize its unique potential, and the great influence this natural artery has had and continues to exercise upon the development of London.

The river determined the city's very existence and position, at the crossing point of London bridge, from Roman times. As the city evolved its commercial greatness resulted from the port facilities that developed to the east of the City, with the rest of London spreading westward in a linear form around the great bend in the river. The river, therefore, bonded together the two cities of Westminster and the City, the two worlds of constitutional and commercial power. This linear development of London is expressed within the street pattern by a series of major streets that run parallel to the river - from Whitehall, up the Strand, up Fleet Street, along Newgate to St Paul's. This route actually continues along Lower Thames Street, connecting Westminster Abbey to the Tower. All the sites along this bend, between this major route and the river, were the prime sites of the great city, and all the buildings addressed both, with front doors onto the major thoroughfares and watergates onto the Thames. These buildings represented the great institutions of power, and dominated the familiar riverscape of London, as depicted by Canaletto.

The river has also strongly influenced the form of London, by acting as a barrier, separating and making distinct the areas of north and south London. The inhabitation on the banks lies at the point of tension between land and water - and the river dictated the nature of this development. The south bank has evolved with quite different uses to the north bank, and its topography has dictated a very different urban pattern to the linear form of the north bank. The land to the south of the river was subject to continual flooding due to its flatter terrain, and was consequently only occupied periodically by invaders such as the Nordic people, who settled across the river from the fortified city. In the late 16th century the area drained naturally and the south bank became the site for uncontrolled and illegal activities beyond the control and laws of the city. A string of places of

*Opposite*: Vauxhall Cross; *Left*: The River Thames looking west across East Greenwich

VAUXHALL CROSS EFFRA

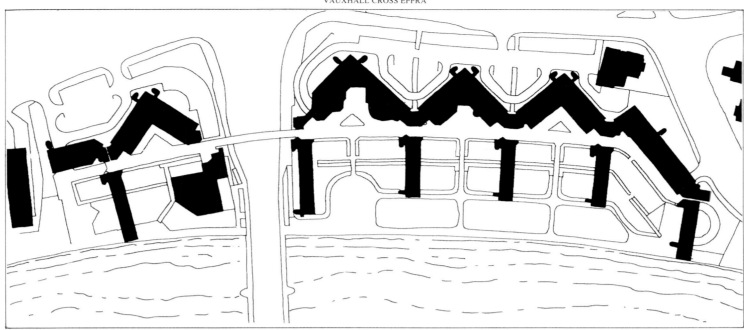

SEBIRE ALLSOPP 1982

NICHOLAS LALEY 1982

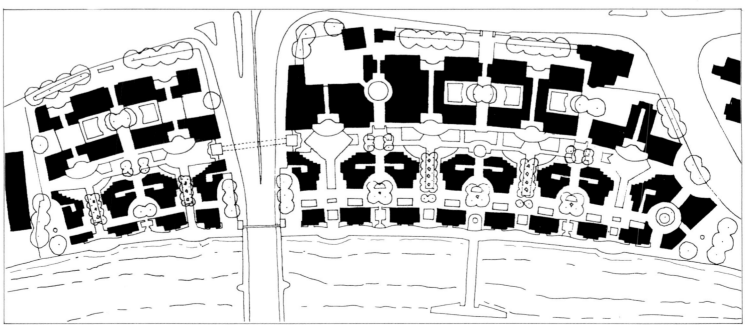

FARRELL 1982

entertainment ran from the Globe Theatre to the gardens at Battersea and Vauxhall. The area's role as a place of pleasure for the city continued into the 18th century with inns, bowling greens, gardens and concerts. But this role, as an anarchic and lively counterpart to the more regulated city on the north bank ended with the arrival of the railways. The urban pattern of the south bank was generated by a number of elevated viaducts that issued from Charing Cross, and the patchwork pattern of residual sites was abandoned to industries, such as lead-working and brewing. The area became crowded with wharfs and factories, and deteriorated into a polluted slum. The servant role of the south bank continues to this day and the land on the inside of the great bend in the river provides the routes and access which the north bank needs. The south bank has an urban pattern which is more radial than the dominantly linear form of the north bank, with the land criss-crossed by roads and viaducts.

The bulk of Farrell's work connected with the river lies along the stretch from Vauxhall to Waterloo Bridge. This central stretch has also been the focus for discussion on the underuse of the river, with a number of proposals exploring the possibilities for the regeneration of the river and its banks. Farrell's approach to such development is once again grounded in the desire for continuity and an understanding of the unique relationship between the river and the buildings and urban fabric along its banks. It also involves his commitment to reinstating the Thames as an accessible part of London, and a unique resource for Londoners.

On the site of Vauxhall Cross, Farrell's original mixed-use scheme sought to create a new riverside community, based upon the traditional linear form of development along the river. The realized version of the proposals, a bespoke office building, instead echoed the heroic structures of Bankside and Battersea power stations and their relationship to the river as an urban feature. Similarly Farrell's scheme at Charing Cross, which centred on an air-rights office building for the developers, Greycoats, established itself as a new landmark, at the hinge of the bend in the river, a prominent site forming part of the riverscape of emblematic buildings along the north bank. The building rises above the tracks of the station, in the form of two vast barrel-vaulted elements, this new facade reinstating the tradition of buildings which address the river and the Strand. As at Alban Gate, Farrell took the opportunity to use the building to repair the surrounding fabric, with improvements to the station forecourt, Villiers Street, and Embankment Gardens. Particular attention was paid to the enhancement of routes and views to the river, enlivened by the creation of an active hinterland around the station.

On the South Bank, Farrell once again seeks to repair the urban fabric and

*Left*: Charing Cross

HUNGERFORD BRIDGE

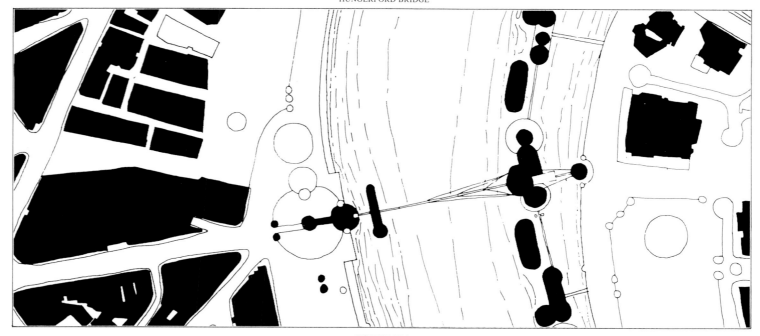

ROGERS 1986

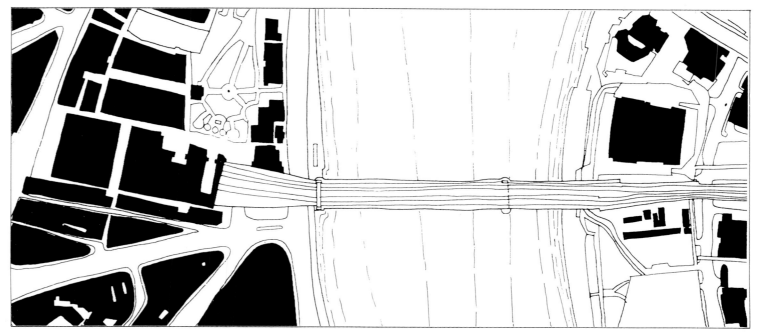

EXISTING 1987

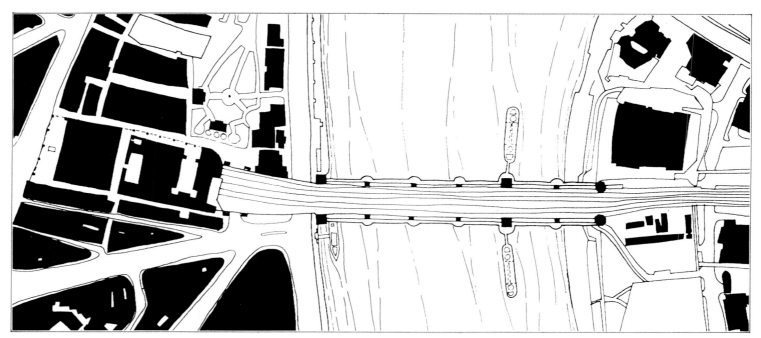

FARRELL 1988

alleviate the problems from which the complex suffers. For Farrell, its mono-functional nature provides ample provision for the higher forms of cultural activity, but lacks the most elementary features of normal urban life. The existing scheme also commits the urban design 'cardinal sin' of removing pedestrians from the ground level, which becomes the domain of the vehicle. Pedestrians are relegated to an upper-level network of walkways which generate disorientation and exposure to a bad microclimate - the perceived tripartite logic of urban form is destroyed. Hungerford Bridge forms a connection between these two schemes, and Farrell's proposal replaces the existing mean pedestrian route with a grand pier, which echoes Brunel's bridge of 1845.

Taken together these three schemes run continuously from Trafalgar Square to Waterloo. Unlike other, more dramatic proposals, each project is based upon existing structures, re-used whenever possible; and existing redundant public spaces and routes are enlivened with new activities which attempt to integrate the river as part of the urban scene.

Farrell's involvement with the river extends beyond this inner London stretch. The invitation from the Royal Fine Arts Commission to lead a Thames Study project, provided the opportunity for Farrell to explore a number of urban design interests, particularly the role of urban designer as co-ordinator. This role involves the creation of a coherent environment and framework which generates opportunities for different kinds of expression and solutions to be developed. As at Paternoster, Farrell was asked to bring together a number of architects and professionals with a shared commitment - the redevelopment and regeneration of the river. Each of the ten designers involved took a site and environment and developed schemes which sought to enhance the riverside environment. For Farrell the project emphasized the role of urban designer as being very much involved with persuasion and propaganda; the resultant exhibition was designed to provoke interest in the future of the Thames, and to provide a focus for feedback and debate.

Farrell's earlier schemes for Bankside, Brentford Dock and East Greenwich similarly sought to enliven redundant pieces of the riverside environment and architecture by building on the specific characteristics of each site and its relationship to the river.

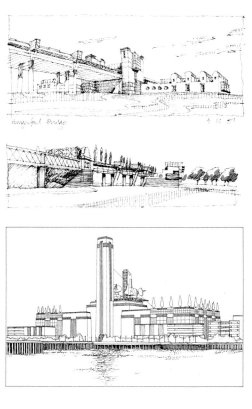

*Left*: Thames Study, excursions guide;
*Above*: Hungerford Bridge and Bankside

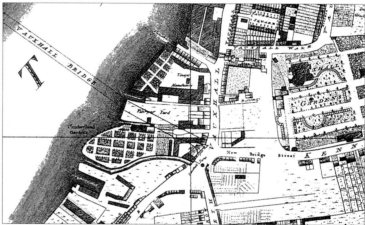

HISTORICAL VIEWS OF THE SITE

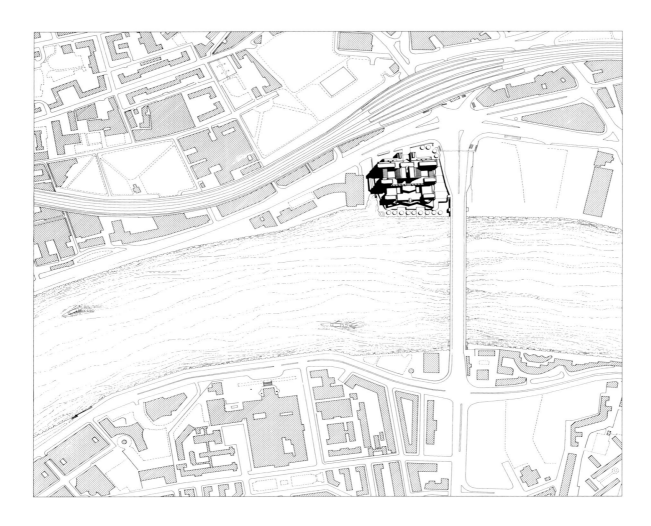

# VAUXHALL CROSS
## *LONDON BOROUGH OF LAMBETH 1982-1992*

*The unrealized Effra scheme evolved into the built scheme Vauxhall Cross, which embodies Farrell's belief that the urban designer/architect must be flexible and capable of adapting his designs, instead of being driven by dogmatism. The major revisions to the original scheme were a change from a mixed to a government office development, and the reduction in site area to the portion to the east of Vauxhall Bridge. But the new scheme contained many of the urban design features developed for Effra.*

*The network of routes designed for the original scheme was translated into atria and internal spaces which were used to break up the mass of the building. These spaces, articulated with terraces and balconies, provided an inner sheltered low-level domain for office workers and created a sense of place and focus within the building itself. The lower floors housed a number of social and communal facilities, including a restaurant, auditorium, sports room, and library, to generate activity at these levels.*

*The new scheme is again a pyramidal, tiered composition, in section and elevation. Consisting of three longitudinal blocks parallel to the river, the building rises in height to the edge of the site along the road, where the main entrance is positioned. This massing maximises views of the river but also allows daylight into all the internal cellular offices. The solid plinth element is retained, from which the taller elements emerge.*

*Rather than the urban village ethos that underpinned the Effra project, at Vauxhall Cross Farrell chose to make a new powerful building that contributed to the area. He drew inspiration from buildings such as Bankside and Battersea power stations - the vast scale and dramatic form of the buildings heroically addressing the river and opposite bank. At Vauxhall Cross the solid central element is flanked on either side by tiered glazed elements composed to create a massive yet articulated building form. The contrast between the pale concrete cladding and the darker wall glazing emphasizes the layered nature of the composition. The three-dimensional qualities of the building are enhanced by deep-set windows and openings and by a series of balconies which face the river. The single central chimney element of Gilbert Scott's Bankside power station is translated into two solid towers which crown the building, providing the dramatic skyline and recognizable silhouette.*

*The evolution of the scheme through three separate clients' briefs from mixed use, to housing, to government offices was achieved whilst still maintaining the essentials of the original urban design principles. Farrell's belief is that urban design relies first upon physical form and secondarily upon land use. The mass and void, the public river walk and pyramidal forms have survived all the changes.*

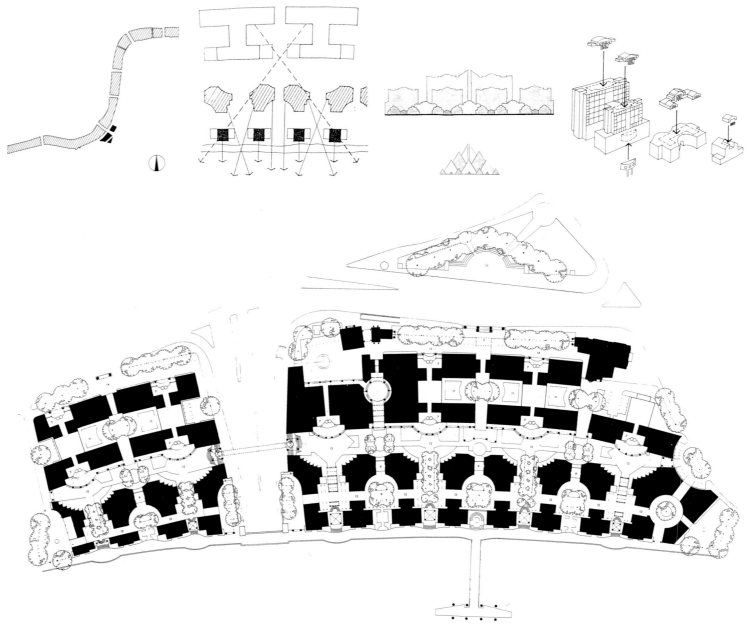

THE 1982 EFFRA COMPETITION SCHEME

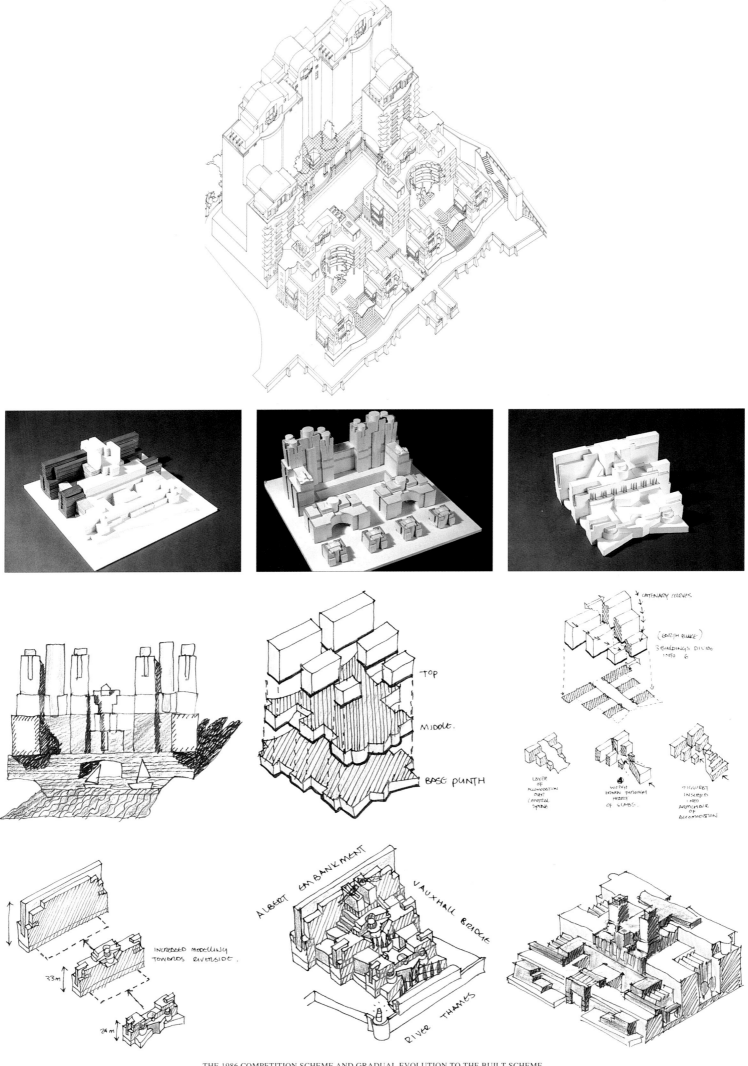

THE 1986 COMPETITION SCHEME AND GRADUAL EVOLUTION TO THE BUILT SCHEME

RIVER FRONTAGES

SOUTHERN ENTRY FRONTAGE

RIVER FRONTAGE

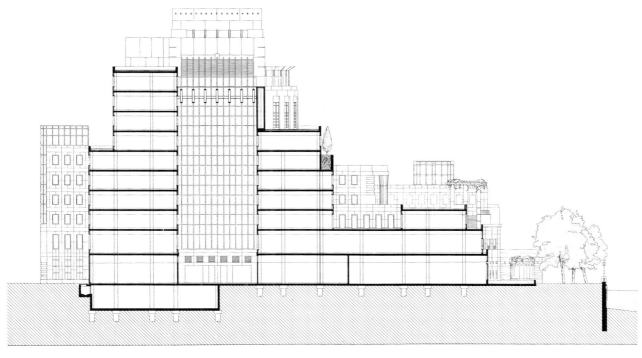

NIGHT ILLUMINATION DESIGNED BY TERRY FARRELL'S OFFICE, AND CROSS SECTION

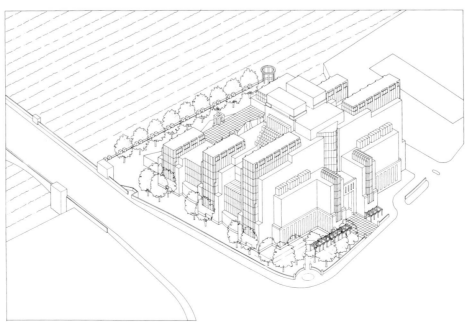

NEW PUBLIC WALKWAY AND AXONOMETRIC FROM ALBERT EMBANKMENT

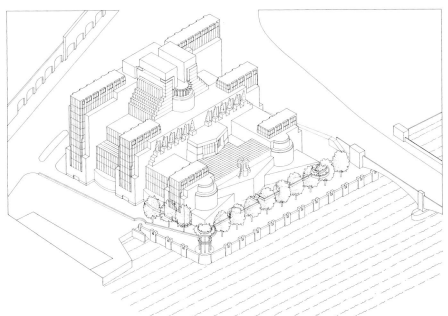

NEW PUBLIC WALKWAY AND AXONOMETRIC FROM RIVER THAMES

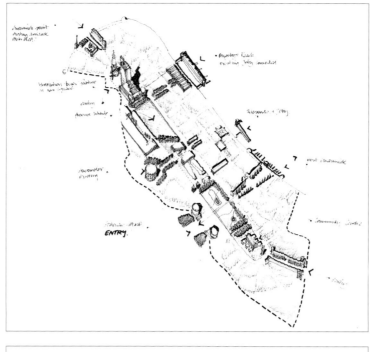

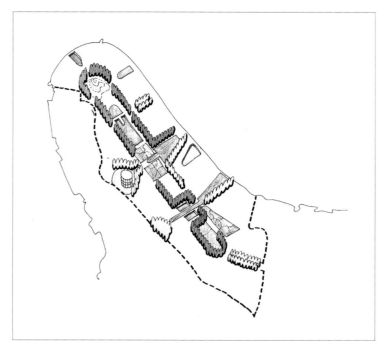

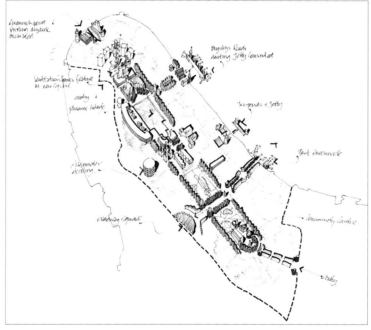

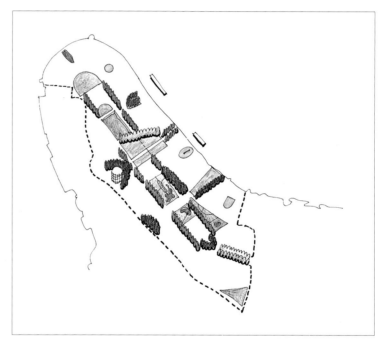

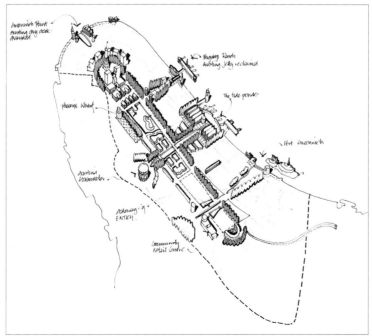

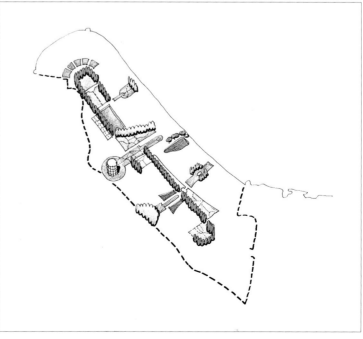

TOWNSCAPE AND LANDSCAPE STUDIES

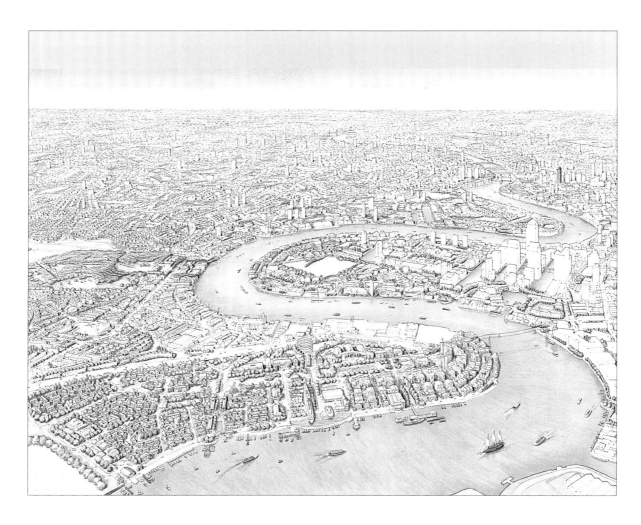

# EAST GREENWICH
## *LONDON BOROUGH OF GREENWICH 1988*

In designing a masterplan for the redevelopment of this long north-south peninsula in Greenwich, Farrell had to resolve the problem of creating a new urban framework for this unusual site. The main urban design concept was to establish a green hinterland in the middle of the peninsula to create a second focus for the site, as well as the river itself. A similar principle was used on the Effra scheme, to provide a land and waterside front. The built elements of the design were organized around this central park, extending the traditional green spaces and ordered urbanity of Greenwich into the site, to establish the scheme as an integral part of Greenwich, and not just an extension of Docklands.

Farrell used the remnants of the area's history - the

jetty, a pier and drydock, and the giant No. 2 gas holder - to provide focal points of interest within the masterplan and create a sense of continuity with the site's history. The peninsula had remained essentially rural until the arrival of the South Metropolitan Gasworks in the 1880s. Development continued with the opening of the first Blackwall Tunnel and the immense coaling jetty, and most recently with the River Wey Power Station, the second Blackwall Tunnel and the world's biggest gas and oil plant in the 1960s. The scheme sought to repair this redundant industrial river site and reintegrate it with the river and adjoining areas by building upon the history of the site and its traditional relationship with the river and the urban features of Greenwich.

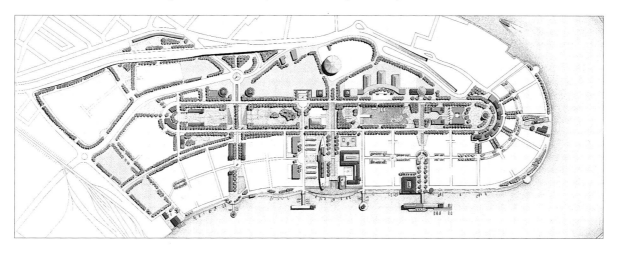

RIVER WALL
BLACKWALL TUNNELS
ROUTES OF MAJOR GAS MAINS

EXISTING TENANTS
OTHER OWNERSHIPS

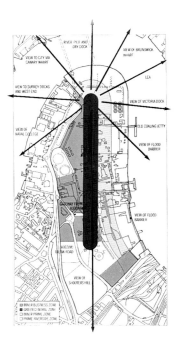

MERIDIAN LIGHTSHIP AND PUB. SMALL
LEISURE CENTRE BASED ON THE RECLAIMED
DRYDOCK AND ITS OLD LIGHTSHIP, ALL
NAMED AFTER THE LINE FROM GREENWICH
THAT CIRCLES THE GLOBE

GREENWICH POINT. RESIDENTIAL
ACCOMMODATION OF THE HIGHEST
STANDARD. FINE VIEWS FROM LOW LEVEL
ACROSS THE RIVER. SPECTACULAR VIEWS
FROM HIGH LEVEL IN ALL DIRECTIONS
INCLUDING THE CITY, DOCKLANDS,
BLACKHEATH AND EAST BEYOND THE NEW
LONDON CITY AIRPORT

TIDE MILL PARK. RESIDENTIAL
ACCOMMODATION OF A VERY HIGH
STANDARD. FINE VIEWS FROM BOTH HIGH
AND LOW LEVELS ACROSS THE RIVER AND
THE PARK

TIDEWAY. A VARIETY OF BUSINESS PARK
UNITS DESIGNED TO FIT HARMONIOUSLY
INTO THE CHARACTER OF THEIR SURROUND-
INGS

EXISTING GAS HOLDER. THE LARGEST IN
BRITAIN

PORT GREENWICH PARK. A CENTRAL OPEN
SPACE ANIMATED BY A FLOWING NETWORK
OF WATER FEATURES AND PROVIDING
PLEASANT VIEWS FOR DWELLINGS IN THE
HEART OF THE SITE

PORT GREENWICH GATEWAY. THE MAIN
ENTRANCE TO THE DEVELOPMENT, WELL-
LANDSCAPED AND FRAMED BY A SMALL
SHOPPING AND LOCAL SERVICES CENTRE ON
ONE SIDE AND COMBINED PUBLIC HOUSE AND
RESTAURANTS ON THE OTHER

WESTCOMBE GREEN. LEAFY NEIGHBOUR-
HOODS WITH THEIR OWN VILLAGE GREEN

TUNNELS
HEAVY FOUNDATIONS
LIGHTER FOUNDATIONS

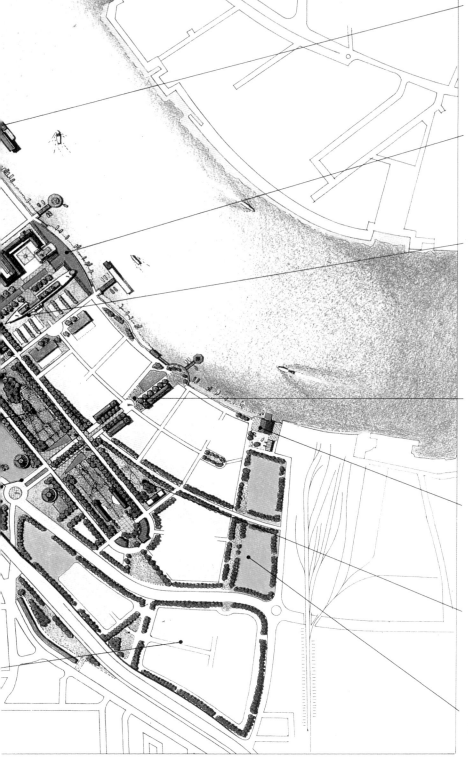

PALM HOUSE PIER AND HOTEL. A CONSERVA-
TORY STRUCTURE BUILT ON THE EXISTING
PIER TO HOUSE HIGH-QUALITY SHOPS,
RESTAURANTS, CLUBS AND A CASINO, AND
TO BE OPERATED AS PART OF AN ATRIUM
HOTEL PERCHED ON THE RIVER BANK. THE
PIER IS ALSO TO BE A RIVERBUS STOP

STEAMER YARD. AN IMPRESSIVE SPECIALITY
RETAIL AND LEISURE PARK THEMED AROUND
TWO REPLICA STEAMSHIPS AND A RECON-
STRUCTION OF THE ORIGINAL TIDE MILL ON
THE SITE. TWO PIERS (ONE OF WHICH IS ALSO
TO BE A RIVERBUS STOP) AND A CANAL HELP
COMPLETE THE SETTING. SPECIAL FEATURES
INCLUDE A MARITIME EXPERIENCE CENTRE
AND AN OMNIMAX CINEMA

AVENUES AND CANAL TO BRING THE THAMES
VISUALLY INTO THE SITE, GIVE VIEWS OUT
AND STRUCTURE THE PHASES OF DEVELOP-
MENT

GREENWICH HITHE. LEAFY NEIGHBOUR-
HOODS AND STYLISH APARTMENTS AROUND
AN ELABORATE VILLAGE FOCUS WHERE
HITHE STREET MEETS THE THAMES. THE
LOOKOUT PUBLIC HOUSE WITH BROAD VIEWS
FROM THE RIVER'S EDGE

BOATHOUSE AND YARD TO PROVIDE A NEW
HOME FOR THE LOCAL SAILING CLUB

SCHOOL CONVENIENTLY LOCATED AT THE
SOUTH EASTERN END OF THE PARK

RIVER WAY BUSINESS TENANTS RELOCATED
TO FORM A BUFFER ZONE BETWEEN THE NEW
RESIDENTIAL NEIGHBOURHOODS AND THE
INDUSTRIAL ACTIVITIES TO THE SOUTH EAST

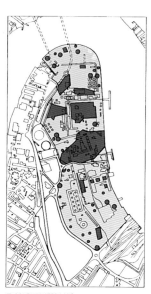

CONTAMINATED LAND
HEAVILY CONTAMINATED LAND

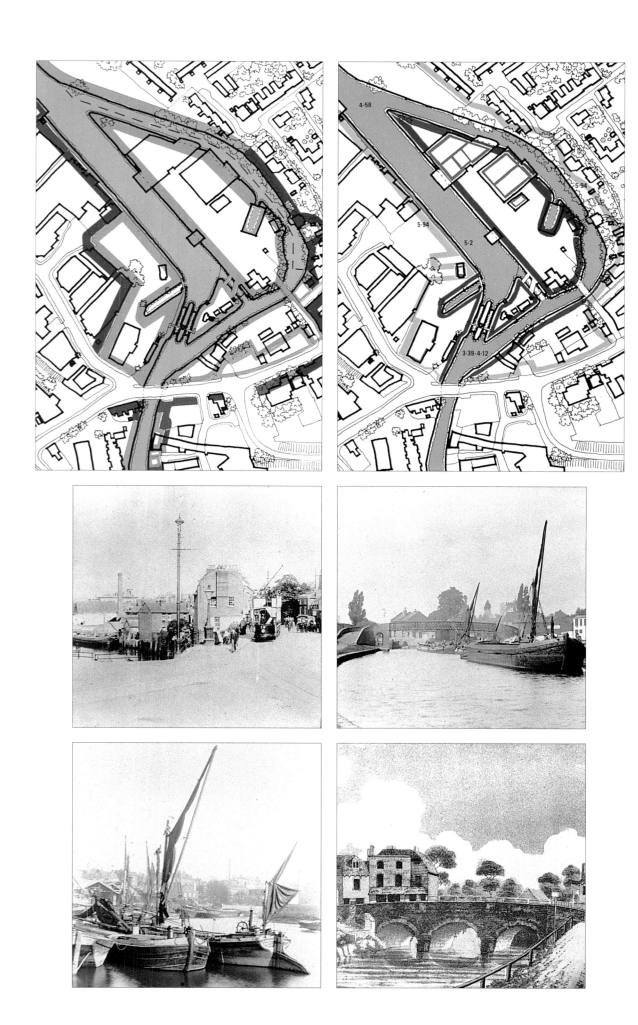

MAPS OF THE SITE AND HISTORICAL VIEWS

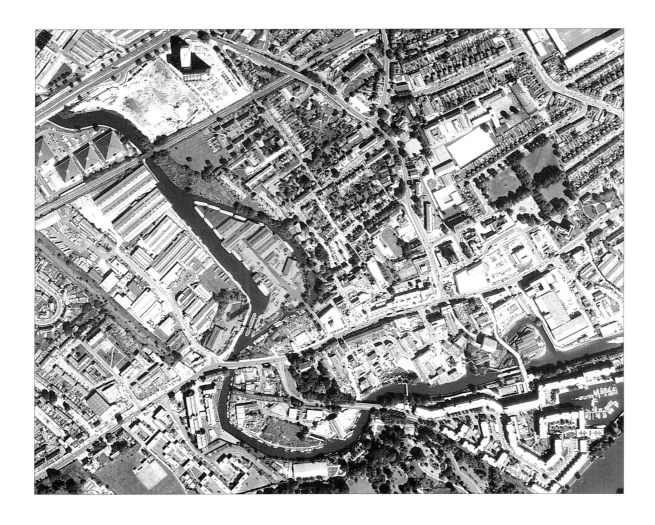

# BRENTFORD DOCK
## *LONDON BOROUGH OF HOUNSLOW 1988*

*Farrell's proposals for the redevelopment of Brentford Dock contain the familiar themes of continuity and re-use of existing historical artefacts to build upon the existing character of a site. The mixed-use scheme contained the wide range of facilities that Farrell views as essential to establish the traditional diversity of urban life.*

*The scheme for Brentford Dock drew upon the site's rich history, principally associated with canal architecture and engineering. The canal opened in 1794, and the lock, formerly known as 'Gauging Lock' was an important commercial point where cargoes were transferred from Thames lighters to narrowboats. Although the area had deteriorated into an isolated disused enclave, its unique nature remained with the survival of the locks, weirs, and bridges. Farrell's scheme retained the worthwhile struc-*

*tures and buildings which were interwoven into the new urban fabric.*

*Farrell emphasized the potential of the unique site surrounded by canals, by creating a dense framework of routes that provided maximum permeability through the built fabric to the water's edge. A sequence of spaces - paved pedestrian courts, towpaths, and quaysides - related the inside of the site to the edges and enhanced the canalside environment, creating places for public and social activity.*

*By reinforcing the existing character of the area and creating a new focus for leisure and activity, with a unique identity, Farrell sought to reintegrate the site into the surrounding context, and re-establish the traditional relationship between the canal and the local communities.*

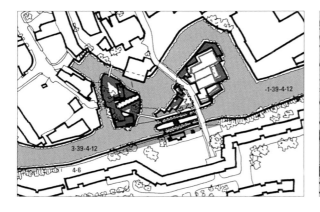

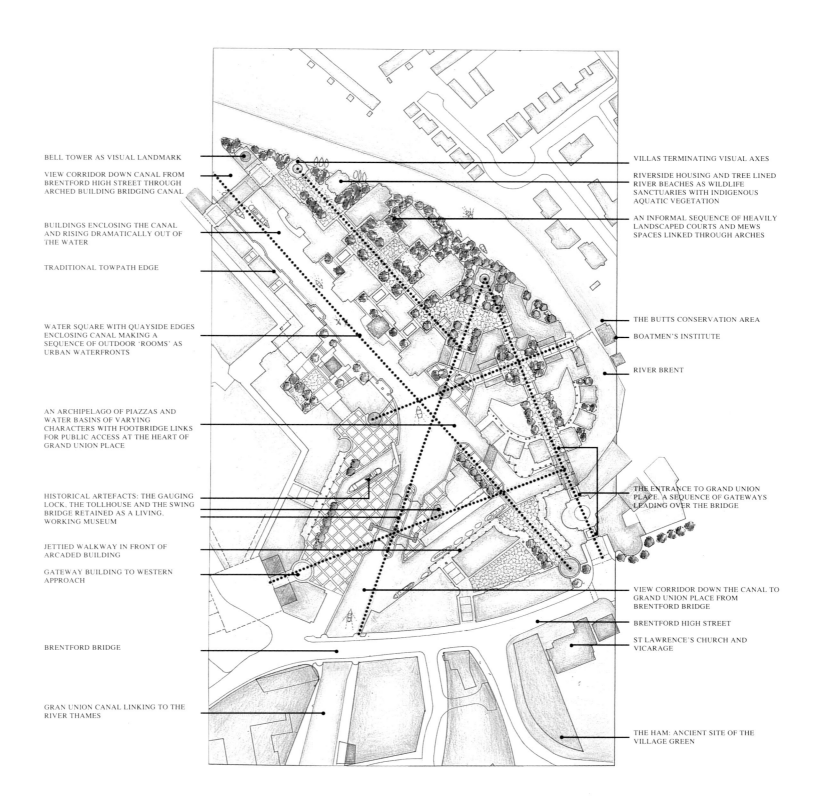

BELL TOWER AS VISUAL LANDMARK

VIEW CORRIDOR DOWN CANAL FROM
BRENTFORD HIGH STREET THROUGH
ARCHED BUILDING BRIDGING CANAL

BUILDINGS ENCLOSING THE CANAL
AND RISING DRAMATICALLY OUT OF
THE WATER

TRADITIONAL TOWPATH EDGE

WATER SQUARE WITH QUAYSIDE EDGES
ENCLOSING CANAL MAKING A
SEQUENCE OF OUTDOOR 'ROOMS' AS
URBAN WATERFRONTS

AN ARCHIPELAGO OF PIAZZAS AND
WATER BASINS OF VARYING
CHARACTERS WITH FOOTBRIDGE LINKS
FOR PUBLIC ACCESS AT THE HEART OF
GRAND UNION PLACE

HISTORICAL ARTEFACTS: THE GAUGING
LOCK, THE TOLLHOUSE AND THE SWING
BRIDGE RETAINED AS A LIVING,
WORKING MUSEUM

JETTIED WALKWAY IN FRONT OF
ARCADED BUILDING

GATEWAY BUILDING TO WESTERN
APPROACH

BRENTFORD BRIDGE

GRAN UNION CANAL LINKING TO THE
RIVER THAMES

VILLAS TERMINATING VISUAL AXES

RIVERSIDE HOUSING AND TREE LINED
RIVER BEACHES AS WILDLIFE
SANCTUARIES WITH INDIGENOUS
AQUATIC VEGETATION

AN INFORMAL SEQUENCE OF HEAVILY
LANDSCAPED COURTS AND MEWS
SPACES LINKED THROUGH ARCHES

THE BUTTS CONSERVATION AREA

BOATMEN'S INSTITUTE

RIVER BRENT

THE ENTRANCE TO GRAND UNION
PLACE. A SEQUENCE OF GATEWAYS
LEADING OVER THE BRIDGE

VIEW CORRIDOR DOWN THE CANAL TO
GRAND UNION PLACE FROM
BRENTFORD BRIDGE

BRENTFORD HIGH STREET

ST LAWRENCE'S CHURCH AND
VICARAGE

THE HAM: ANCIENT SITE OF THE
VILLAGE GREEN

PLAN SHOWING MASSING TOWNSCAPE AND LANDSCAPE

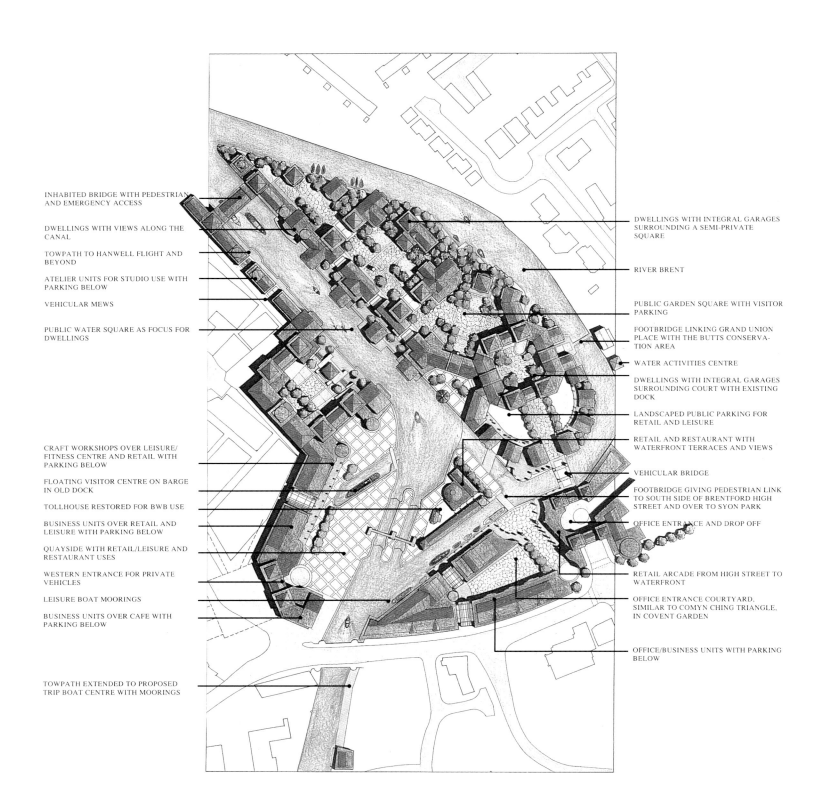

INHABITED BRIDGE WITH PEDESTRIAN AND EMERGENCY ACCESS

DWELLINGS WITH VIEWS ALONG THE CANAL

TOWPATH TO HANWELL FLIGHT AND BEYOND

ATELIER UNITS FOR STUDIO USE WITH PARKING BELOW

VEHICULAR MEWS

PUBLIC WATER SQUARE AS FOCUS FOR DWELLINGS

CRAFT WORKSHOPS OVER LEISURE/ FITNESS CENTRE AND RETAIL WITH PARKING BELOW

FLOATING VISITOR CENTRE ON BARGE IN OLD DOCK

TOLLHOUSE RESTORED FOR BWB USE

BUSINESS UNITS OVER RETAIL AND LEISURE WITH PARKING BELOW

QUAYSIDE WITH RETAIL/LEISURE AND RESTAURANT USES

WESTERN ENTRANCE FOR PRIVATE VEHICLES

LEISURE BOAT MOORINGS

BUSINESS UNITS OVER CAFE WITH PARKING BELOW

TOWPATH EXTENDED TO PROPOSED TRIP BOAT CENTRE WITH MOORINGS

DWELLINGS WITH INTEGRAL GARAGES SURROUNDING A SEMI-PRIVATE SQUARE

RIVER BRENT

PUBLIC GARDEN SQUARE WITH VISITOR PARKING

FOOTBRIDGE LINKING GRAND UNION PLACE WITH THE BUTTS CONSERVA- TION AREA

WATER ACTIVITIES CENTRE

DWELLINGS WITH INTEGRAL GARAGES SURROUNDING COURT WITH EXISTING DOCK

LANDSCAPED PUBLIC PARKING FOR RETAIL AND LEISURE

RETAIL AND RESTAURANT WITH WATERFRONT TERRACES AND VIEWS

VEHICULAR BRIDGE

FOOTBRIDGE GIVING PEDESTRIAN LINK TO SOUTH SIDE OF BRENTFORD HIGH STREET AND OVER TO SYON PARK

OFFICE ENTRANCE AND DROP OFF

RETAIL ARCADE FROM HIGH STREET TO WATERFRONT

OFFICE ENTRANCE COURTYARD, SIMILAR TO COMYN CHING TRIANGLE, IN COVENT GARDEN

OFFICE/BUSINESS UNITS WITH PARKING BELOW

PLAN SHOWING PRINCIPAL USES AND COMMUNICATIONS FRAMEWORK

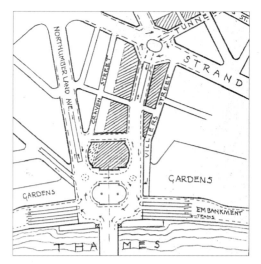

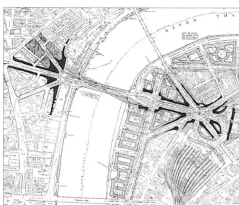

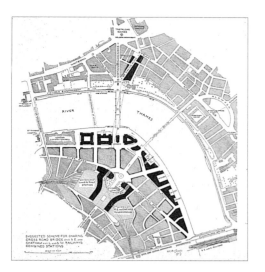

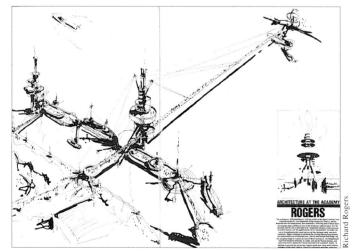

EARLIER PROPOSALS AND RELATED PROJECTS

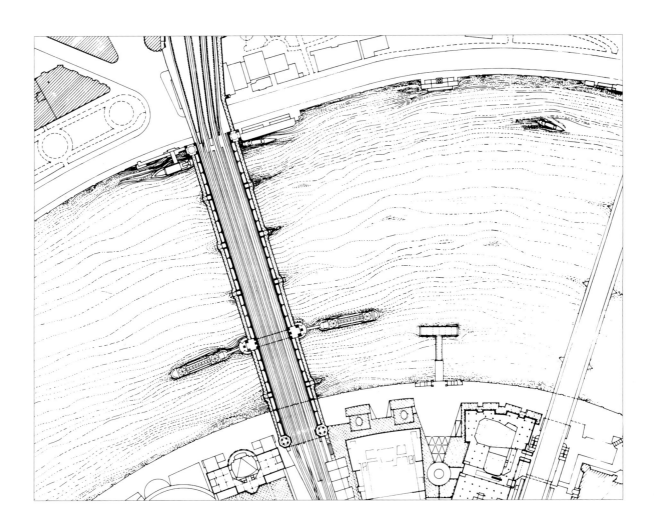

# HUNGERFORD BRIDGE
## *CITY OF WESTMINSTER AND LONDON BOROUGH OF LAMBETH*

*As a result of Farrell's involvement with Charing Cross and the South Bank Arts Centre, British Rail asked him to put forward a proposal for improvements to the existing 19th-century Hungerford Bridge, essentially a railway bridge with an inadequate pedestrian walkway attached on the downstream side. For Farrell, the bridge creates an unusual urban design opportunity: the bridge acts as a linear connector, but at the same time acts strongly as a physical object in its own right. What fascinates Farrell is the possibility of the bridge as a building, of using the space above the river to provide public amenities of a unique character.*

*The proposals embodied the recurring theme of priority given to the pedestrian over the car-user in the city, and formed part of the vision for improving the pedestrian link between the Strand and Waterloo, an essential link between the north and south banks - integrating the river into the city. The history of the bridge contained a number of threads that were common to Farrell's own approach - continuity and re-use of the existing.*

*Brunel himself had taken the idea for his scheme for a vast pedestrian route from the old Hungerford Bridge, and Farrell proposed to reinstate a bridge that drew inspiration from Brunel's. As well as this historical continuity, Hungerford Bridge was an example of the physical continuity of elements. When Brunel's suspension bridge was replaced in 1867, the new railway bridge made use of the existing stone pylons, which were supplemented by new*

*piers. Brunel himself re-utilized the chains from the demolished Hungerford structure on his subsequent Clifton Suspension Bridge at Bristol.*

*Farrell's scheme similarly re-uses the existing, with the addition of two new structures either side of Hungerford Bridge. Half of the new 8m wide pier to the east, facing the City, would be a widened, sheltered version of the walkway now in place. On the west side, facing Westminster, a new route would be created, lined with shops and leisure facilities. The new structure would be punctuated by towers, built on Brunel's stone pylons, and echoing the design of Brunel's elegant structure. The towers would reinstate the panoramic views from the bridge, at present blocked by the rail bridge, and would provide access to vessels moored to either side, which could be used for a museum or public attraction.*

*Brunel's original commission for the bridge was an attempt by the owners of Hungerford Market on the north bank to attract custom from across the river. Brunel's solution created a physical link but its elegance also made it a physical attraction in its own right. Farrell also views this project as an opportunity to give the bridge a greater civic role in the reintegration of the river. The scheme by Sir Richard Rogers involves the expensive removal of the bridge, and the relocation of Charing Cross on the south bank. Farrell instead provides a simpler and more feasible solution, which tests the designer's skill in creating something of quality out of what is given.*

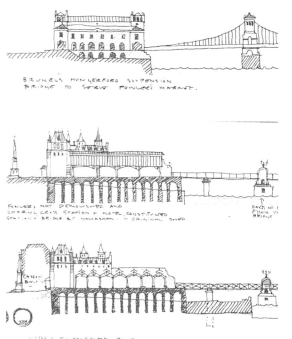

BRUNEL'S HUNGERFORD SUSPENSION
BRIDGE TO STEVE FOWLER'S MARKET.

FOWLER'S MKT DEMOLISHED AND
CHARING CROSS STATION & HOTEL CONSTRUCTED
STATION BRIDGE BY HAWKSHAW. — ORIGINAL SHED

PART OF
PIGEON VI
BRIDGE

VICTORIA EMBANKMENT BUILT
MORE SPAN HUT SCRAPPED REPLACED WITH PRETTY CONSTRUCTION
LINNEA. X BRITISH HAMISPHERE RAILWAY OFFICE

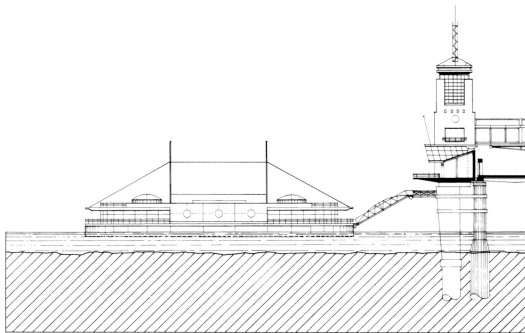

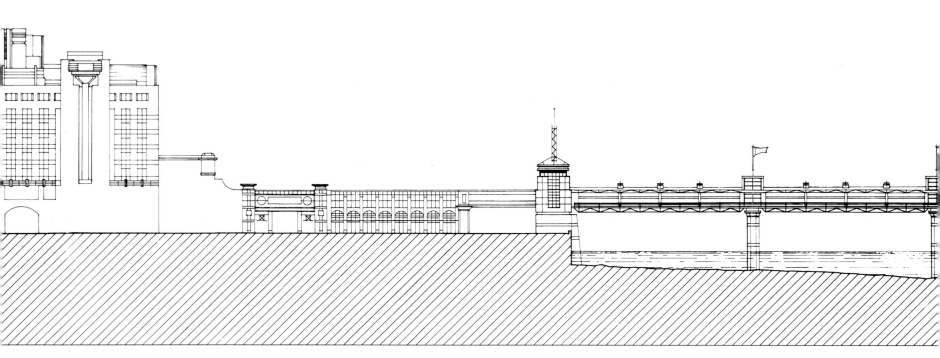

MODEL, CROSS SECTION, DRAWINGS SHOWING THE

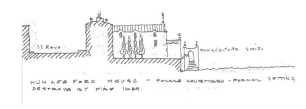

HUNGERFORD HOUSE - PAVILS COURTYARD - FORMAL SETTING
DESTROYED BY FIRE 1669.

HUNGERFORD MARKET 1682
MEAT FISH FRUIT - 1ST STARTED IN GROUNDS OF HOUSE
AND FULLY ESTABLISHED UPON DESTRUCTION OF H. HO.

FORMER MARKET (MEAT FISH VEG FRUIT) IN
DIRECT COMPETITION WITH COVENT GARDEN

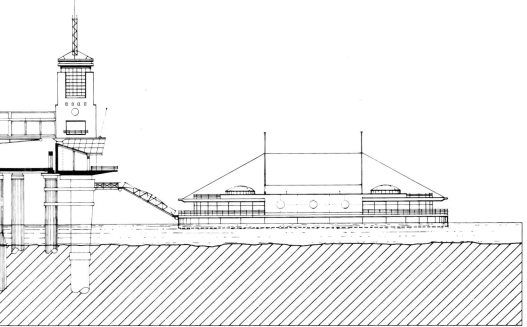

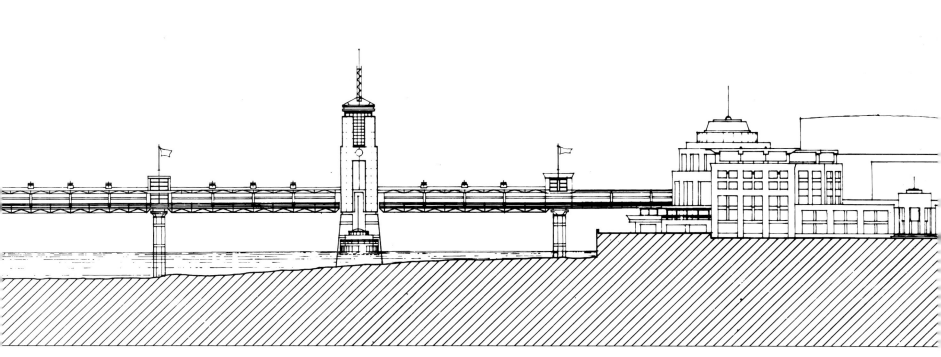

EVOLUTION OF THE SITE AND ELEVATION OF THE PROPOSALS

# MARKET HALLS

The market hall and the market square present a number of generic characteristics which at once offer the architect/urban designer a unique opportunity but also a unique set of problems. As an urban feature the market square has a particular role in the fabric of the city. It differs from the dense pattern of streets and blocks - it is the open space, the agora, and often forms the very heart of a neighbourhood.

Originally it was a multi-purpose space used for gatherings, festivals, religious and sporting events. These spaces were also often used for the selling of produce, goods that were more freely sold in the open air from temporary stalls, rather than shop-based items. In the 19th century these stalls were replaced with large structures constructed from steel and glass, which created an open air condition beneath a large protective roof. The permeability of these structures to the pedestrian routes through the agora maintained the sensation of open space within the squares, as does Archer's building in Smith Square, Westminster.

The market as a constituent part of the city acts strongly upon its surroundings - it sets the pattern of the connecting streets and the uses of the buildings, and also dictates the whole character of an area. These areas are usually very congested, though traditionally traffic did not penetrate into the middle of the neighbourhood, which remained predominantly a pedestrian domain. The market building itself reflects the urban characteristics of the large institution, which acts as a mini-community containing many different uses and activities within a single built entity. As an urban object the market hall acts as a complex with offices, shops, its own little streets and pattern of circulation, all beneath one roof.

The evolution of these urban markets involved the process of specialization from the sale of general goods to the more specific - Smithfield for meat, Billingsgate for fish. This transformation resulted in the emergence of the very specialized and private building type, the bonded warehouse, open only to specialist buyers and vendors. Tobacco Dock is an example of this type of market

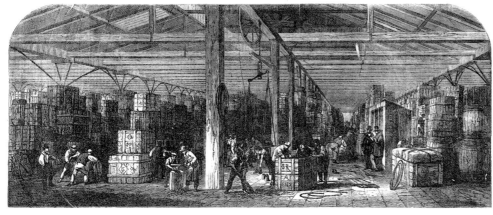

*Opposite*: Tobacco Dock; *Left from above*: Tobacco Dock engraving, historical photographs of Smithfield Market and Covent Garden

TOBACCO DOCK

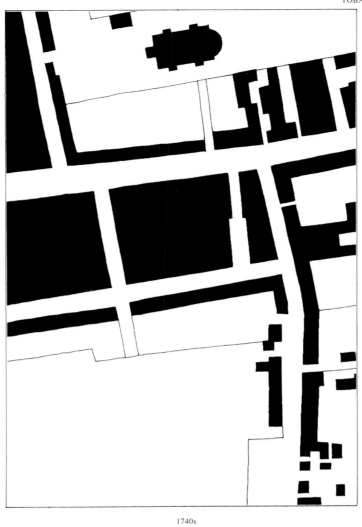

1740s

1850s

1970s

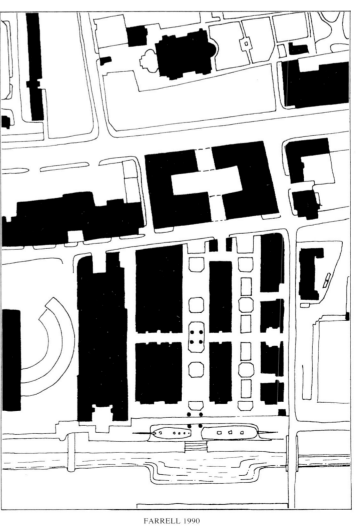

FARRELL 1990

building, which replaces the traditional permeability of the market hall with enclosure and security.

Many of these market buildings have now become obsolescent. Problems of congestion and refuse, and the great intensity of activity have led to the degeneration of the surrounding fabric. As attitudes to health and food hygiene have changed these markets have moved to new modern buildings on the edge of the city, stripping the remaining buildings and the neighbourhood of their raison d'être. For the urban designer this presents the particular problem of rejuvenating and finding a new use for not only a vast building but also its surrounding area. At Covent Garden there were initial reservations about the possibility of re-using the buildings and many viewed demolition as the only feasible option.

The history of Covent Garden reflects this evolution of the urban market type. Originally the square, laid out by Inigo Jones, was used to sell general produce from the Bedford Estate, but gradually developed into a specialized fruit and vegetable market. The area serviced the needs of the market, and by the 20th century Inigo Jones's elegant residential area had become a working area, with problems of congestion and deterioration. When the market moved out to New Covent Garden, American developments, such as Quincy Market in Boston, were used as a precedent for its regeneration as a multi-purpose shopping area, and a social, retail and fashion centre. The surrounding fabric was transformed to office and leisure use, with a mixture of studios, offices, shops and restaurants.

Farrell's involvement with Covent Garden began with the commission to design a temporary retail building for Clifton Nurseries on the vacant site to be used for the Royal Opera House extension. For Farrell this project presented an interesting urban design exercise in using landscape gardening to make a redundant site usable, but also in designing a small temporary building that could relate to the surrounding formality. Aligned centrally on the axis of King Street to terminate the vista along this route, the building took its form from the porticos of the market buildings and Inigo Jones's St Paul's Church. The classical details were interpreted with the expressive qualities of the new technology of light-weight demountable structures. The portico facade was split along its central axis, one half serving as the entrance to the shop, the other half acting purely as a screen to the car-parking.

But in urban design terms Farrell's proposals for the Royal Opera House extension, developed in 1980-1984, were an opportunity to explore a number of generic problems presented by the site. For Farrell the main objectives were to restore the square to something of the completeness intended in the scheme by Clutton, and to reinstate the physical and formal relationship between the two large

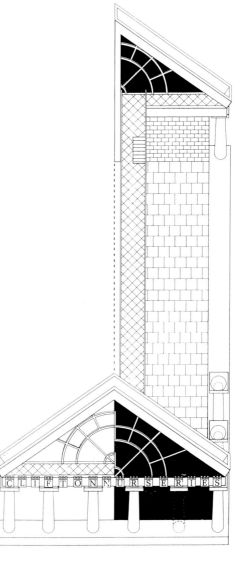

*Left and above*: Clifton Nurseries, Covent Garden

SPITALFIELDS MARKET

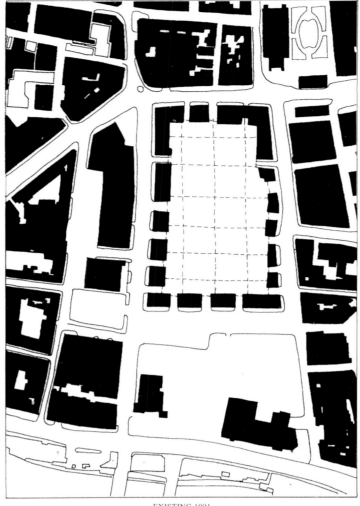
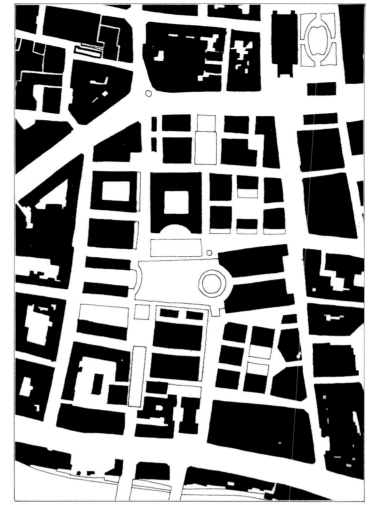

EXISTING 1991

KRIER 1986

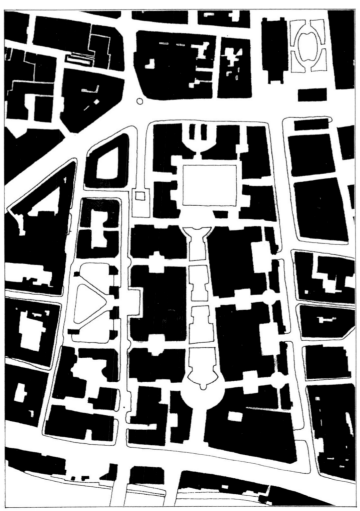

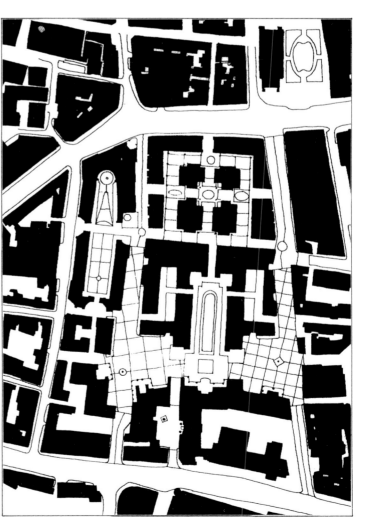

MacCORMAC 1990

FARRELL 1991

*Left*: Tower Hill Wine Vaults

COVENT GARDEN: OPERA HOUSE

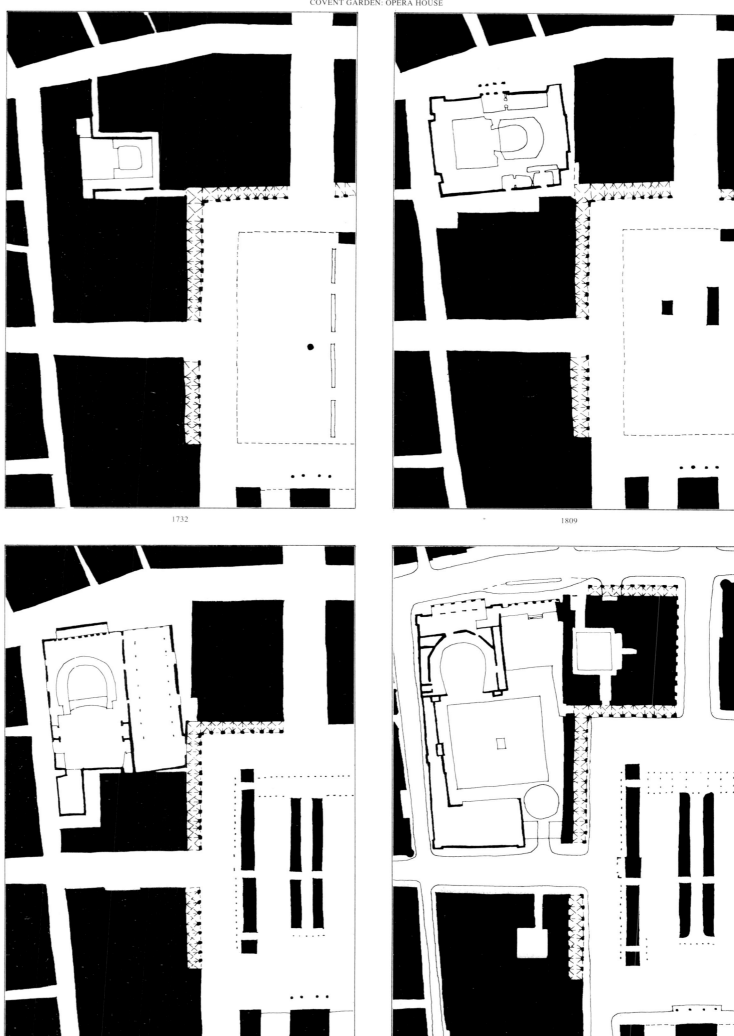

1732

1809

1858

FARRELL 1981

buildings that dominated the area - the market hall and the Opera House. Both buildings acted as mini-neighbourhoods, housing many uses and activities in a single built element, and Farrell was particularly fascinated that the Opera House expressed the different functions on each of its facades. It offered a blank facade to the piazza, and another urban design problem was how to relate the large scale of the Opera House to the more intimate scale of the buildings around the piazza.

Farrell designed a building, replicating Clutton's Bedford Chambers, to complete the square and restore the arcade. This block, which contained five separate office buildings, acted as an appropriate scale screen to the Opera House extension. Behind this building, a restored Floral Hall was transformed into an atrium with three levels of shopping, which related to the dominantly pedestrian and sheltered shopping experience within the existing market buildings. This enclosed arcade provided important new pedestrian routes by connecting the piazza to Bow Street, but also provided a link from the piazza to the Royal Opera House foyer areas - a connection lost when Barry re-oriented the Opera House to address Bow Street rather than the piazza, as had the previous five versions. Within this central element Farrell made provision for a new experimental theatre, and the wedge of space between the new and the existing building allowed the creation of generous booking and foyer space for the Opera House, as well as desired improvements to the side stage, rehearsal, technical and administration accommodation.

Another important aspect of the Royal Opera House proposals, in urban design terms, was Farrell's involvement with the concept of planning gain - how the public could benefit from private initiatives, but also how the extension to the Opera House could be funded by the office and retail provision on the site. Many of the design features that Farrell developed were to form the basis for the subsequent competition brief and the winning proposal.

Farrell's masterplan for Paternoster Square, as the name suggests, was based on the reinstated urban form of the market square. The original Paternoster Square had been filled with the purpose-built Newgate Market building after the Great Fire. Although Holford's scheme had retained the form of a square on the site, this 1960s' version was an open space of limited function and enclosure, in contrast to the manner in which the agora had evolved, being used more intensively with a market building in the centre. Farrell's square was based on this tradition, and attempted to re-invent the market building type, firstly with three small elements - the Loggia, the Pavilion, and a loggia attached to Building Group 5 - and in a later revision with a single building. These elements provided outdoor shelter and were not only permeable to the pedestrian routes across the site at ground level, but also formed vertical circulation between the two levels of the square, providing a link to St Paul's tube station via the underground shopping arcade.

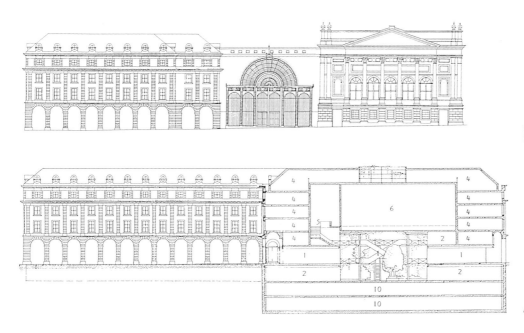

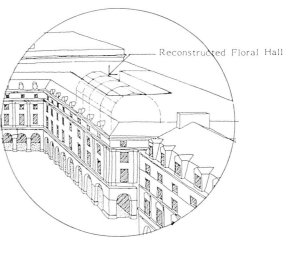

*Left and above*: Royal Opera House, Covent Garden

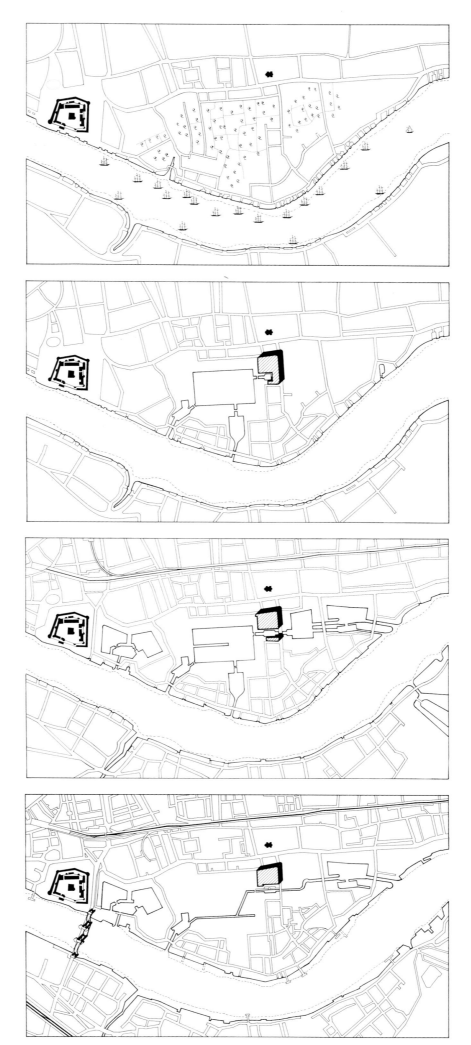

PLANS SHOWING HISTORICAL EVOLUTION OF THE SITE

# TOBACCO DOCK
### *LONDON BOROUGH OF TOWER HAMLETS 1985-1990*

The redevelopment of Tobacco Dock presented Farrell with a number of specific urban design problems particular to the building's original function as a highly-specialized bonded warehouse for the sale of tobacco, wines and spirits, and later sheepskins. Designed primarily to ensure security, the warehouse was a private and introverted space. The re-use of the building presented difficult problems, firstly due the general state of degeneration of the Docklands, and also because the building itself presented no connections or continuity with the area around it. The traditional permeability of the market hall was replaced by an impenetrable wall around the site.

The Grade 1 listed building, designed by architect David Asher Alexander and engineer John Rennie, was a revolutionary structure in which cast-iron constructions were integrated with stone and timber elements to create a component building that pioneered many principles of high-tech architecture. Farrell's initial task was two-fold: to restore and repair the existing fabric, and to invent a new viable use for the building which would ensure its conservation. The idea that emerged was to transform this specialized market building into a shopping village, similar to the concept adopted at Covent Garden.

Farrell's philosophy on the conversion of historic buildings is essentially one based on pragmatism - to utilize as much as possible of the existing fabric and inherent characteristics as the basis for new work. In the main space or 'Skin Floor' level, to fulfil light and ventilation requirements, Farrell extracted columns in groups of four to create courts, which created a sequence of open spaces between inserted retail accommodation. The façades of these elements were constructed from a modular system of light-weight steel components and glazing, to relate to the building's structure, and obstruct the open flow of space as little as possible. The retail units inserted into the vaults below were treated differently to relate to the heavier structure of this subterranean area. To save it from demolition, one of the original standing bays on the west façade was dismantled and reconstructed on the eastern façade.

It was vital too for Farrell to relate the scheme to the existing street pattern and pedestrian routes, and reverse the building's inherently internalized nature. New arches were cut through the perimeter wall, creating an entrance to Wapping Lane to the east, and two to the north along Pennington Street, setting up visual links to Hawksmoor's church, St George-in-the-East. The entrances related to the series of internal courts which formed routes through the building, accessing the new promenade and landscaped canal walk to the south.

Another interesting urban design feature of the scheme for Farrell was the creation, within this single-use building, of a project that contained the urban characteristics of the market hall: a complex or village with many diverse uses and activities under one roof. Tobacco Dock contained offices, shops, galleries, studios and attractions to recreate the role of the market hall as focal point of activity and leisure within the neighbourhood.

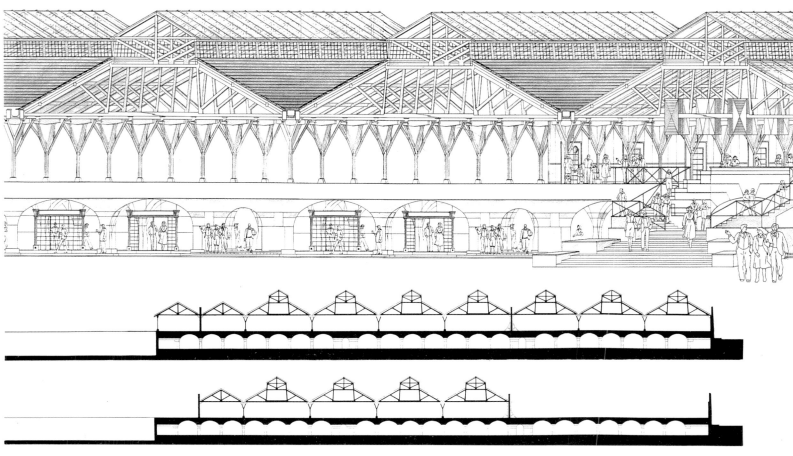

NEW SHOPS IN THE UPPER LEVEL SKIN FLOOR, AND GRADUAL RATIONALISATION AND CONSTRUCTION OF THE ORIGINAL STRUCTURE

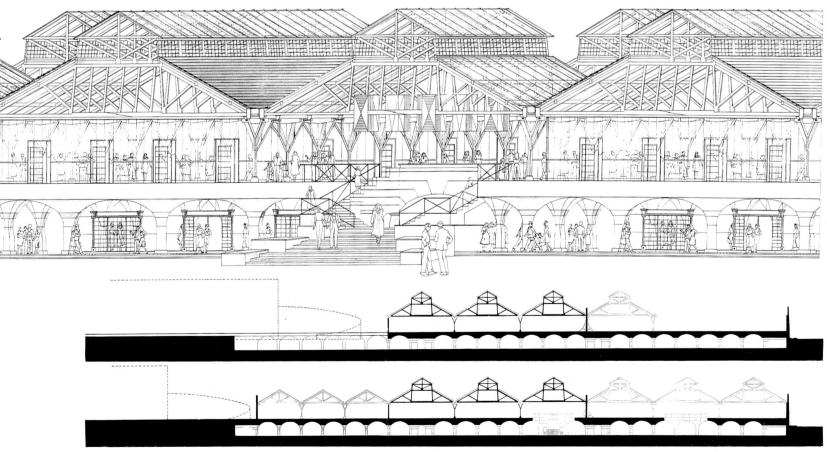

NEW SHOPS IN THE LOWER LEVEL VAULTS, AND GRADUAL RATIONALISATION AND CONSTRUCTION OF THE ORIGINAL STRUCTURE

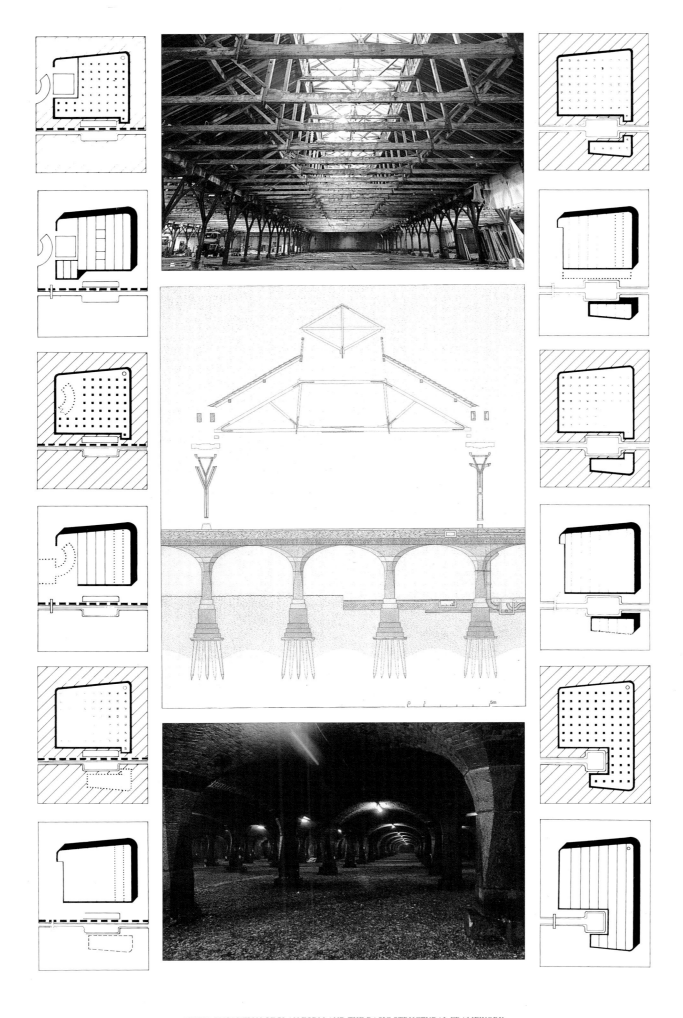

*ABOVE*: EVOLUTION OF PLAN FORM AND THE BASIC STRUCTURAL FRAMEWORK
*OPPOSITE*: THE CENTRAL MEETING POINT WITH OPENED ROOF AND VAULTS

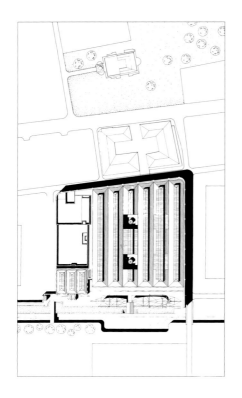
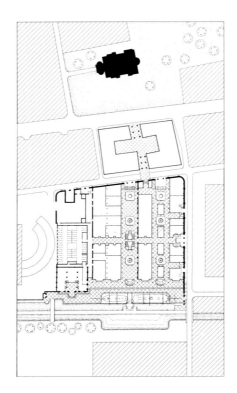
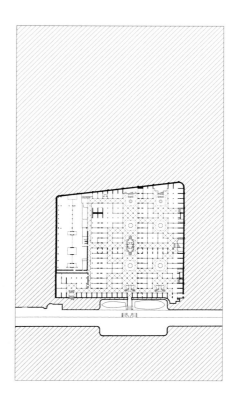
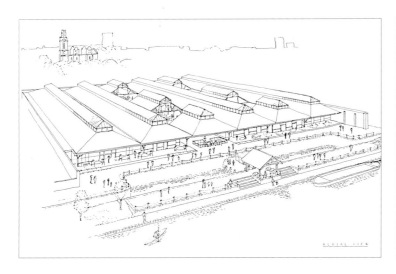

*ABOVE*: PLANS AND SKETCHES OF THE COMPLETED RECONSTRUCTION
*OPPOSITE*: VIEW FROM DOCKS WITH RESTORED GABLE ENDS TO MAIN BUILDING

99

THE MARKET USED FOR VICTORY CELEBRATIONS, HAWKSMOOR'S CHRIST CHURCH AND THE EXTERIOR OF THE MARKET AND MODEL OF PROPOSALS

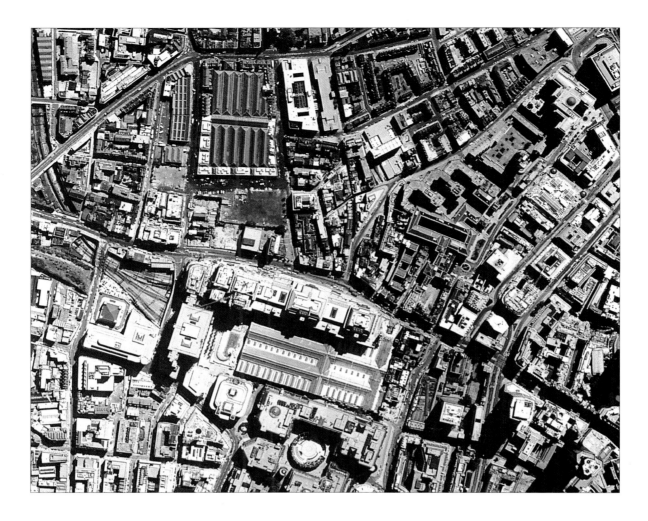

# SPITALFIELDS MARKET
## *LONDON BOROUGH OF TOWER HAMLETS 1991*

The urban design project for the redevelopment of Spitalfields Market was of great interest to Farrell because it so clearly illustrated the particular problems suffered by such areas after the market, the very heart of the neighbourhood, has relocated. What remained for Farrell to work with were the specific relationships of the surrounding streets to the large market square and to the major routes of Bishopsgate to the east and Commercial Street to the west, and a very large group of market buildings, some of which were listed.

As at Mansion House, the project, commissioned by Save Britain's Heritage, evolved from concern generated by an earlier proposal to replace all the existing buildings with massive office blocks. Farrell's proposals were based on the familiar theme of re-using and adapting the existing buildings, to reinstate them as the centre of activity within the local community. The inherent characteristics of the market building type, as a mini-neighbourhood containing a variety of small elements and uses, was taken as the model for redevelopment. Small units suitable for shops and restaurants were located along Brushfield Street and Lamb Street, and the large market hall housed an undercover retail market with mezzanine level for additional shops, and a central space for public performances and activities.

Farrell's desire for historical continuity was further addressed in the design of the new-built elements on the site. In contrast to the massive scale of the proposed office development, which related only to the new buildings over Liverpool Street Station, Farrell designed a series of separate office blocks that responded in scale and character to the existing fabric. Placed at the western end of the site, the buildings were arranged around a central court that provided a route from Bishopsgate to the retail facilities at the centre of the site. Farrell's particular concern was to establish a high level of penetrability through the site, and an irregular non-orthogonal plan was developed that related to and reflected the layout of the existing streets. The traditional pattern of movement across the site from east to west was crossed by subsidiary routes that accessed the centre of the scheme. These new routes linked a series of open spaces and squares that created vistas and focal points for the pedestrian within and beyond the site. The scale of the new buildings retained the view of Hawksmoor's Christ Church, framed by the low market buildings and the Georgian houses opposite.

Another important feature of the scheme, as an urban design approach, was that the masterplan provided a framework for development that could occur gradually over time, with new buildings commissioned only when demand arose. This also allowed for a number of architects to be involved, which would generate a variety of architectural responses, that for Farrell would recreate the qualities of diversity and interest found in traditional urban architecture.

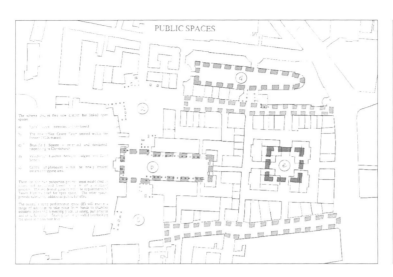

PUBLIC SPACES

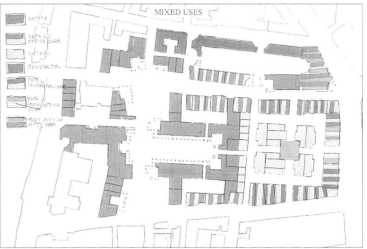

MIXED USES

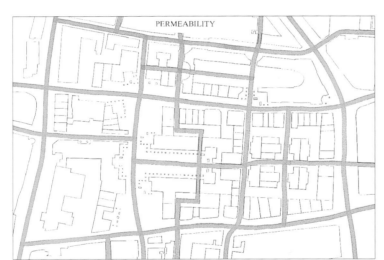

PERMEABILITY

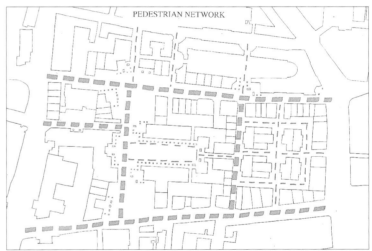

PEDESTRIAN NETWORK

PROPOSED SCHEME

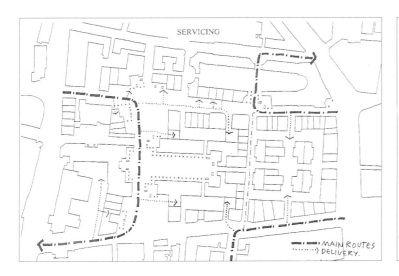

SERVICING

MAIN ROUTES
DELIVERY.

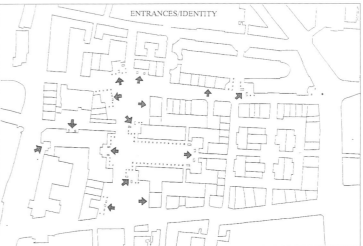

ENTRANCES/IDENTITY

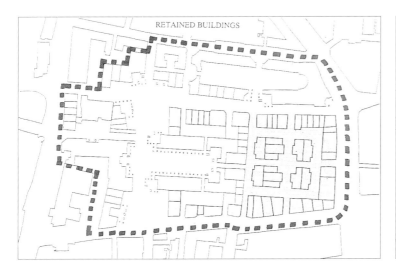

RETAINED BUILDINGS

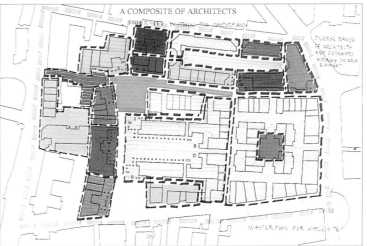

A COMPOSITE OF ARCHITECTS

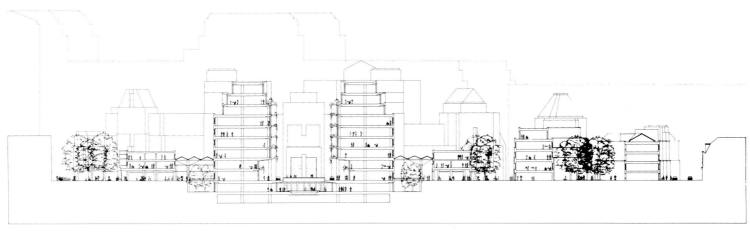

PROPOSED SCHEME

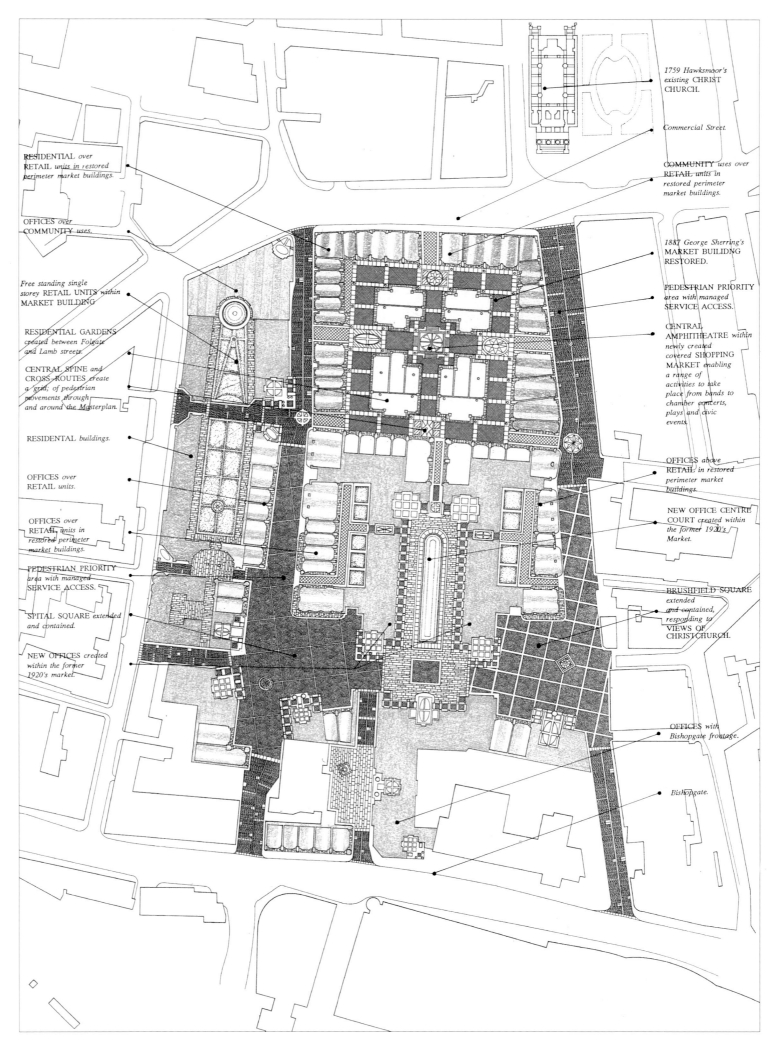

1759 Hawksmoor's
existing CHRIST
CHURCH.

Commercial Street.

COMMUNITY uses over
RETAIL units in
restored perimeter
market buildings.

1887 George Sherring's
MARKET BUILIDNG
RESTORED.

PEDESTRIAN PRIORITY
area with managed
SERVICE ACCESS.

CENTRAL
AMPHITHEATRE within
newly created
covered SHOPPING
MARKET enabling
a range of
activities to take
place from bands to
chamber concerts,
plays and civic
events.

OFFICES above
RETAIL in restored
perimeter market
buildings.

NEW OFFICE CENTRE
COURT created within
the former 1920's
Market.

BRUSHFIELD SQUARE
extended
and contained,
responding to
VIEWS OF
CHRISTCHURCH.

OFFICES with
Bishopgate frontage.

Bishopgate.

RESIDENTIAL over
RETAIL units in restored
perimeter market buildings.

OFFICES over
COMMUNITY uses.

Free standing single
storey RETAIL UNITS within
MARKET BUILDING

RESIDENTIAL GARDENS
created between Folgate
and Lamb streets.

CENTRAL SPINE and
CROSS ROUTES create
a grid; of pedestrian
movements through
and around the Masterplan.

RESIDENTAL buildings.

OFFICES over
RETAIL units.

OFFICES over
RETAIL units in
restored perimeter
market buildings.

PEDESTRIAN PRIORITY
area with managed
SERVICE ACCESS.

SPITAL SQUARE extended
and contained.

NEW OFFICES created
within the former
1920's market.

THE MASTERPLAN

104

VIEWS DOWN BRUSHFIELD STREET AND LAMB STREET: RETAINED MARKET BUILDINGS IN THE FOREGROUND, BISHOPSGATE DEVELOPMENT IN THE DISTANCE

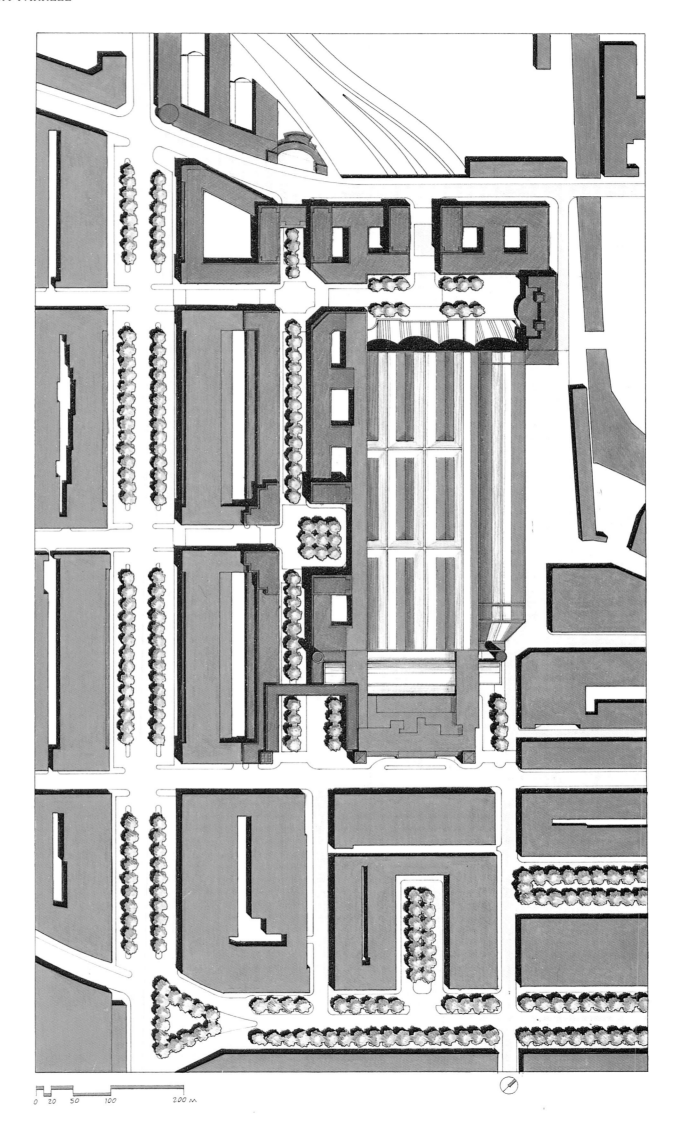

# RAILWAY STATIONS AND RAILWAY LAND

Farrell's interest in railway stations and railway lines is at two levels: at the macro-scale as a series of powerful geometries and network of routes superimposed on the almost medieval fabric of London in the 19th century; and at a micro-level relating to the station as an urban element and the effect it exerts upon the surrounding area.

The urban form of London was radically altered with the development of the railways that connected the capital to the rest of the country. The simple geographic fact that London lies at the base of the country meant that routes from the industrial north were primarily used to transport goods to the docks and to the large market of London itself. The stations terminating these routes from the north were primarily goods stations which did not penetrate into the heart of the city, but were instead positioned at distribution points along the peripheral line of the canal system that circled London from Brentford to the docks at Lime House. Such stations include King's Cross, Euston, Marylebone and St Pancras, with routes from the west terminating at Paddington, and from the east at Liverpool Street.

In contrast, the lines from the south were primarily passenger lines, transporting commuters from dormitory towns serving London. Consequently, it was essential for these stations to be placed nearer the centre of London. For the rival private companies this meant crossing the river and involved the struggle to find sites on the north bank, as occurred at Charing Cross, Victoria, Blackfriars and Cannon Street. Waterloo stopped short, but an underground railway was built to connect the terminus with the City. London Bridge station also remained on the south bank, as its proximity to the existing bridge provided easy access to the north bank. Crossing the Thames also involved raising the lines long before they reached the river, to connect to the higher level of the north bank. The construction of a number of elevated viaducts created enormous urban intrusion that dominated the pattern of development on the south bank. Due to greater competition between the railway companies, the routes from the south lacked the coherence of those entering from the north and new lines frequently crossed those already existing.

The first underground railway, the Circle Line, was constructed to link the stations placed around the edge of the city. The extensive underground system that developed was predominantly a north-London-based commuter system providing direct access into the centre of London from the stations.

At the micro-scale, the stations went through several phases of development. Generally the stations themselves were fine buildings, with dramatic train halls behind. The north London stations expanded with large goods yards placed beside the original terminus. For Farrell the station as an urban element embodies the mono-functional characteristics of the large institution, but unlike the museum or opera house, the station created problems of dirt and intense activity of movement which had a detrimental effect upon the environment. In particular the stations

*Opposite*: Paddington Basin masterplan; *left*: Historical photographs of Paddington Station and King's Cross Station

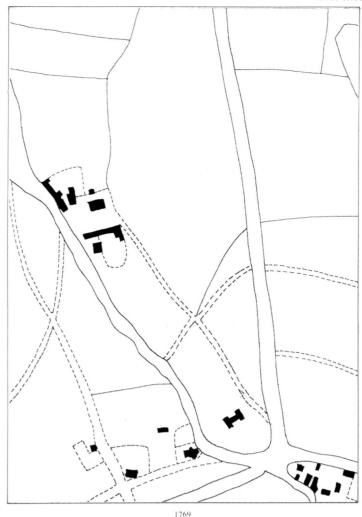

1769

1846

FOSTER 1987

FARRELL 1987

along the Marylebone Road, from Paddington to King's Cross, severely disrupted connections to the north of this main artery, with disastrous effects upon the economic fortunes of the areas around the station.

As an urban designer in London, Farrell pinpoints the importance of healing the wounds and damage inflicted on numerous areas by the arrival of the railways. The regeneration of the station and its hinterland has been a major focus of attention, particularly in the last ten years. For Farrell this involves primarily understanding the relationship of the station, as large mono-functional monster, to the surrounding fabric, and the problems specific to this urban element. For the great northern stations the problem involves the redevelopment of vast tracts of surfeit land where goods yards and industrial activities were once located; whereas for the stations to the south, built on very small pieces of land, expansion is necessarily upwards, in air-rights developments, as at Charing Cross or Cannon Street.

At a smaller scale, the underground station replicates the characteristics of the large terminus, as point of connection, often forming the heart of a neighbourhood. Farrell has been involved with proposals for two underground stations which emphasize this pivotal role, at South Kensington and Hammersmith Broadway.

South Kensington was originally the nucleus of the area, at the crossroads of various routes. The area gained importance with the building of the museums and cultural buildings to the north, and the construction of the Circle and District Lines station, in 1868, provided access to this important area. Farrell's main task, in urban design terms, was to build upon the station's raison d'être as the principal point of access and circulation, and enhance its relationship to the surrounding area. It was also important to recognize that the open-air station was regarded as an asset by passengers. The underground line had been cut through the existing street pattern and formed a barrier between the area to the north and south of the station. Farrell began by reconnecting severed routes across the site with a new glazed shopping arcade between the three new-built elements. This formed a sheltered route from north to south, but also westwards to a new public space at the corner of the triangular site. A new station concourse connecting to the museums and parks to the north was linked to the improved subway. A new entrance, crowned by a tower element, announced the station at the end of the Exhibition Road axis.

The scheme for Hammersmith Broadway was developed in 1984 and Farrell's primary concern was to create a coherent pedestrian route network out of the existing chaos. The site, originally the village centre, had become an isolated transport interchange on a traffic island. Farrell established a pedestrian ground domain of gardens, shops and cafés that connected routes across the site, with the

*Left*: Charing Cross Station and East Putney Station

SOUTH KENSINGTON

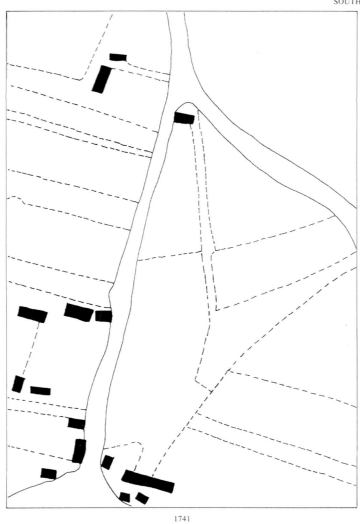

1741

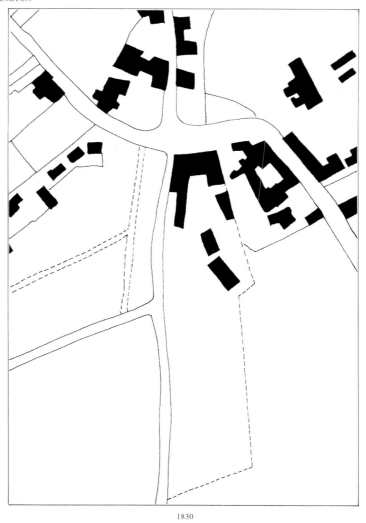

1830

EXISTING 1991

FARRELL 1991

transport facilities of the new bus station and improved Underground station. This convergence of activity reinstated the site as a working element within the fabric of Hammersmith. The restored existing buildings formed a backdrop to a new point of connection and movement. For Farrell this scheme demonstrates that a piece of urban design can have an extensive life that continues through changes of client and use, as with the Effra scheme. The important elements of urban design projects are connected with infrastructure and underlying principles, such as concern for the pedestrian, and these can often be independent of use.

For Farrell the proposals for Crossrail and Thameslink are particularly fascinating because the projects will radically alter the traditional pattern of terminus stations and radiating routes within London. Instead, with connections through the Channel Tunnel, London would become part of a larger network of rail routes connecting the rest of the country to Europe. Farrell was commissioned by British Rail to study the effects of the Thameslink project on major locations in central London and to devise a series of studies for the proposed Thameslink stations.

At Blackfriars, Farrell designed a double-ended station that created a dramatic point of connection between the City to the north and the more isolated south bank. The existing 1960s' air-rights buildings over the station on the north bank limited the scope for comprehensive redevelopment, but Farrell created an impressive station hall, within the existing buildings, that connected the station to the Circle and District Line. On the south bank, the presence of the old goods station was re-established, with a new station building placed over the existing underground car park. The requirements of the new line and the geometry of the north bank station meant that the Thameslink platforms had to be located on the bridge itself. By adding a new superstructure to the existing listed bridge, Farrell seized the opportunity to transform the bridge into a unique architectural element that would bring activity and lighting onto the river, as Paul Gibson had proposed in the Thames Study initiative. Pedestrian movement across the river was facilitated by a travelator and grand concourse that ran beneath the platforms.

In order to create a coherent domain for pedestrian movement at London Bridge, Farrell had to radically redesign the unsatisfactory circulation routes through the station that were a consequence of incremental expansion over a number of years. A new concourse, at the original ground level, was created in the vaults beneath the platforms connecting the proposed Jubilee line extension and Thameslink to existing Network Southeast and bus services. Additional space for waiting areas, shops and cafés created provision for small private sector involvement which for Farrell is essential within vast mono-functional developments to form a relationship between new public spaces and the normality and activity of the streets beyond. To overcome the isolation of the station on the south bank, Farrell positioned the new main entrance on London Bridge to create a presence from across the river, with an underground travelator providing a physical connection to the City.

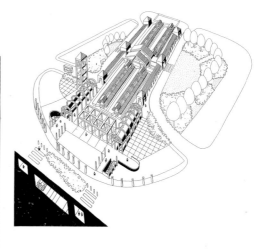

*Left and above*: Hammersmith Island

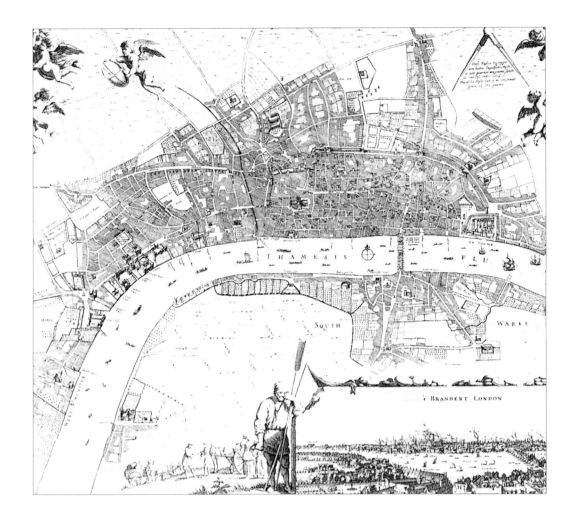

## CHARING CROSS
### *CITY OF WESTMINSTER 1985-1990*

*Situated on the north bank at the point of greatest curvature on the great bend in the river, Charing Cross station holds an important position of prominence within the urban fabric of London. The urban characteristics of the site which informed Farrell's approach were established by the great aristocratic houses that ran along the Strand in the 17th century. The result of this early development was large plot sizes, and the tradition of buildings with two facades, one addressing the road, the other the river. Although many of the existing buildings along the Strand were built between the wars they continued this urban tradition.*

*The railway version of Charing Cross had abandoned its river frontage, only addressing the Strand with the hotel facade. For Farrell, one of the most important aspects of the new scheme was to reinstate the river facade, and repair a gap in the sweeping riverscape of the north bank. Farrell was very interested in how to create a powerful building that would be primarily viewed at long distances from across the river, and drew upon the design features of the surrounding fabric. The building rises above the railway tracks in a layered composition of two-stepped elements. The dramatic facade consists of two vast glazed barrel vaults, which echo the original train shed, flanked by four solid towers. The form of these central elements is emphasized by the pale projecting lip which contrasts with the darkened glass within the arches. Farrell studied a number of buildings along the river, and noted that the architects, such as Waterhouse, used the*

*contrast between Portland stone and dark lead or zinc roofs to articulate the facade and produce an effect of layering. Farrell used the contrast between pale grey Sardinian granite and black powder-coated aluminium to emulate the features of the existing buildings and produce a dramatic effect of depth without the need for sunlight.*

*The Charing Cross scheme also provided the opportunity for Farrell to emphasize the inherent relationship between urban design and major buildings, and highlight the great effect which such schemes can have upon their surroundings. Unlike the north London stations, Charing Cross is predominantly a passenger station, without a massive goods yard beside it. The volume of activity, both vehicular and pedestrian, generated around this important transport interchange had left its surroundings in a state of degeneration. Farrell's scheme included provision for the major redevelopment of the areas around and beneath the station, and the enhancement of the routes through and alongside the building to the river and across to the south bank.*

*The fascination for Farrell of such schemes as Charing Cross is the manner in which the tripartite activity of form of urban buildings is heightened to an enormous degree of intensity. The scale of all the elements is exaggerated, the vast arched structure crowning the enormous volume of office accommodation, and the station itself, surrounded by its large ground-level hinterland of gardens, streets, shops and theatres, with its immense concentration of activity and movement.*

HISTORICAL DRAWINGS AND PHOTOGRAPHS

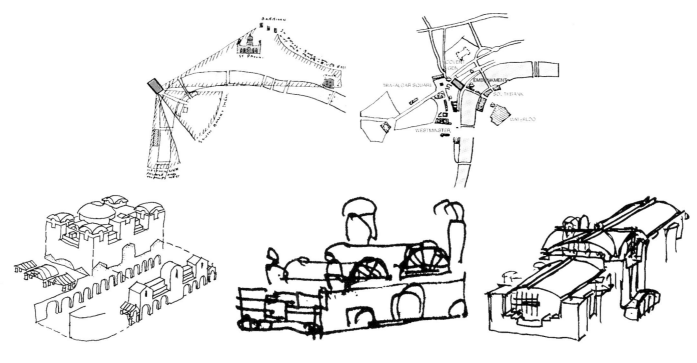

A EXTENSION OF HUNGERFORD PEDESTRIAN BRIDGE TO
   STATION CONCOURSE
B COVERED ESCALATOR LINK TO VILLIERS STREET
C PART PEDESTRIANISATION VILLIERS STREET
D CONCOURSE LEADING TO RELOCATED THEATRE,
   SHOPPING, SPORTS CENTRE AND TO THE SOUTH BANK
E VAULTS CONVERTED TO SHOPPING AND CATERING
   COMPLEX
F WEST SIDE OF VILLIERS STREET BUILT UP AS SHEET
   ARCHITECTURE WITH PEDESTRIAN ARCADE

G EAST SIDE OF VILLIERS STREET IMPROVED AND
   PART ARCADED
H IMPROVED SERVICE VEHICLE ROUTES
J SHOPS AND COLLECTORS MARKET
K ENTRANCE GATEWAYS EMBANKMENT PLACE
L OPENING UP AND IMPROVEMENT OF GARDENS
M REINSTATEMENT OF BARRY'S ORIGINAL RAILINGS
   AND LIGHTS TO STATION FORECOURT

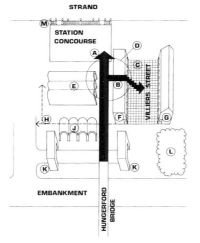

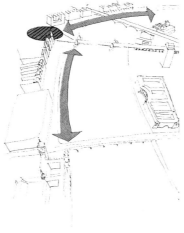

EARLY DESIGN STUDIES, EXISTING VIEWS AND PLANNED URBAN IMPROVEMENTS

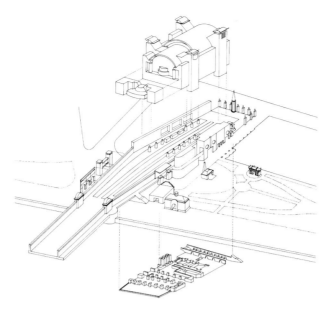

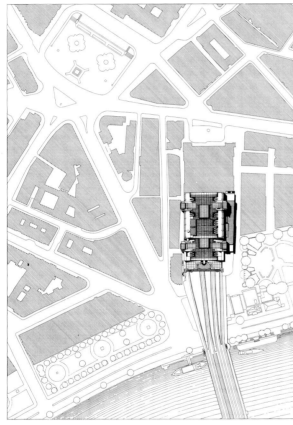

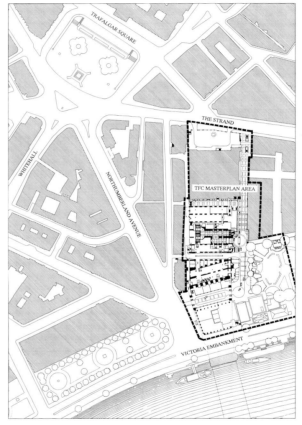

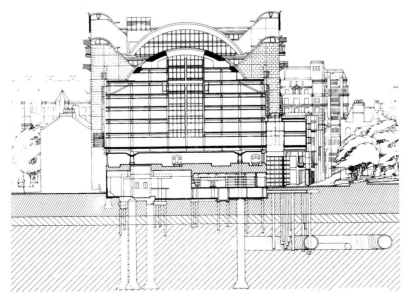

DRAWINGS OF OVERALL COMPLETED BUILDING AND CONTEXT

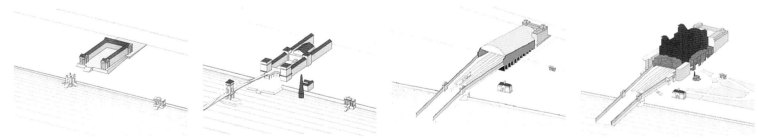

EVOLUTION OF THE RIVERSIDE SITE

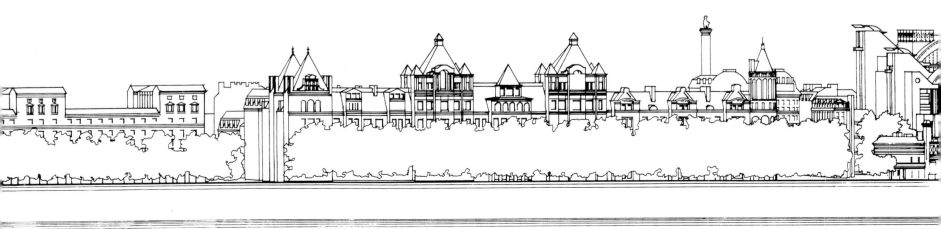

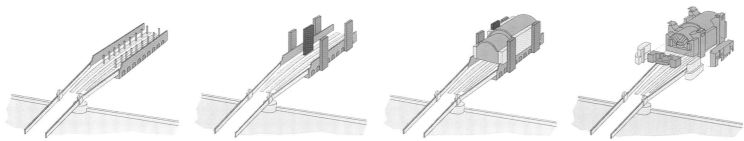

EVOLUTION OF THE BUILDING'S STRUCTURE AND FORM

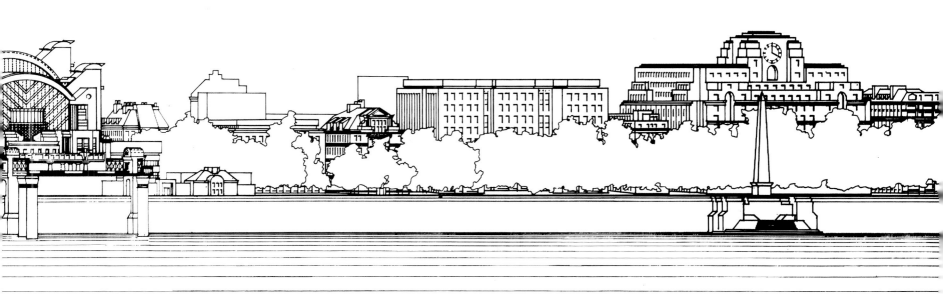

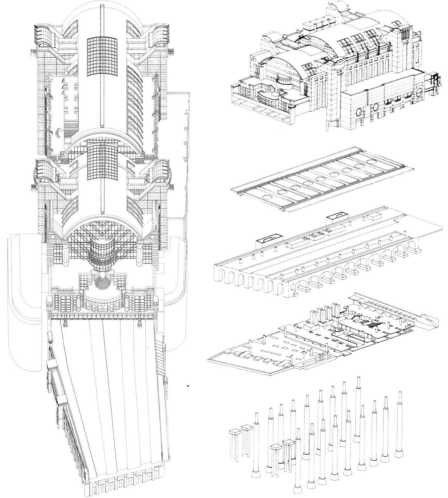

*ABOVE*: DRAWINGS OF FINISHED BUILDING
*OPPOSITE*: RESTORED RAILINGS IN FRONT OF THE VICTORIAN STATION WITH THE CHARING CROSS MONUMENT

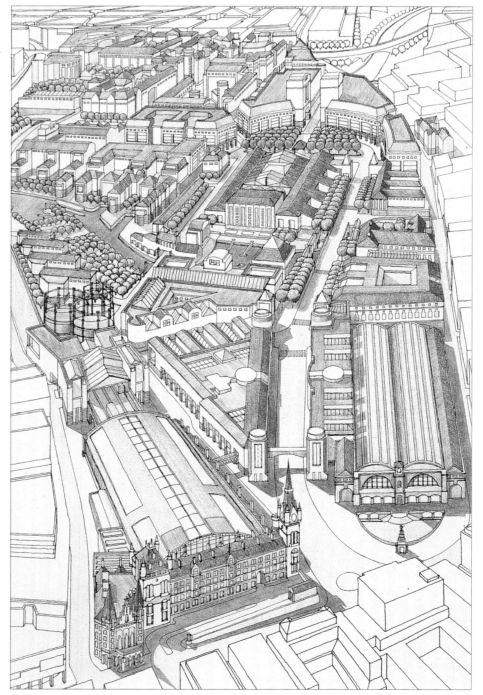

EARLY PHOTOS OF ST PANCRAS AND KING'S CROSS, AND AERIAL VIEW OF MASTERPLAN

# KING'S CROSS RAILWAY LANDS
## *LONDON BOROUGHS OF CAMDEN AND ISLINGTON 1987*

The competition for the redevelopment of King's Cross presented Farrell with the opportunity to design a more extensive masterplan for a site in central London than he had been involved with before. The main problems of the site were two-fold: the vast size of the derelict land that needed to be regenerated, and the isolation of the site created by the barriers of the great walls of the viaducts and storage areas, and the enormous scale of the stations themselves.

The main aim of the scheme was to recognize the enormous value and resource of the historical background of the site. The area not only contained the magnificent stations of King's Cross and St Pancras, but a number of artefacts and buildings, such as the gasometers, the canal and the granary buildings built by Lewis Cubitt in 1851. Farrell used these elements as the basis for the scheme, which sought to retain and build upon the specific identity and character of the area. Due to the depth of the site, seen in terms of the walking distance from the back of the site to Euston Road, Farrell created a centre for the scheme, based on the restored granary buildings, around which were placed a library, community centre and the main shopping area. This integrated the historical buildings, not as museum pieces, but as working elements within the community.

As a result of Farrell's concern for the pedestrian and the experience at ground level, particular attention was paid to distances while walking, but also to the visual relationships of built elements that were positioned to provide orientation, incentive and points of familiarity within the site. Farrell used buildings and little towers to end vistas and denote routes. The planning of the scheme also sought to decrease the isolated nature of the area, by generating improved penetrability of routes that extended beyond the boundaries of the site.

Between the two stations, Farrell created a new street, in contrast to other proposals that plugged the gap with a new building. Also a travelator directly linked the stations to the central main square, throwing the centre of gravity of the scheme northwards, and drawing activity into the heart of the site.

The character of the new-built fabric drew upon the qualities of 18th and 19th century town planning of squares and streets which Farrell believes have a great deal to offer the urban designer of today. The development of medium-rise buildings maintained a certain grain and consistency with the surrounding areas. The development of deep office plan buildings with atria generated the required amount of office accommodation, without resort to the tower block type, which creates problems of visual intrusion and disrupts the traditional infrastructure at ground level. In contrast to Foster's scheme, which offered a radical new vision of city living, Farrell's scheme was based upon a belief that urban design should be concerned with improving and enhancing urban life, rather than revolutionizing it.

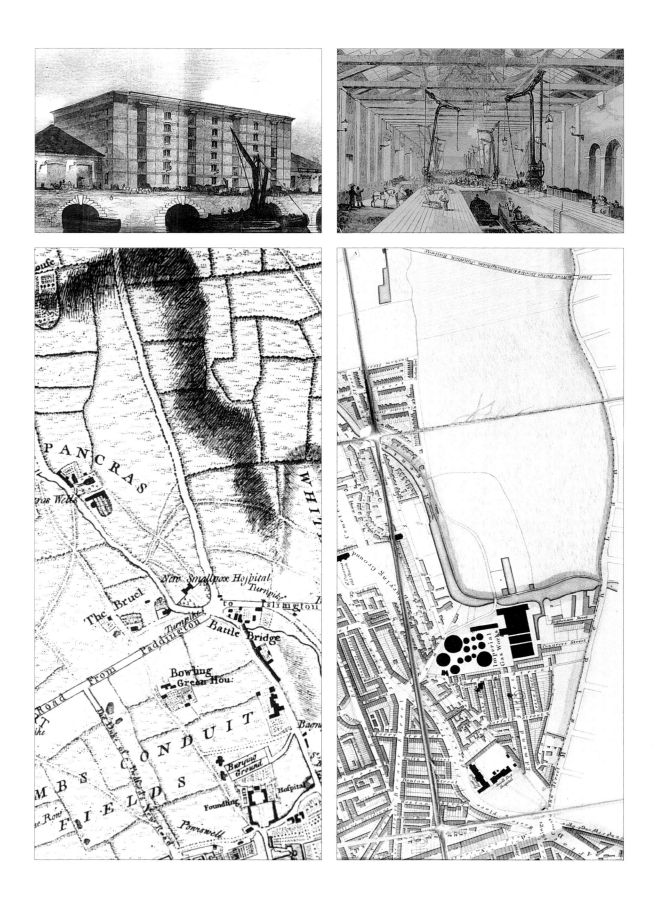

EARLY SITE PLANS AND DRAWINGS

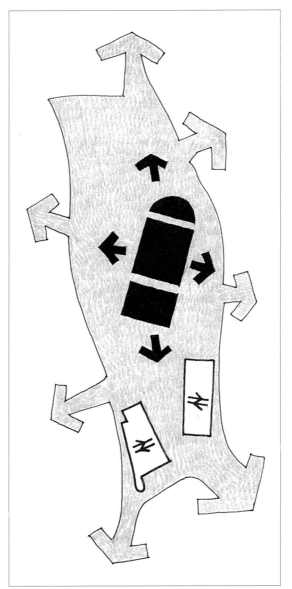
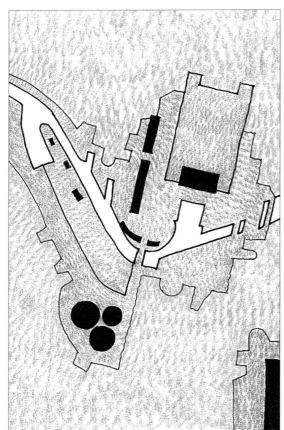
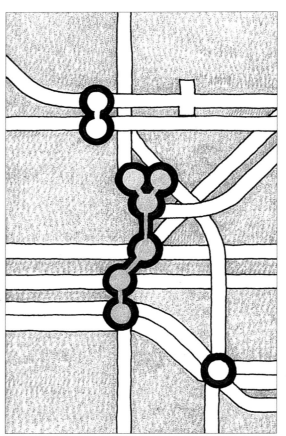

CONCEPT PLANS, AND DETAILED PLANS OF CANAL INTERCHANGE AND RAILWAY INTERCHANGE

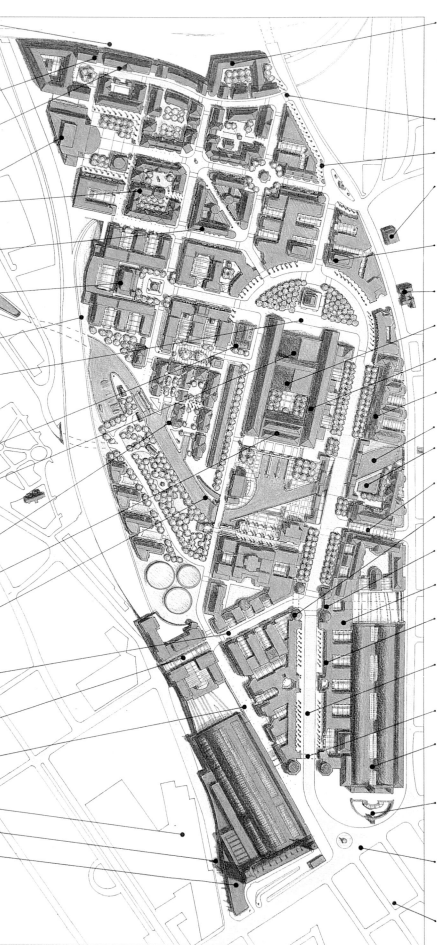

NORTH LONDON LINE presents strong boundary to site: over time roads and pathways will extend out of site

Multiple links for pedestrians and cycles to North and West

LIGHT INDUSTRIAL UNITS form buffer between railway and housing

LEISURE CENTRE

Development over new EAST COAST MAIN LINE RAIL LINK to St Pancras

Low rise mixed use buildings, housing, leisure, community uses and open spaces

OFFICES around atria and conservatories with mid-rise feature tower

FOOTPATHS AND CYCLE LINKS to Camley Street

NORTH SQUARE linked to King's Cross and St Pancras by low level travelator and to North London Station and Piccadilly Tube Station

Relocated GERMAN GYMNASIUM

THE CIVIC CENTRE: Council District Offices Library, Arts Centre Advice Bureau

HOUSING situated around new canal inlets

HERITAGE CENTRE with residential over

NEW BELOW GROUND RAIL LINK to Midland main line and to new King's Cross Low Level Station

NEW EAST-WEST CROSS-SITE ROAD linking Midland Road and York Way

OFFICES above railway and road junction

St Pancras pedestrian priority route and restricted hours service road

BRITISH LIBRARY

Midland Road

ST PANCRAS STATION including hotel and specialist shopping centre

21  Master Plan showing principal uses and communications framework

Reinstated NORTH LONDON LINE STATION linked by covered arcades to Civic Centre and Piccadilly Line Tube Station and integrated with Maiden Lane development

York Way viaduct over new East Coast main line rail link

Four road access points to York Way

Re-opened YORK ROAD UNDERGROUND STATION on Piccadilly Line connected into site

OFFICES with mid-rise feature tower over arcades and shops

Local existing COMMUNITY CENTRE

'THE CENTRE': shopping and leisure

WORKSHOPS above shopping and leisure

OFFICES around atria and conservatories

GRAND UNION CANAL

NEW CANAL BASIN with adjacent housing

CROSS-SITE ROAD replacing Goods Way

TRAVELATOR links King's Cross with 'The Centre'

Possible alternative cross-site road connection to York Way

NEW LOW LEVEL STATION below King's Cross Station

OFFICES over 2 storeys British Rail accommodation and retail

MAIN NORTH-SOUTH STREET lined at ground level with shops

MAJOR GATEWAY and first floor link between stations

KING'S CROSS STATION with restored façade, enlarged Concourse and increased passenger facilities

Sunken lower level LRT UNDERGROUND STATION improved passenger facilities around open square

EUSTON ROAD: surface level road crossings in addition to those at lower LRT concourse level

Future redevelopment of existing low rise buildings to south of Euston Road

PLAN OF USES AND COMMUNICATIONS

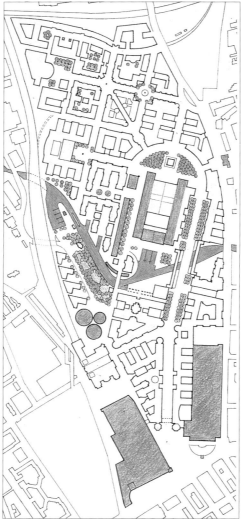

PLANS OF SHOPPING, PUBLIC BUILDINGS AND OFFICES, AND VIEWS OF THE MODEL

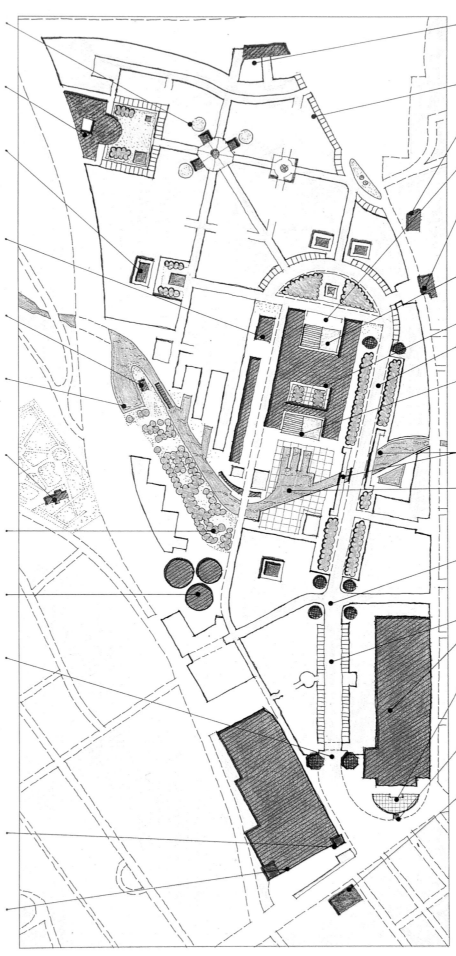

HOUSING *enclosing residents' private squares with corner shops*

LEISURE CENTRE *with local shops and public square as focus for residents*

FOUR MID-RISE TOWERS *of business use with penthouse roof tops rising to 12-13 storeys, are the only buildings in the scheme above 8 storeys*

1864 GERMAN GYMNASIUM *building with fine roof structure relocated as part of civic complex*

*Restored listed* Lock Keeper's *Cottage and existing* Canal Basin

MAJOR ENVIRONMENTAL IMPROVEMENTS TO CANAL *to form an ecological corridor and recreation centre*

*Ancient site c600 AD of* ST PANCRAS CHURCH. *Present 1350 building with well tree-ed graveyard*

*Preserved and protected* CAMLEY STREET NATURAL PARK

1834 *Historic decorated* GAS HOLDERS, *retained and restored*

*The plan suggests the removal of the Great Northern Hotel and one listed gas holder to give a wide and* IMPRESSIVE APPROACH TO THE NEW ARCADED STREET *and giving functional and visual access to the site. If the removal of the hotel is not achieved, the access can be modified accordingly*

*St Pancras Gothic Landmark* TOWER *on axis with gateway entrance to New King's Cross*

1868 *Sir George Gilbert Scott's existing Gothic* ST PANCRAS STATION *restored*

*1887-1917 Reinstated* MAIDEN LANE STATION *with paved square to forecourt with small shops*

ARCADED LINK *from railway station to tube station along York Way*

*Re-opened Edwardian tiled* UNDERGROUND STATION

NEW SQUARE *surrounded by civic buildings, shopping and arcades*

*Imposing and attractive Edwardian* SCHOOL BUILDING *visually linked to centre of New King's Cross*

*Formal* CIVIC CENTRE, *set between existing wings of Cubitt's granary*

'THE CENTRE'

*Generous tree-lined wide* AVENUE

1851 *Handsome* CUBITT GRANARY, *refurbished and re-establishing access for boats to Regents Canal forming Heritage Centre*

*Covered arcaded 'Palladian'* PEDESTRIAN BRIDGES

SOUTH SQUARE *with re-opened canal basin with pedestrian promenades surrounded by shops and housing*

TOWER *elements mark major change in streets and link the scheme's three main public street forms*

ARCADED MAIN STREET

*Cubitt's 1852 existing engineering masterpiece:* KING'S CROSS STATION

NEW PUBLIC SQUARE *at King's Cross with sunken space opening up underground station area*

*Recreated* MONUMENT *of King's Cross to George IV 1830*

*Existing* CAMDEN BOROUGH COUNCIL OFFICES *linked at ground, lower ground and upper levels across Euston Road to stations and New King's Cross square.*

22 *Master Plan showing massing, townscape and landscape. Important long and short distance views are unimpaired*

PLAN OF CONTEXT AND URBAN DESIGN

132

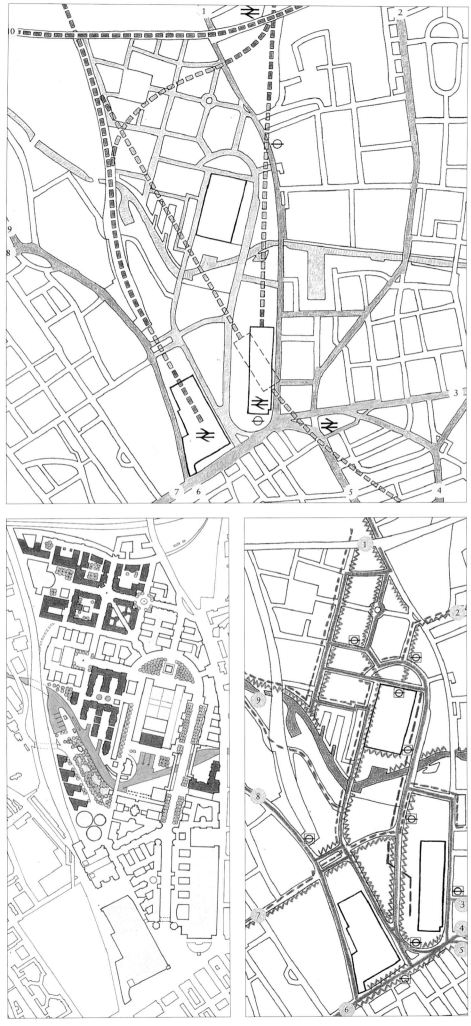

PLANS OF ROAD NETWORK, RESIDENTIAL USE AND PUBLIC TRANSPORT

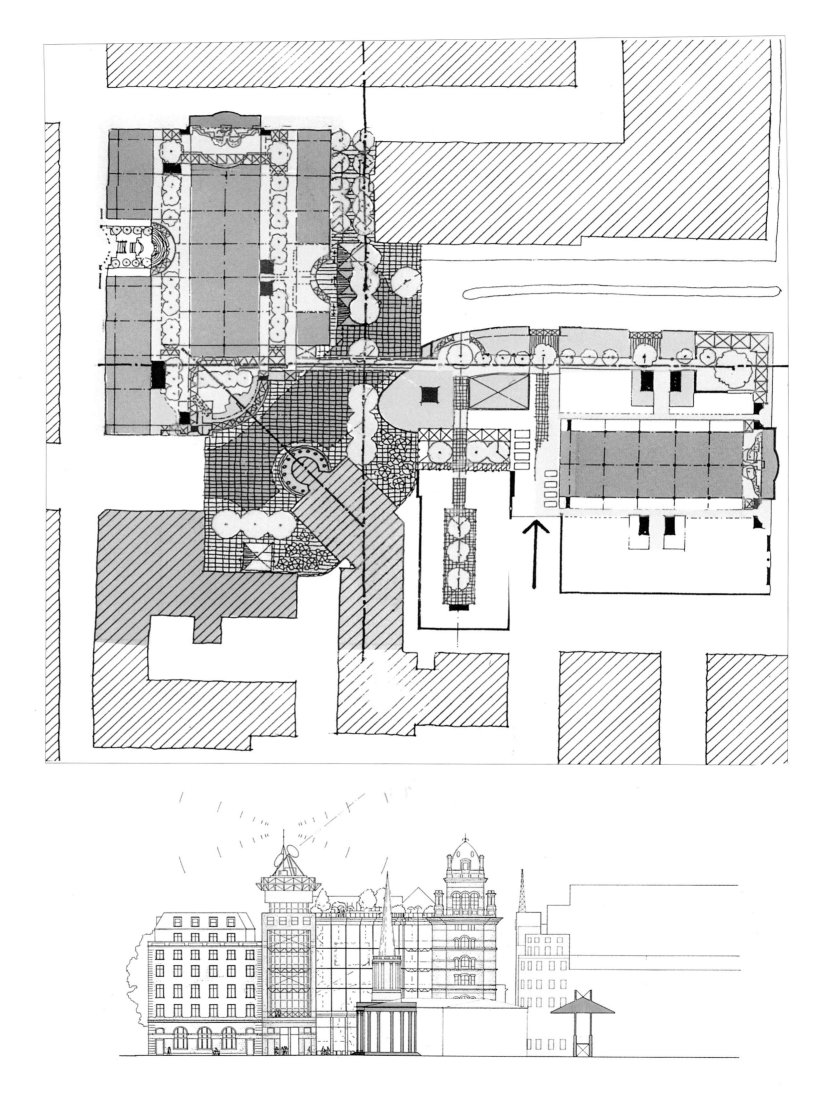

# LARGE INSTITUTIONS

The city as a single entity is made up of a multitude of small and diverse activities that give city life its unique vitality and specific nature. Within the urban fabric, buildings range from the smallest shops to large institutions. For Farrell the fascination of the institution, as an urban type, is that as it expands it takes on the characteristics of the city. It becomes a mini-city, or a village in itself, containing its own systems, infrastructure and amenities that service its many parts.

Another characteristic of the British institution - the BBC, the Oxbridge colleges - is the architectural expression of the village structure as a group of inter-related elements, rather than a great single architectural statement. A classic example of this urban element is the Palace of Westminster and Westminster Abbey, the government and religious complex which forms the centre of national power. The Houses of Parliament, seen as a single entity, is formed from a village of buildings of different periods, with the buildings designed by Barry and Pugin added to the original Westminster Hall, with the chapel below. Westminster Abbey consists of a number of elements for different functions: the church yard, the ecclesiastical offices, the cloisters, the Abbey itself and St George's Chapel. What interests Farrell is the contextual awareness of the architects such as Barry or Hawksmoor who added to the complex, using perpendicular gothic to express the concept of the buildings forming a coherent single entity. For Farrell, the Houses of Parliament is the large institution as 'gentle giant'. Vast in scale but broken down into component parts, it integrates with the surrounding fabric, and as an entity contains elements, such as the clock tower 'Big Ben', that provide a focal point of recognition for the institution as a whole.

The institution appears in many forms and includes many types: the market hall, the university campus, the hospital, the museum complex as in South Kensington, and the cultural complex as on the South Bank. The traditional development of the single-function institution or complex involves the absorption of other activities, including housing, shopping and transport connections. It is this inherent infra-structure and diversity of uses that Farrell believes is the key to the success of the mono-cultural complex as an urban element within the city. His proposals for a number of institutions are therefore based on the general themes of his urban design approach which begins with a concern for the public domain, a notion of spaces and scale, a distribution of building elements within a context, an understanding of a building type in the city, without necessary reference to use and function. For Farrell, historical examples such as the Bedford Estate, reinforce his belief that good urban design and planning can accommodate and go beyond changes in use. The squares and Georgian houses were originally built as a residential estate, but over time the buildings have absorbed educational and

*Opposite*: BBC Radio Headquarters; *Left*: Historical photographs of the Houses of Parliament and the Natural History Museum

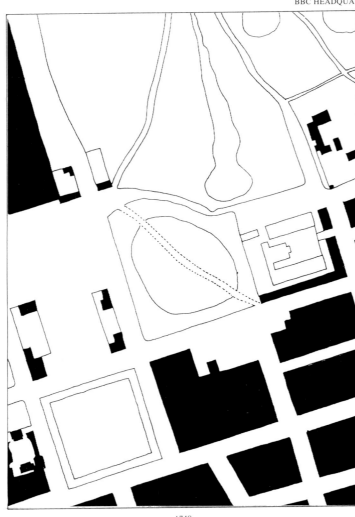

1740

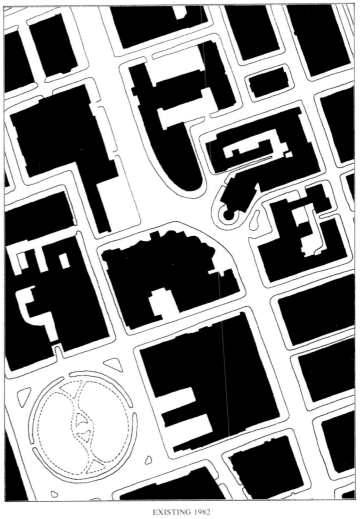

EXISTING 1982

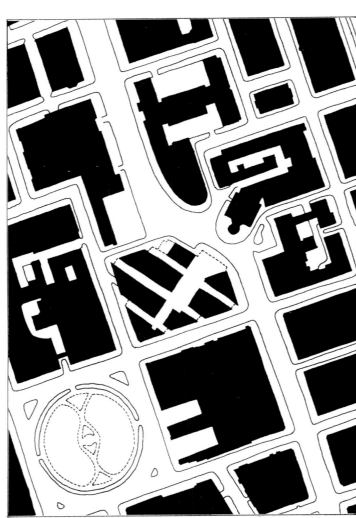

FOSTER 1982

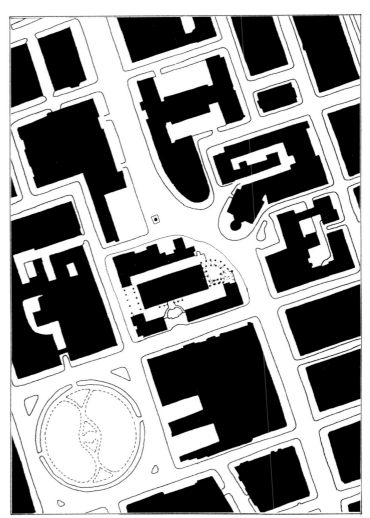

FARRELL 1982

hospital functions and small-scale offices. The recent desire for mono-cultural design and for casting areas, plots and buildings as fixed-use types runs counter to the British tradition of piecemeal evolving development. For Farrell diversity and flexibility are essential features of the changing urban scene, and the institution as urban element should relate to traditional aspects of a mixed-use city environment.

In 1982 Farrell was selected as one of ten practices to make a submission for the redevelopment of the BBC's Radio Headquarters, on the site of the Langham Hotel in Portland Place. Farrell was particularly interested by the BBC's self-image as a village of inter-related activities, and the scheme was based upon two concepts of the institution. The first was the major national institution as 'gentle giant', which rejected the ostentatious display of the mighty single architectural statement in favour of an incremental and multi-layered solution that integrated with the context around it. The second concept was for a 'city within a city', consisting of a structure of spaces and built elements whose inherent organization and relation-ships contributed to the understanding of the city as a whole. The scheme was based around a new circulation system with a central public space, or 'High Street' link, beneath the existing street. This connected Broadcasting House to a series of indoor spaces and doorways within the new core building placed in the centre of the new site. With limited demolition, this new-built element contained the broadcasting activities, with the retained Langham Hotel and the properties along Cavendish Place and Chandos Street providing ancillary facilities and a contextual wrapping for the technical facilities that related to the scale of the surrounding buildings. Farrell designed a number of new elements which related and harmo-nized with the existing elements to create a total composition. An electronic information window and atrium, placed opposite All Souls church, provided a modern counter-point to Nash's clever corner device, and with the new Langham tower in the restored Langham Hotel, Farrell made reference to All Souls spire and the original BBC Tower on top of Broadcasting House.

The educational institution of the Polytechnic of Central London, now the University of Westminster, was investigated by Farrell as part of an Urban Design Group initiative. For Farrell it was another interesting example of urban designer as coordinator, as in the Thames Study. Farrell developed a simple brief for the redevelopment of the site and buildings as a framework within which a number of architects, including Ron Herron, Francis Machin and David Gosling, could develop different responses. For Farrell the problems of the site and institution were a result of post-war planning, dictated by zoning and a mono-functional approach. The existing scheme symbolized the rejection of context, both historical

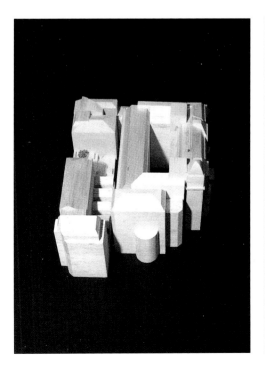
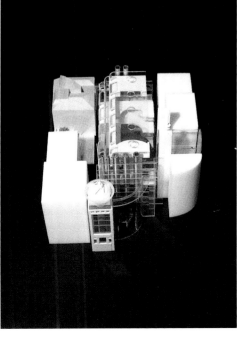

*Left*: BBC Radio Headquarters

137

SOUTH BANK ARTS CENTRE

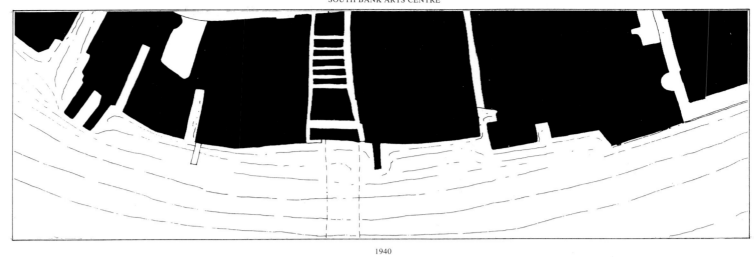

1940

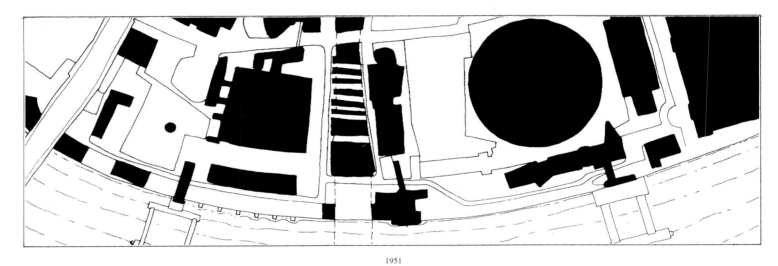

1951

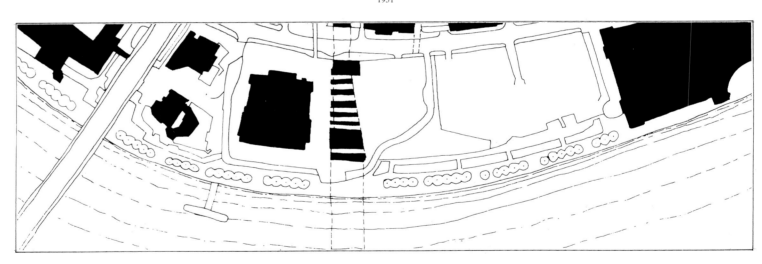

EXISTING 1989

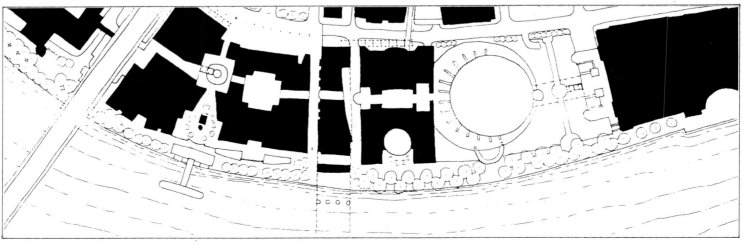

FARRELL 1989

and physical, and as an urban element characterized the worst features of the large institution which generates no relationship with the surrounding areas. In particular, the buildings provided no interest at street level, with the main entrance positioned back from the building line. The internal courtyards and open spaces, isolated from the city beyond, are bleak and underused areas. Farrell's proposal primarily addressed the problems of isolation at ground level by integrating activities, such as shops and cafés, along a number of new pedestrian routes that connected the site to the surrounding fabric. The primary route, with a new main entrance, linked the activity on Marylebone Road, through the existing courtyard areas, to the park at the south end of the site. Devices, such as atria and terraces, were used to break down the mass of the existing buildings as isolated elements, and relate them to the pattern of circulation and activity, as found in the traditional urban scene. The scheme by Ron Herron was reminiscent of the Archigram ideas from the 1960s. Again inspired by ideas of connection and inter-relation, the proposal was for a large-scale intervention that linked Regent's Park to the park to the south of Paddington Street. The new buildings extended from the existing, literally reaching out into the city, and were designed to facilitate change and promote events and activity on the site.

For Farrell the area to the north of South Kensington, 'museum-land' or 'Albertopolis', is a mono-cultural area that presents the modern day urban planner with a unique area of unexplored potential. Following the Great Exhibition of 1851, Prince Albert instigated plans for the area to the south of Hyde Park, known as the Imperial College campus, to be developed as a centre of cultural and educational interest. Whilst history has provided the great resource of the collection of museums and cultural buildings, Farrell noted that the area lacked the sophisticated infrastructure of routes and amenities, such as cafés and shops, that would enhance the experience of the visitor to this important area. Farrell's particular involvement was at South Kensington Station, but the area as a whole is the focus of one of Farrell's proposed 'grand projects' for the evolution of London. The scheme reinstated the original vision that linked the park, the Royal Albert Hall, down through Imperial College, to the Science and Natural History Museums and the Victoria and Albert Museum, down to South Kensington. The importance of this unique part of London would be reinforced by the enhancement of pedestrian routes, particularly across the divisive Cromwell Road, and the greater provision of cafés, shops, and public amenities, that would break down the mono-cultural nature of the area, and integrate it within the city fabric.

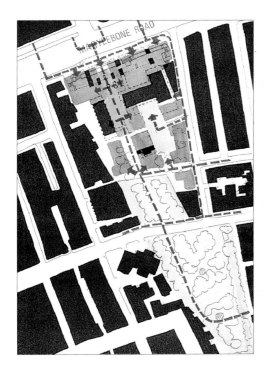
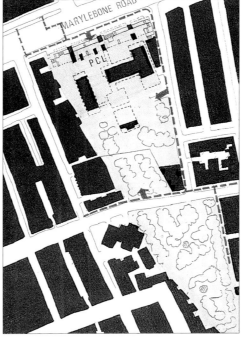

*Left*: Polytechnic of Central London Farrell's proposals; *Above*: Polytechnic of Central London Ron Herron's proposals

EARLY AND EXISTING VIEWS OF THE SOUTH BANK AND ANALYSIS OF SITE GEOMETRY

## SOUTH BANK ARTS CENTRE
*LONDON BOROUGH OF LAMBETH 1984-1992*

The South Bank Arts Centre represents the mono-culture of culture itself. Farrell attributes the difficulties of the site to what he regards as the anti-urban era of modernism. The scheme makes little reference to the city and its surrounding context, and merely serves to reinforce the isolated nature of this part of the south bank, severed by railway viaducts from the surrounding communities.

The South Bank, which boasts the largest collection of arts venues in Europe, lacks some of the basic characteristics of the city and the provision for subsidiary amenities is severely limited. At present in a state of incoherence, the site has little by way of recognizable streets or squares, shops or places to eat. For Farrell, an important part of his involvement with the South Bank, was a study of the phenomenon of mono-cultural institutions, and how within the city no purely single-use activity exists. He also investigated shopping areas in London that had reputations for specific products, such as Hatton Garden for jewellery, Bond Street for fine art galleries, and noted that they had a mixture of other facilities creating the normal diversity and activity of urban life. In 1976 Farrell wrote an article which proposed addressing the deficiencies of the South Bank by restoring a balance between the artistic intensity generated within the venues and the activity of the areas outside, by adding hotels and shops to the site.

The early ideas for the South Bank were used in Farrell's later proposals and the desire to make the isolated arts complex a more integrated part of London dictated the design in a number of ways. Farrell began with the familiar theme of creating a ground-level pedestrian domain from the existing incoherent network of elevated walkways. This new circulation system, articulated by squares, arcades and courtyards, evoked the traditional grain of the city and established connections with existing patterns of movement forming routes into and across the site. Farrell used the resource of the existing buildings as a framework in which he placed a number of new built elements. Provision for restaurants, pubs, studios, and shops, selling a variety of products connected with the arts, was made at ground level, with accommodation for small business and office use placed above. In place of a rarefied single-purpose city, Farrell proposed a more familiar mix of human activity, that would enliven the area at all times of the day.

Farrell's proposals for the South Bank were based upon a desire to break down the mono-cultural isolation of the area. As with the proposals for South Kensington, the existing facilities were supplemented by other everyday services that would attract people into an area they might not normally visit. An improved infrastructure of circulation and amenities was established to broaden the enjoyment of this, at present, under-used part of the city.

CONCEPT DIAGRAMS

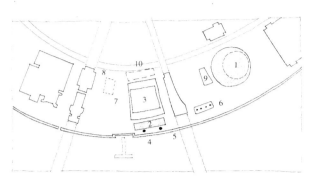

MEMORIES OF THE FESTIVAL OF
BRITAIN
1 DOME OF DISCOVERY
2 THE SEASIDE PAVILION
3 THE ROYAL FESTIVAL HALL
4 THE RIVER WALL
5 MASTS AND BALCONIES
6 THE WALL OF FOUNTAINS
7 ORIGINAL ENTRANCE REINSTATED
8 POSSIBLE FESTIVAL OF BRITAIN MUSEUM
9 MOAT GARDEN
10 RETURN OF THE OPEN PUBLIC SQUARE ON
  BELVEDERE ROAD

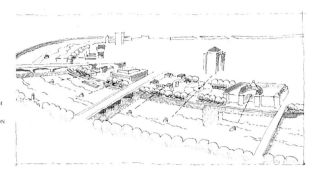

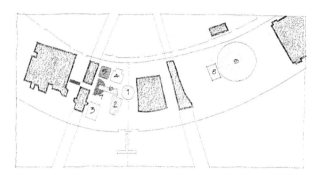

THE ARTS BENEFITS
1 CENTRALISED TICKETING
2 NEW QUEEN ELIZABETH HALL FOYER
3 NEW BACKSTAGE TO QUEEN ELIZABETH
  HALL AND PURCELL ROOM
4 IMPROVED SERVICING TO HAYWARD
  GALLERY
5 ENLARGED FOYER TO HAYWARD GALLERY
6 COVERED PUBLIC SPACE BETWEEN
  BUILDINGS
7 IMPROVED ACCESS TO MOMI
8 ORCHESTRAL REHEARSAL SPACE
9 IMPROVED OUTDOOR PERFORMANCE SPACE

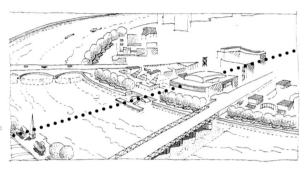

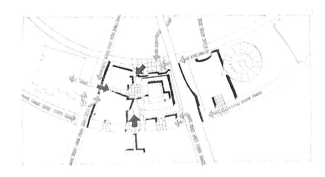

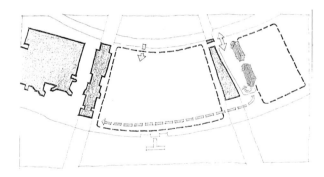

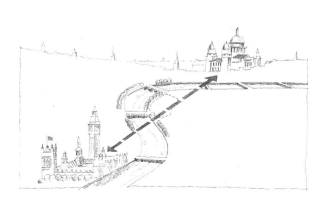

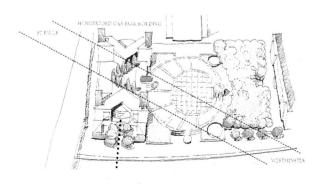

CONCEPT DIAGRAMS

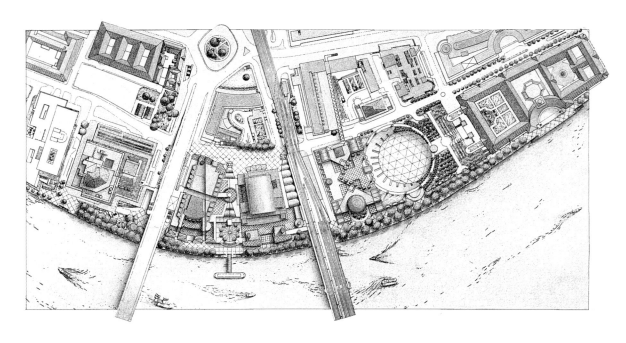

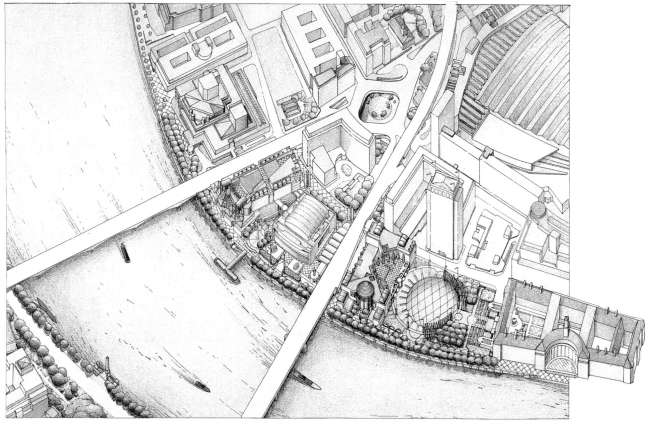

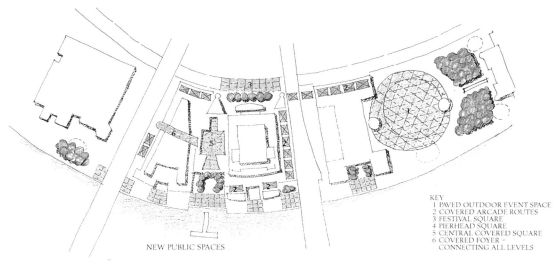

NEW PUBLIC SPACES

KEY
1 PAVED OUTDOOR EVENT SPACE
2 COVERED ARCADE ROUTES
3 FESTIVAL SQUARE
4 PIERHEAD SQUARE
5 CENTRAL COVERED SQUARE
6 COVERED FOYER –
CONNECTING ALL LEVELS

THE MASTERPLAN

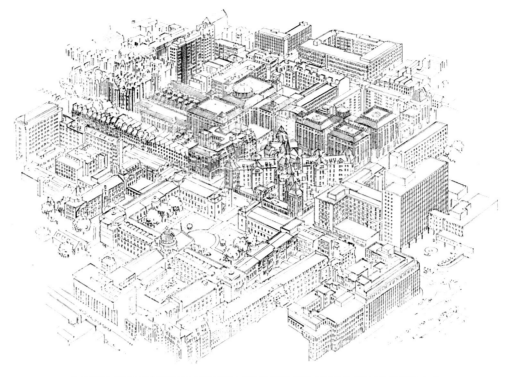

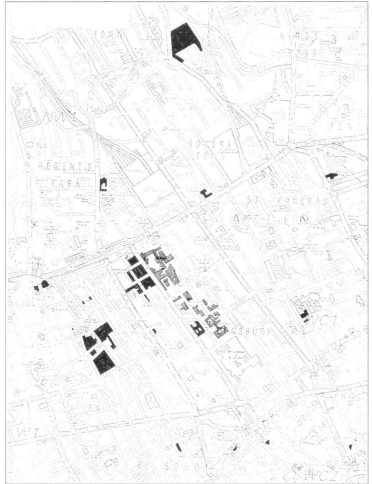

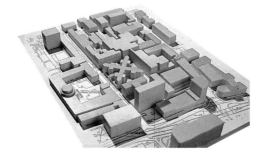

AERIAL VIEW, LOCATION AND MODEL VIEW OF MASTERPLAN

# BLOOMSBURY HOSPITALS

*CITY OF WESTMINSTER AND LONDON BOROUGH OF CAMDEN, 1988*

*Farrell was commissioned by the Bloomsbury and Islington Health Authority to examine options for two hospital sites - the Middlesex and University College - and various scattered sites that involved the rationalization of health facilities in the area. Farrell acted as overall coordinator working with a number of specialists to produce a submission presented to the Department of Health.*

*The hospital, as a public institution, suffers the worst problems of mono-culturality, with its typecast image as a faceless system for the sick, the building containing a world associated with illness. Based upon a study of different aspects of hospital culture, as a number of separate, if inter-related facilities and elements, Farrell proposed to emphasize the institution as mini-community or village. The scheme established a campus-style hospital on the site adjacent to Waterhouse's University College Hospital, that redeveloped many listed buildings already owned by the health authority. By developing a number of new-built elements, integrated with existing structures, the urban image of the hospital as large forbidding building, was replaced by Farrell's concept of the institution as 'gentle giant' which sits unobtrusively within the urban fabric. The Waterhouse building was converted into a teaching hospital, with the new hospital elements designed to relate in scale to the listed buildings.*

*In order to encourage the integration of the institution,*

*Farrell concentrated upon creating an infrastructure of circulation and activity that mirrored the normality of the city street. The new pedestrian ground domain was developed around a network of routes into and across the site. The main entrance was placed on the north-south axis that took the line of Huntley Street and extended it to link Grafton Way to Torrington Place. This main route was crossed by two east-west routes, connecting Gower Street to Tottenham Court Road. By relating the internal circulation system of the hospital to the existing street pattern, the institution contributes to the city by providing new pedestrian routes through a once impermeable city block.*

*Farrell also provided a number of amenities that were placed along the main circulation routes and public spaces in the centre of the scheme. Outpatient and other public-use facilities were placed at this ground level, with more private and specialized wards placed on the floors above. Some years earlier, Farrell had been struck by a children's hospital in Philadelphia that had a McDonald's in the main foyer area. Making provision for shops, restaurants and a cinema within the scheme, blurred the distinctions between the world within the hospital and the city outside. By introducing everyday facilities for people to meet and socialize, Farrell provided a centre for the community of the hospital, but also encouraged the use of the institution by others working and living locally.*

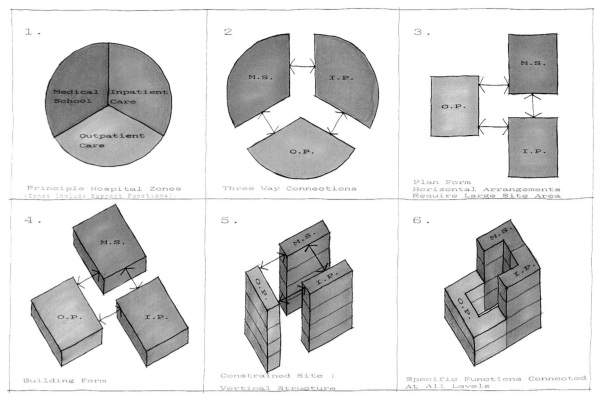

1. Principle Hospital Zones
(Zones Include Support Functions).

2. Three Way Connections

3. Plan Form
Horizontal Arrangements
Require Large Site Area

4. Building Form

5. Constrained Site :
Vertical Structure

6. Specific Functions Connected
At All Levels

HOSPITAL ZONES : CONCEPTS

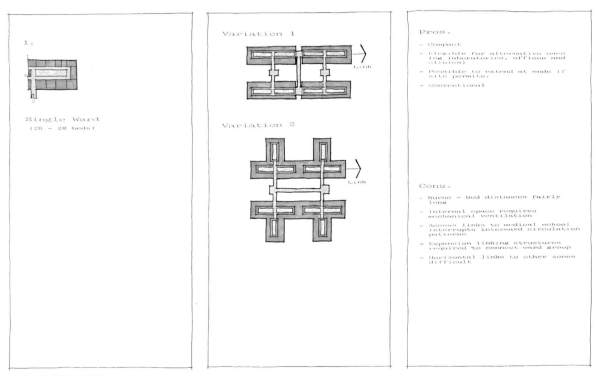

1. Single Ward
(26 – 28 beds)

Variation 1

Variation 2

Pros.

– Compact
– Flexible for alternative uses
  (eg laboratories, offices and
  clinics)
– Possible to extend at ends if
  site permits.
– Conventional

Cons.

– Nurse – Bed distances fairly
  long
– Internal space requires
  mechanical ventilation
– Access links to medical school
  interrupts interward circulation
  patterns
– Expansion linking structures
  required to connect ward group
– Horizontal links to other zones
  difficult

RACETRACK

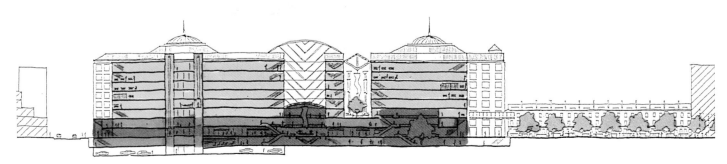

SECTION

LISTED BUILDINGS &
CONSERVATION AREA

▓ Listed buildings

▢ Conservation area

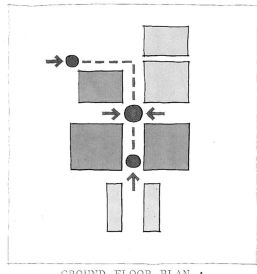

GROUND FLOOR PLAN :
Organisation

▓ Clinical zone

▢ Other hospital zones

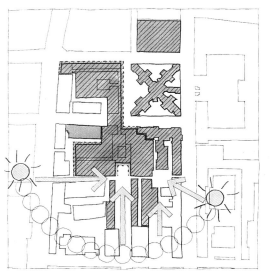

BUILDING ORIENTATION & SUNLIGHT

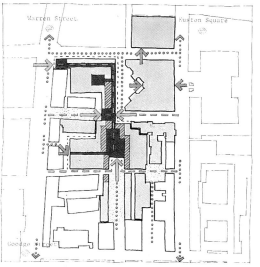

PEDESTRIAN ZONES

▢ Principal pedestrian routes
within site

▢ Shopping zone

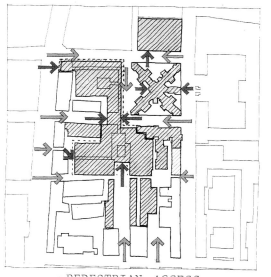

PEDESTRIAN ACCESS

▓ To Buildings

▢ To Site

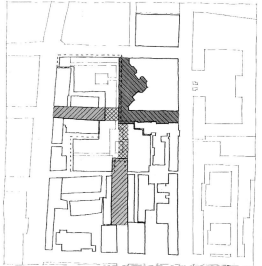

HIGHWAY CLOSURE

▨ Highway pedestrianisation

▨ Highway closure

▨ Hospital traffic only

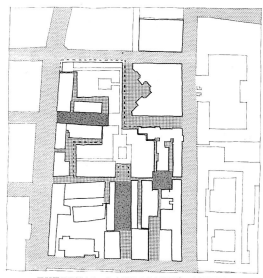

EXTERNAL LANDSCAPED AREAS

▓ Primary Landscaped Space

▨ Secondary Landscaped Space

▨ Roads

MASTERPLAN DIAGRAMS

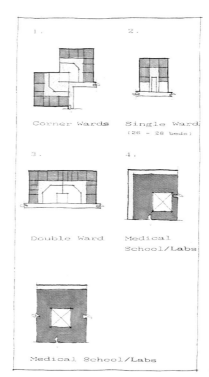

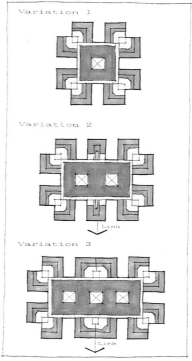

Pros.

- Good observation of patients
- Short nurse – bed distance providing patient confidence and staff efficiency
- Simple movement patterns
- Service core incorporated
- Enables direct horizontal links to medical school and laboratories
- Easy internal communication
- Wider views for patients
- Potential for giving zones

Cons.

- Variation 1: difficult for direct expansion
- Inflexible for some future alternative
- Internal space requires mechanical ventilation
- Possible only on larger more regular shaped sites
- Greater external wall area (with some cost implications)

CLUSTER

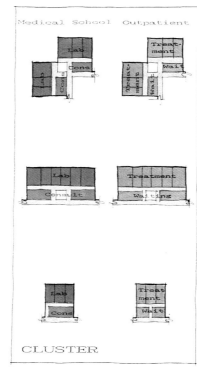

Statement :

CLUSTER

Inpatient areas shown on the plans could accommodate Medical School space, albeit in the corner wards or double ward design rather less straightforwardly than in the more regular racetrack or double ward design.

RACE TRACK

The race track wards could more easily accommodate laboratory space of the Medical School or outpatient treatment areas.

CLUSTER

RACETRACK

FLEXIBILITY

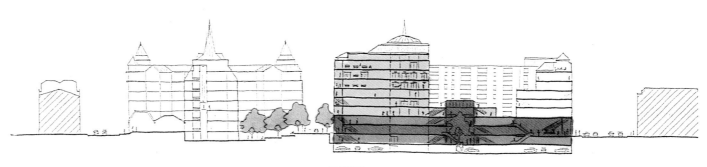

SECTION

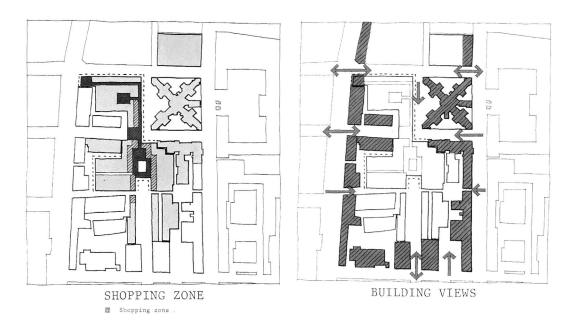

SHOPPING ZONE

▨ Shopping zone .

BUILDING VIEWS

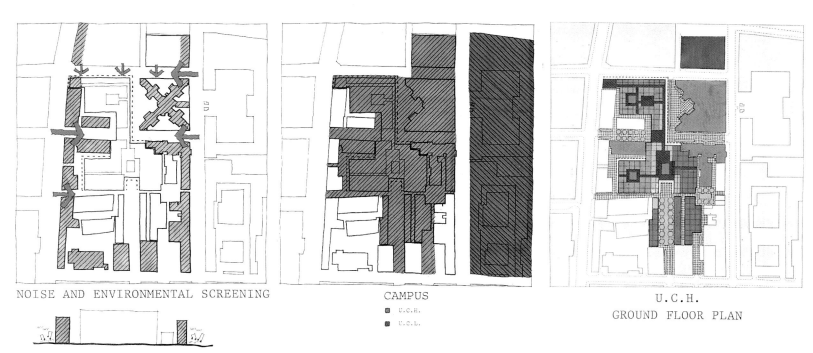

NOISE AND ENVIRONMENTAL SCREENING

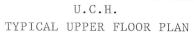

CAMPUS

▨ U.C.H.

▨ U.C.L.

U.C.H.
GROUND FLOOR PLAN

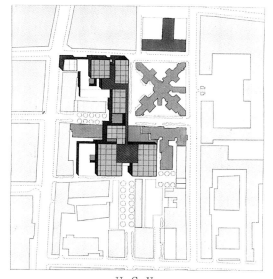

U.C.H.
TYPICAL UPPER FLOOR PLAN

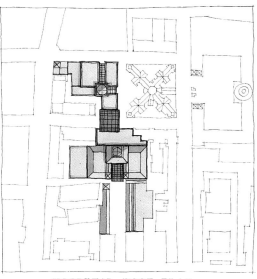

HOSPITAL ROOF PLAN

MASTERPLAN DIAGRAMS

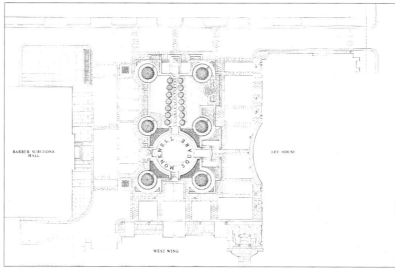

# GREEN LONDON: PARKS, SQUARES, GARDENS

For Farrell the concept of 'space positive' is fundamental to urban design. Developed by Rowe and Koetter in the book *Collage City*, this concept highlighted the contrast between the traditional Italian city, where space is created as a positive urban element defined by the built fabric around it, and the Corbusian vision of buildings as objects in themselves, standing in fluid open space.

Within the traditional grain of the city, the buildings provide the major element of ground coverage. The space between - the public domain - is therefore the lesser element, the scarce resource, that must be prized, enclosed and preserved. The very nature and character of urban space in London differs from those in places such as Milton Keynes, where space is abundant, and buildings, placed within the open landscape, are the rarity. The great tradition of urban space evolved from ancient times, with the market square, the agora, the street, the arcade and colonnade. All great European cities incorporated these generic types and developed indigenous interpretations. In London, these traditional prototypes, the square, the arcade and colonnade were used particularly from the 17th to the early 19th century.

But during the 19th and 20th centuries Britain developed its own way of looking at urban spaces, and Nash was one of the earliest and most original thinkers in urban design. Nash developed many of his ideas from the great landscape architect, Humphrey Repton. Repton's approach to landscape design, distinctly non-European, was that existing features should be retained, and adapted to create a total composition which emphasized the natural qualities of the landscape. Nash adapted this 'contextual' approach - as it would be known today - to the city. Working with Repton on the layout of Regent's Park, Nash designed perhaps the most famous piece of urban design in London. The route from Carlton House to Regent's Park, along Regent Street, was built around existing thoroughfares and houses, transforming old buildings into focal points and creating new ones, such as All Souls Church, a device used to divert the route from Upper Regent Street to the

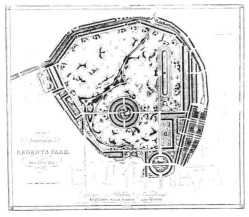

*Opposite*: Monkwell Square; *Left above*: Historical photographs of Embankment Gardens and Marble Arch; *Left below*: J. Nash and T. Shepherd's plans for Regent's Park

1691

1746

1973

1986

line of Portland Place. By developing a piece of urban design that recognized the characteristics of London's parks as areas of rural land within the city, the sequence of streets and spaces which joined these parks added a dimension to urban planning that was unique to London. This piecemeal and pragmatic approach was historically nothing new: London has developed in a fragmentary nature as the two cities of Westminster and the Square Mile were joined. This gradual development also dictated the character of the great London parks, as entrapped pieces of countryside within the city, quite different from the formal, consciously urban parks in cities such as Paris and New York. For Farrell the history of the parks and their evolution into urban and planning type was particularly interesting and has been a powerful force in the development of London.

Farrell's involvement with the open spaces of London has included a variety of scale and forms: from tiny developments such as the square at East Putney and the small garden next to Clifton Nurseries; to larger urban squares such as Paternoster Square, Horseferry Road and Monkwell Square; to work on the great parks of London as part of the Royal Parks Study Group. Both Monkwell Square and Embankment Gardens were part of the larger developments for office buildings, and highlight Farrell's belief in the essential role space plays within the city, and how it must be preserved and enhanced as a limited resource. As part of the Alban Gate project, Farrell seized the opportunity to transform the post-war creation of Monkwell Square from a car park access and service yard into a landscaped space in the tradition of London squares. The importance of enclosure was addressed by a four-storey residential block, which protected the square from London Wall to the south. All the entrances of the new built elements opened onto the square to generate an intensified level of use and activity. At Embankment Gardens, the main task was to enhance the character of the space by restoring various original features that had fallen into disrepair, such as the York Water Gate, built in 1626, and the bandstand. The restoration of the gardens was just one of a sequence of improved spaces, which formed a new hinterland of activity around the station.

The importance of the parks of London in contributing to the unique character of the city was first addressed by Farrell in 1972, with proposals for a series of green links from Regent's Park, along Regent's Canal to Paddington Basin, connecting to Hyde Park, and through to Green Park and St James's. More recent proposals for Hyde Park and Kensington Gardens were based upon a historical study of the development of the parks - how their unique nature resulted from origins as areas of natural landscape used for hunting by the English kings. Although the parks were gradually opened to the general public, the royal family retained ownership,

*Left*: Embankment Gardens

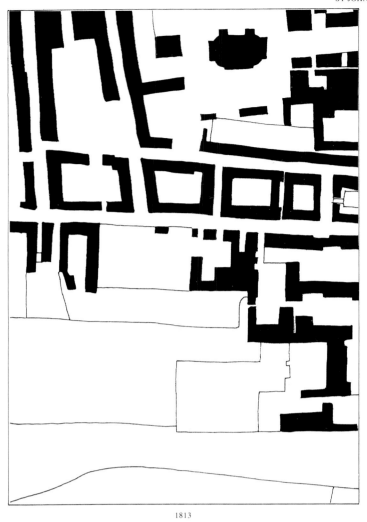

1813

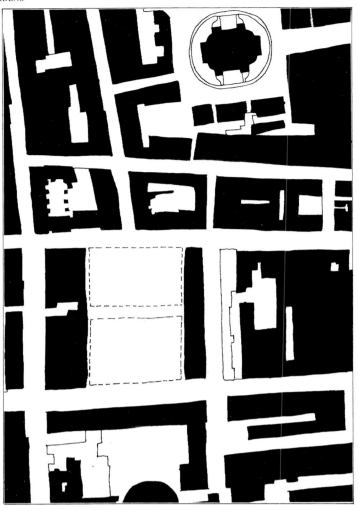

1869

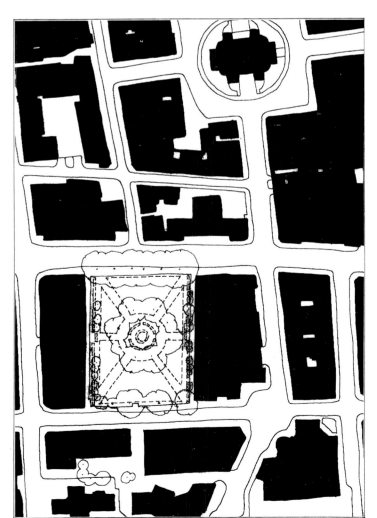

EXISTING 1991

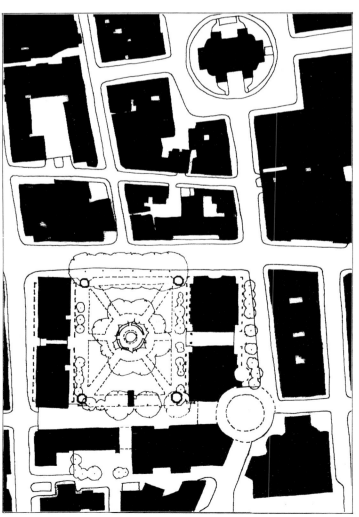

FARRELL 1992

thus preserving them from comprehensive redevelopment. In urban design terms, the main concerns were to preserve and enhance the specific characteristics of the parks as essentially pieces of countryside, with particular attention paid to the definition of the edges between park and city. Both Hyde Park and Kensington Gardens have been eroded by roads at their edges, with the loss of formal points of entry; and others have been badly affected by the priority given to the vehicle over the pedestrian. For Farrell this encroachment showed a lack of understanding of the notion of boundary, which acts as much symbolically as functionally, reinforcing the contrast between two worlds - the world of urbanity and the world of natural landscape - that serves as an escape and release.

Farrell proposed a number of features to enforce this point of transition, including new grand gateways with lodges placed on new pedestrian routes which created formal entrances, and also accommodation for amenities, such as kiosks and toilets. New railings, evoking the detail and generous civic scale of original examples, replaced existing inadequate barriers. The issue of enclosure was linked with traffic control at the edges and in the park itself, and solutions to alleviate the traffic problems of the city invariably damaged the integrity of the park. Farrell proposed the reintegration of Marble Arch, Park Lane and Hyde Park Corner into the park, to liberate these important areas as pedestrian priority traffic areas and to provide access to isolated monuments and gateways, such as Marble Arch. The existing entrances and system of underground subways beneath the two roundabouts at each end of Park Lane were replaced with formal new entrances that linked to ground level routes from the city.

As well as establishing this important feature of boundary, Farrell's concern to conserve the specific character of the parkland dictated proposals for future developments within the park itself. As a natural environment, a piece of open countryside, the main theme was to reduce built elements, and limit them to buildings traditionally found in such a landscape - conservatories, lodges, and follies. Around the lake the restaurant was removed, leaving the lido and boat-house as elements that had relevance to the lakeside context. For reasons of pragmatism and historical continuity, Farrell rejected the need for new buildings, proposing instead to restore existing buildings and use them for necessary amenities. The Old Arsenal and the Pumping House were brought into public use, and Kensington Palace was made a more integrated and accessible part of the park. The control of building heights around the edges preserved strategic views and the illusion of escape from urbanity into a world of nature. All Farrell's proposals preserved the unique character of the park and sought to reinforce the notion that this urban element was of high value, and an essential resource within the city.

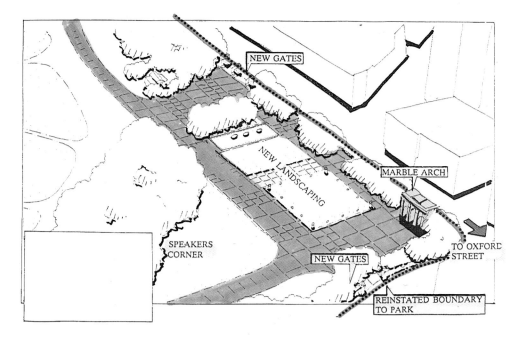

*Left*: Royal Parks Review

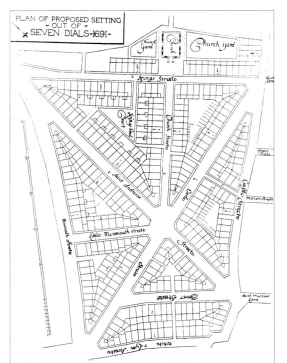

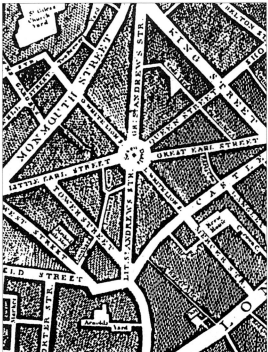

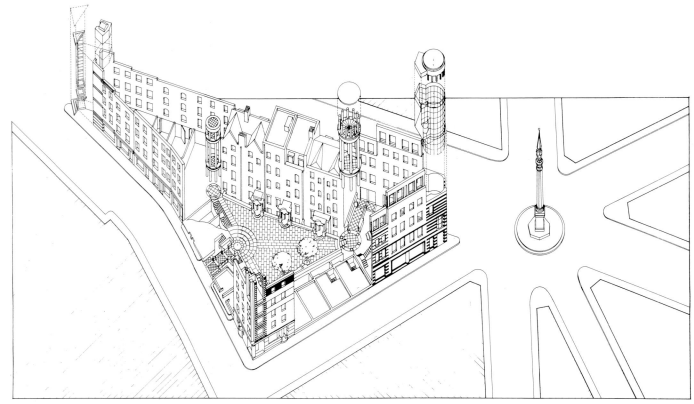

HISTORICAL PLANS, AERIAL VIEW IN 1975 AND PROPOSED SCHEME

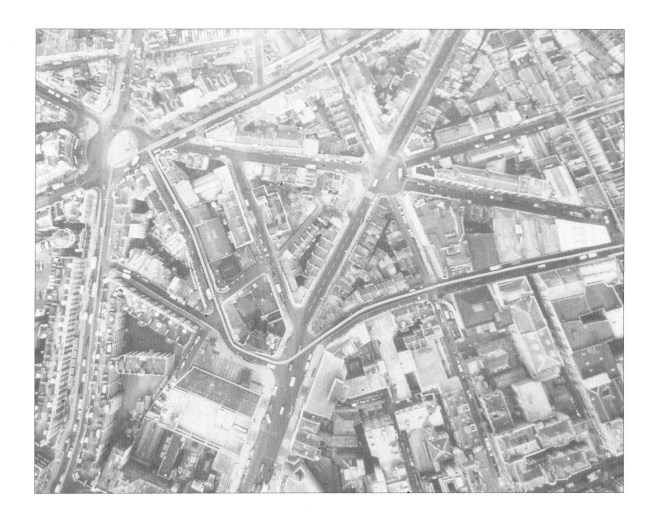

# COMYN CHING TRIANGLE
## *LONDON BOROUGH OF CAMDEN 1978-1985*

*For Farrell the interest of the redevelopment of the Comyn Ching triangle scheme was the nature of the space that was created. The site was one of a number of triangular blocks, created when Sir Thomas Neal laid out the Seven Dials in 1692. Behind the original perimeter terrace buildings the open yard had become entirely built over with a number of extensions and infill buildings.*

*The main feature of the redevelopment of the site for the ironmongery company, Comyn Ching, was the creation of a new public courtyard, Ching Court, carved from the centre of the dense triangular site. This new urban space was in the tradition of space positive, with the buildings as a solid mass out of which the space is created - in contrast to the established areas of the royal parks, around which the city grew. The scheme resembled the Mansion House project in which Farrell proposed the development of a new public space scavenged from the centre core of the existing buildings at Poultry. At Ching Court, by returning the built fabric to the original line of the houses the rear elevations had to be transformed into facades suitable to address the new public space. Also new entrances were established to attract the public into and through an area that had previously been private. The courtyard provided a diagonal public route from Seven Dials to Shelton Street.*

*Much of the fascination for Farrell with this new open public space was at the level of detail, and how its*

*importance was intensified by the scale and enclosed nature of the courtyard. The design was restricted to ground floor level, and a series of events and features were used to generate interest at this level and reduce the potentially oppressive effect of the narrow courtyard space. The courtyard was articulated by a number of elements: three office entrances with large projecting porches arranged against the rear of Monmouth Street, inspired by 18th century design; a rear passage entrance from Shelton Street flanked by large rear windows of shop units; two trees; and Lutyens' seat on the Mercer Street side. The courtyard was paved in York stone, with the edge forcefully defined by a substantial stone kerb, reinforced by railings. Details in the paving pattern, uniting key elements such as doors, were picked out in grey limestone.*

*The existing terraces were restored and Farrell designed three new corner buildings. The scheme contained the traditional diversity of uses found in the city, with one side for residential use, one side for offices, and the other with shops on the ground floor and residential use above. Along the existing streets particular attention was paid to generating interest at street level with new porches and doorways deeply recessed into the rusticated base. For Farrell the mixture of old and new, and the variety of uses were the most important features of the scheme - the public courtyard giving a specific identity and focus of activity to this urban block.*

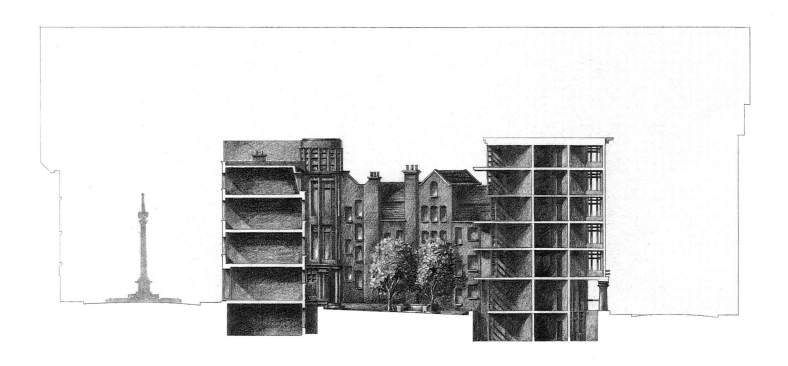

*ABOVE*: SECTION THROUGH COURTYARD

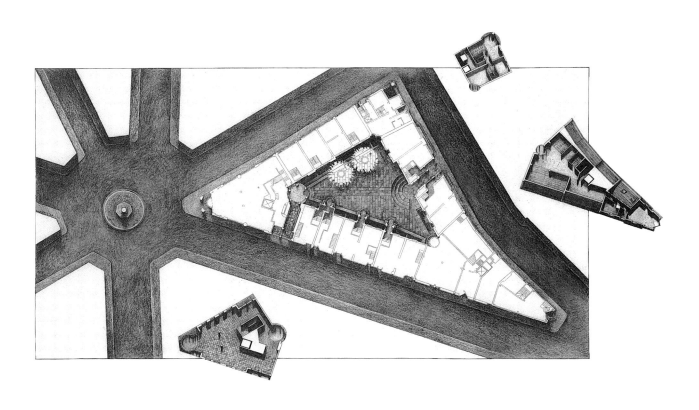

*ABOVE*: GROUND AND UPPER LEVEL PLANS

COMYN CHING

COMMERCIAL (others)

HOUSING OVER (substantially)

OFFICES OVER (substantially)

LISTED BUILDINGS

CLOSING ORDER

*BELOW*: PLANS OF SITE BEFORE ALTERATION

building of poor quality
out of character with
remainder of Seven Dials

dormer workshop windows

victorian warehouse

dormer workshop windows

high    low    high    low pair

fine interior    low pair

19th century tenement
building of very poor
quality, out of
scale and character
with the remainder
of Shelton and Mercer.

high pair

fine interior    low pair

Comyn Ching shopfront
listed grade two star

wide pair    three low varied    high pair

narrow pair

four similar

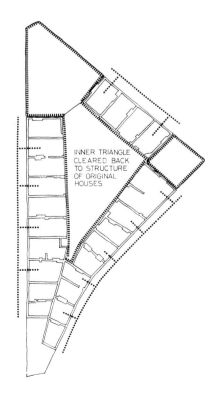

INNER TRIANGLE
CLEARED BACK
TO STRUCTURE
OF ORIGINAL
HOUSES

MAJOR BUILDING OPERATION
REQUIRES ACCESS AND
WORKING SPACE

THESE BUILDINGS RESTORED
BY SPECIALIST CONTRACTOR

*BELOW*: EARLY CONCEPT DRAWING

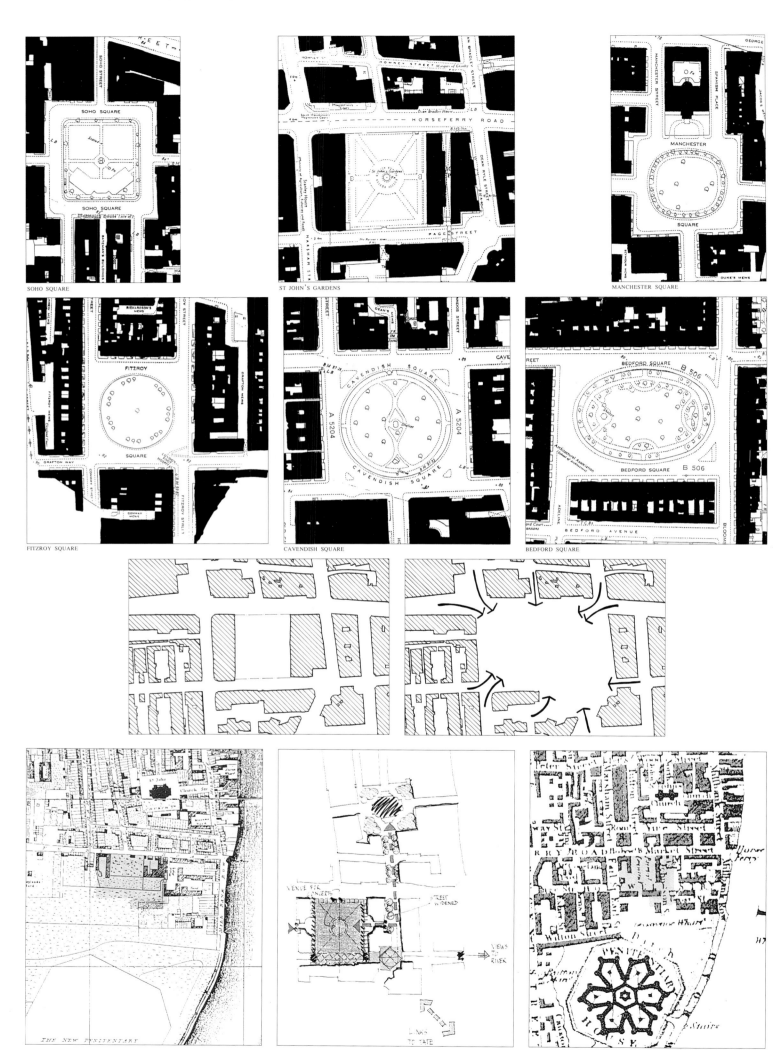

SOHO SQUARE

ST JOHN'S GARDENS

MANCHESTER SQUARE

FITZROY SQUARE

CAVENDISH SQUARE

BEDFORD SQUARE

COMPARATIVE STUDIES, FIGURE GROUND STUDIES, HISTORICAL PLANS AND CONCEPT PLAN

# ST JOHN'S GARDENS
## *CITY OF WESTMINSTER 1991-1992*

*This project at Horseferry Road has similarities with Monkwell Square, in that it is the redevelopment and rejuvenation of an existing open space in the city. The square was originally the site of a graveyard for St John's Church, built by Thomas Archer, within the nearby Smith Square. In 1885 the site was landscaped and opened to the public, as St John's Gardens, and the main task for Farrell was to reinforce the virtues of the existing square. Farrell was particularly interested in improving pedestrian routes through the square, and how this affected the amenity of the space. As a student in Philadelphia, Farrell had made a study of patterns of movement through a number of public squares. In St John's Gardens there was an interesting form of paths, but routes were limited by the position of the entrances, two at the corners along Horseferry Road and one placed centrally along Page Street. This prevented pedestrians crossing diagonally, and making short cuts through the square. By creating an entrance at each corner, signalled by prominent gateways, Farrell encouraged public use by forming more pedestrian-friendly, diagonal patterns of movement. Activity and use of the gardens was also encouraged by the creation of a garden square pavilion, used as a wine bar/café. Placed above an existing tunnel, which connected two of the buildings, the underground passage was transformed into a basement wine bar.*

*A number of devices were used to restore the square to its original size and enhance its nature. The square had been reduced in size by the widening of Horseferry Road, and Farrell reintegrated this part by resurfacing the pavement. The length of Page Street, adjacent to the south side of the gardens, was similarly resurfaced and bollards were introduced to create a pedestrian priority road. The buildings around three sides of the square were redesigned with arcades at ground level to increase the apparent size of the square.*

*All the existing buildings around the square were part of the hospital complex. This single-use activity deadened the square, and Farrell reintroduced a diversity of use, with residential, office and shop accommodation provided in the new buildings. The new buildings also adhered to the tripartite hierarchy of traditional street architecture, with arcades and shops at ground level to generate activity, the restrained and repetitive middle floors crowned by articulated rooftops inspired by the nearby Lutyens' Page Street flats. The project was based on the enhancement and integration of the gardens as the primary urban feature. On the micro scale, attention was paid to the nature of gates, railings and paths, which built upon the existing resource of the gardens, and on the larger scale the new buildings around the square related and responded to the open space they addressed.*

PEDESTRIAN AND SPATIAL STUDIES AND MASTERPLAN

RESTAURANT

REORGANISING STREET FRONTAGES, THE NEW CAFE IN THE SQUARE, AND ENTRANCES AND GATEWAYS

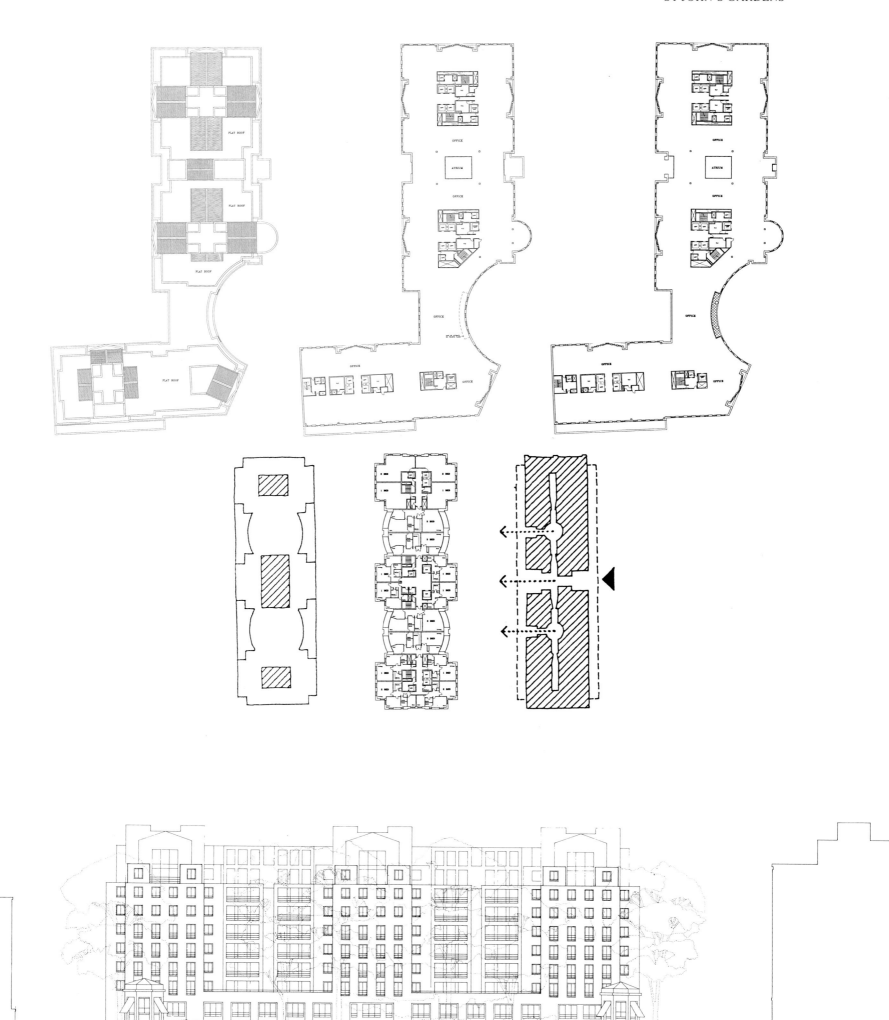

OFFICE PLANS, RESIDENTIAL PLANS AND ELEVATION OF RESIDENTIAL BUILDING

# THE PRIVATE WORLD

If the techniques used by Nolli to represent the plan of Rome are applied to the modern city, within London there is a parallel with the notion of an internal world, a world inside the buildings which constitute part of the public domain of the city. This means of representing the city, its public spaces and the relationships to buildings and streets, reveals a great variety of different types when applied to London, because of its greater size and urban complexity as compared with Rome. Farrell's interest lies in the notion of the extension of the public domain into the interior of a building, linking an inner world to the urban design of the city.

During Farrell's study of the West End and the South Bank, comparisons were made between performance spaces, cultural spaces, theatres and galleries in these two areas, the nature and volume of such spaces, and how they related to the street structure. Unlike the South Bank, in the West End these spaces were integrated and intermingled with the city fabric. Part of this study included Nash's development of the Royal Opera House, on the Haymarket, which for Farrell was of particular relevance for Nash integrated the theatre as part of a larger piece of urban design. Around the existing concert hall performance space, Nash created the foyers and additional accommodation for the larger scheme of the Opera House. A colonnade around the buildings created a ground level ring of protected pedestrian walks for people waiting before or after performances. An arcaded passage through the centre of the block, the Royal Opera Arcade, provided a sheltered route through the block with shops to generate activity in the area and provide alternative interest. Nash also redesigned the street layout that defined the block, as part of the urban design for Regent Street. His proposals regularized street widths and set the layout of Waterloo Place. The masterplan included the elevations to the buildings lining the streets but allowed sites to be developed as desired, so although the buildings on the site have been replaced a number of times, the Royal Arcade and the street layout remains, and the relationship of the block to the surrounding fabric still forms a coherent piece of urban design. For Farrell, Nash's work on the Haymarket contains common themes with the proposals for the South Bank - primarily the use of existing buildings rather than demolition, dictated by a desire to create urban design first and architecture second, a scheme which makes a contribution to the urban planning of the area through the relationship developed between its own internal plan and spaces, and the city as a whole.

Farrell's scheme for the Lloyd's Bank building on Pall Mall formed part of the Royal Opera House block designed by Nash, and during the development of the scheme Farrell became fascinated by this part of London, characterized by the large number of clubs in the area. The West End has two distinct forms of public space contained within buildings - the cinemas, theatres and cultural spaces around Leicester Square; and then along Pall Mall down to Trafalgar Square and Northumberland Avenue there is a private world of clubland, with its controlled semi-public spaces contained behind the imposing facades of the clubs. The facades of Waterloo Place, in particular, were organized around these semi-public, internal spaces. In order to create a solution for the scheme on Pall Mall, Farrell applied the Nolli method of representing the area, and from this discerned a pattern of spaces within this clubland, and the relationship between this inner world and the streets beyond. At an earlier date Farrell had been involved in proposals for flats along Carlton Gardens, one of a growing number of schemes around London which involved the replacement of a 1960s building. The new residential building related to a sequence of public spaces around the gardens and formal set pieces of the area,

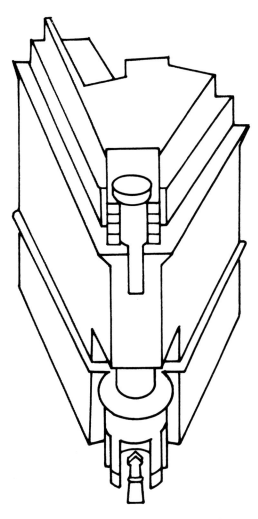

*Opposite and above*: Midland Bank, Fenchurch Street

175

with an internal series of entrance halls that extended the external environment into the interior in a formal way. The project had similarities with the Horseferry Road scheme, which also linked the internal to the external with in-between elements, such as colonnades, relating to entrance foyers and circulation routes within the buildings, which also formed part of the wider urban plan.

In comparison with the West End, the City of London has a completely different pattern of semi-public, internal spaces, which form part of the public domain. The City, as a dense, compacted urban form which can be crossed on foot in twenty minutes, is a place for the pedestrian and this complex network, which acts as a subtle market place, has been a crucial factor in the commercial success of the City. Integral within this network, is a series of semi-public, semi-private rooms, banking halls, narrow alleyways, coffee rooms and pubs in which the business of the City is carried on. Many messengers in the City travel on foot, passing from one internal space to another, taking short-cuts through buildings, delivering or conducting business in the buildings through which they pass. This great network of banking halls includes the NatWest Bank complex, Lutyens' Midland Bank, and Lutyens' Britannic House which, with its new great internal atrium, has become a modern interpretation of the traditional banking hall space. Also the two banking buildings by Farrell at Lombard Street and Fenchurch Street, the great spaces within the Bank of England, the Royal Exchange Public Rooms, recently restored, are all part of the internal public world found in the City. Such networks rely upon the richness of ground level movement and the connections of routes and spaces.

The internal world of clubland in the West End and of the banking halls in the City were all established in the last century, and represented a male-dominated world of leisure and business. For Farrell the creation of the institutionalized male domain, within the city and clubland, holds strong parallels to the nature of education for the 19th century professional male, from public school to Oxbridge college. In particular the Inns of Court replicate the architectural organization of the educational institution, a medieval grouping of hierarchical spaces - the grand procession from entrance hall to great hall, linked to smaller, subsidiary rooms placed around open stairs in corners - which are typical of the Oxbridge college.

The City of London developed its own version of this tradition, loosely adapting classicism to articulate hierarchic progressions, unlike the Gothic style used for the legal world or the parliamentary world of Westminster. The banking buildings of the 19th and early 20th century were dictated by the organizational hierarchy and the desire to express the prestige of the company. Britannic House, designed by Lutyens, contained these severe commercial hierarchies, with the great entrance hall for directors and clients linked to the magnificent boardrooms via a grand staircase. A separate entrance for employees was placed to the side. Farrell proposed an atrium in the centre of the building, creating a new central space within the building, which enhanced the ceremony of the original scheme and unified its grand, opulent spaces with the humble accommodation allotted to the bulk of the workforce. The sequential spaces within the building formed part of the progression for all employees and visitors from the public domain of the street, through the new central atrium, to the more private rooms on the upper floors.

For Farrell this notion of internal space as part of the public domain also relates to great institutional complexes such as hospitals and museums. They are part of the urban design and public domain of the city, and also rely on connections to the network of routes and pedestrian movement. Farrell's projects for the Royal Opera House and the South Bank concentrated on the important relationship of the concert hall or performance space to other public spaces and connections to the city as a whole. On the South Bank the proposals were dictated by the movement of the public in and around the foyer areas of the cultural buildings, and in transforming these areas into an active part of the public domain. New internal spaces offered a protected environment, in which activity was developed - restaurants, cafés, shops - breaking down the isolation of the built elements standing within underused and undefined space, by extending the public domain into the existing buildings.

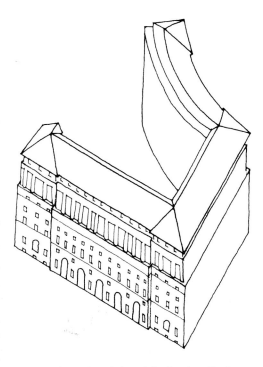

*Opposite from above left to right*: Barclays Bank, Piccadilly; Plymouth House, London W1; Farrell's house; Rules restaurant; Terry Farrell & Company's office; and TVAM; *above*: Lutyens' House

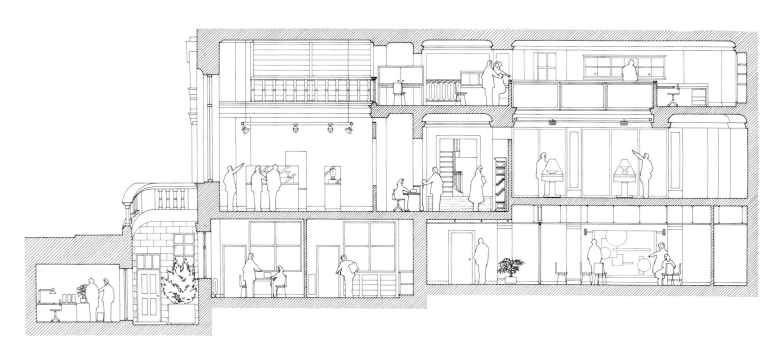

INTERIOR VIEWS, SECTION AND VIEWS OF EXISTING INTERIOR

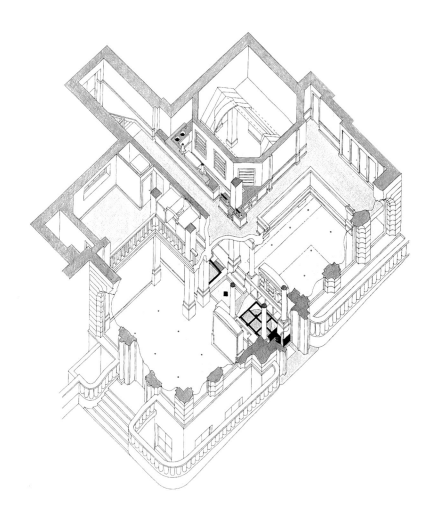

# CRAFTS COUNCIL GALLERY
## *CITY OF WESTMINSTER 1980-1981*

*Farrell uses the Crafts Council project to demonstrate that the principles of pedestrian organisation and hierarchy of space are the same for internal design as for large-scale urban design. Alberti, in his 'On the Art of Building in Ten Books' noted, "If (as the philosophers maintain) the city is like some large house, and the house in turn like some small city, cannot the various parts of the house ... be considered miniature buildings?" For Farrell, a series of interior spaces could be arranged like a small piece of urban design.*

*The project was to combine the three lower floors of two existing buildings on Waterloo Place, generating a range of public and private spaces, from the public galleries through to the privacy of administration and service spaces. To organise quite a complex sequence of spaces and reconcile different floor heights in two buildings, a wheelchair ramp - designed as a main corridor or boulevard - was created in the centre of the plan where the two houses met. This space acted as the central organiser for the whole scheme and was clearly designed as the most important space in the building. By repositioning the main entrance between the premises, lowering the level of this entrance and the reception area, the entry ramp formed part of the new circulation axis which formed a sequence of movement through the two main gallery spaces to the main staircase leading up to the mezzanine information centre.*

*Another interesting feature of the scheme was the debate between Farrell and the Crafts Council about the nature of a gallery - whether it is an anonymous space or whether the gallery itself should have an identity. For Farrell the nature of the small objets d'art and crafts to be displayed demanded a setting with a sense of place, that did not overbear the exhibits but did not act merely as a neutral backdrop.*

*Yet the most public space, and that which was the main focus of design attention, within the scheme was not the gallery space itself, but the spaces between: the circulation space and the route that connected all the spaces. The relationship between these spaces was heightened by opening up the first floor with overlooking balconies and views into the restaurant so that the whole sequence of spaces was interlinked. This hierarchy within the interior of the building, the miniature street ordering the lesser spaces, was designed to relate to Waterloo Place which formed part of Nash's hierarchy of spaces along the triumphal route from Carlton House to Regent's Park. As such, both this scheme and that for Lloyds Bank, responded to and formed part of the urban structure of the area that connects Nash's exterior spaces, defined by imposing street facades, to the grand entrance halls and then onto the public rooms found in the London club. Behind the set piece facade, the Crafts Council building mirrored the immediate world around of clubland, a great sequence of spaces where members meet and socialize united with a common interest or purpose.*

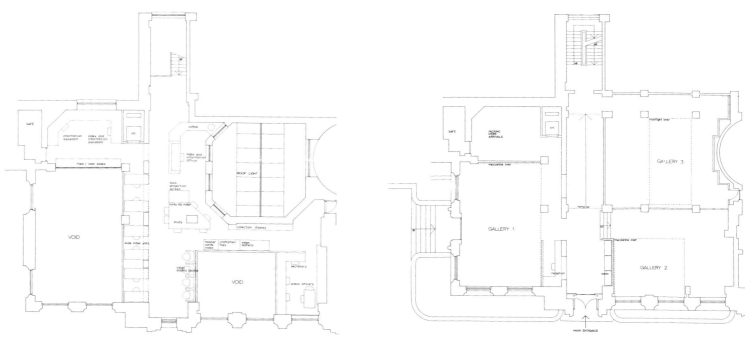

VIEW OF THE RECEPTION AREA, MEZZANINE AND GROUND FLOOR PLANS

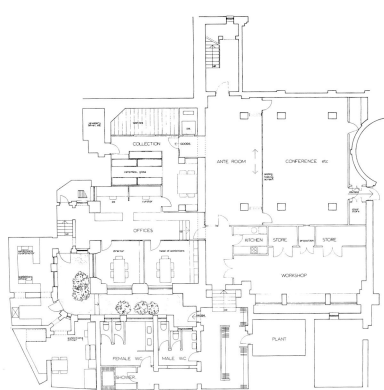

VIEW OF THE RECEPTION AREA AND BASEMENT PLAN

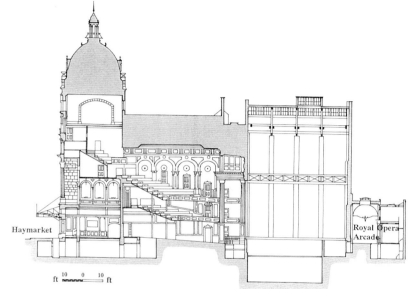

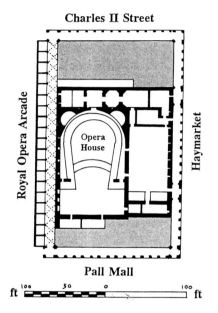

HISTORICAL PHOTOGRAPHS AND DRAWINGS

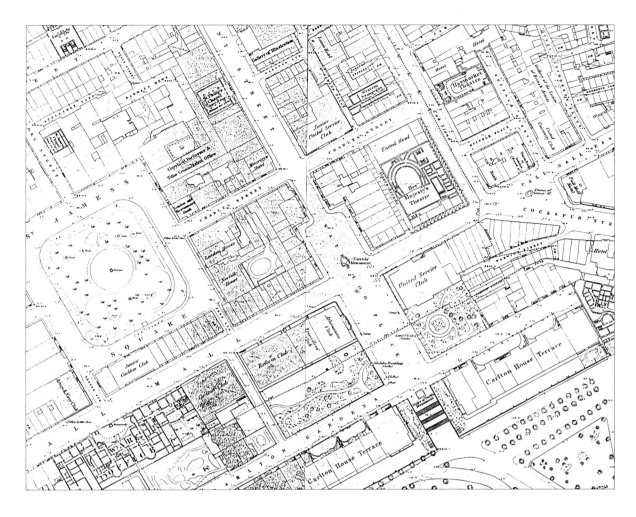

# LLOYDS BANK, PALL MALL
## CITY OF WESTMINSTER 1989-1991

*Within the area of London's clubland Farrell developed a project for the transformation of a listed bank building, owned by Lloyds, into a modern office building and new banking accommodation. Of particular interest to Farrell, in urban design terms, was the development of the area over time by a number of different architects. The original layout of Nash's Waterloo Place, the square and the wide boulevard running from Piccadilly down to St James's Park, was retained when the whole area was redeveloped and redesigned at the turn of the century by Sir William Emerson. The scheme, with facades designed as a symmetrical urban square, was not carried out until after Emerson's death, due to the interruption of the First World War, and the interior of the bank building was therefore the work of another architect, A.E. Thompson.*

*Emerson's scheme therefore mirrored a pattern, established by Nash, of a series of street facades designed in a theatrical way to enclose and define public space. Behind each facade different architects created different kinds of accommodation in a variety of architectural styles according to the taste of the designer and client. This variety was evident between the two schemes with which Farrell was involved. The Lloyd's Bank, formerly Cox and Kings, had extended right across the city block through to adjoining streets, whilst opposite, the Crafts Council building was originally developed as a number of separate, more cellular spaces.*

*The main urban design determinant of the scheme was*

*to create a spatial sequence from the street, through entrance halls to the grand rooms, that related to the interior landscape of the clubs in the area. Farrell was particularly interested in the way the Grand Room of the original bank sat adjacent to the Royal Opera Arcade. The Grand Room overlooked the top of the arcade, and descended two storeys below ground level, to utilize space that had previously been useless basements. This five-storey main internal space provided the access to the new circulation core in the building and related to each of the three entrances which were in turn defined by special double-height entrance halls, created to intensify front door usage. In the main entrance hall the original character of the first banking hall was recreated using elements and features recycled from other spaces in the building.*

*In all, five major spaces were created within the building which was completely reconstructed behind the original facade. For Farrell this reconstruction was not merely immoral facadism, as modernist accusers may claim. Projects of this nature were a direct descendant of the original methods used to generate this kind of building - one architect designing the facades as part of a larger urban design idea and other architects generating smaller spaces and accommodation behind the existing facades. Farrell's scheme for Lloyds Bank continued this tradition and responded to the urban design features of the area - the spatial hierarchies that form the private and semi-public world of clubland.*

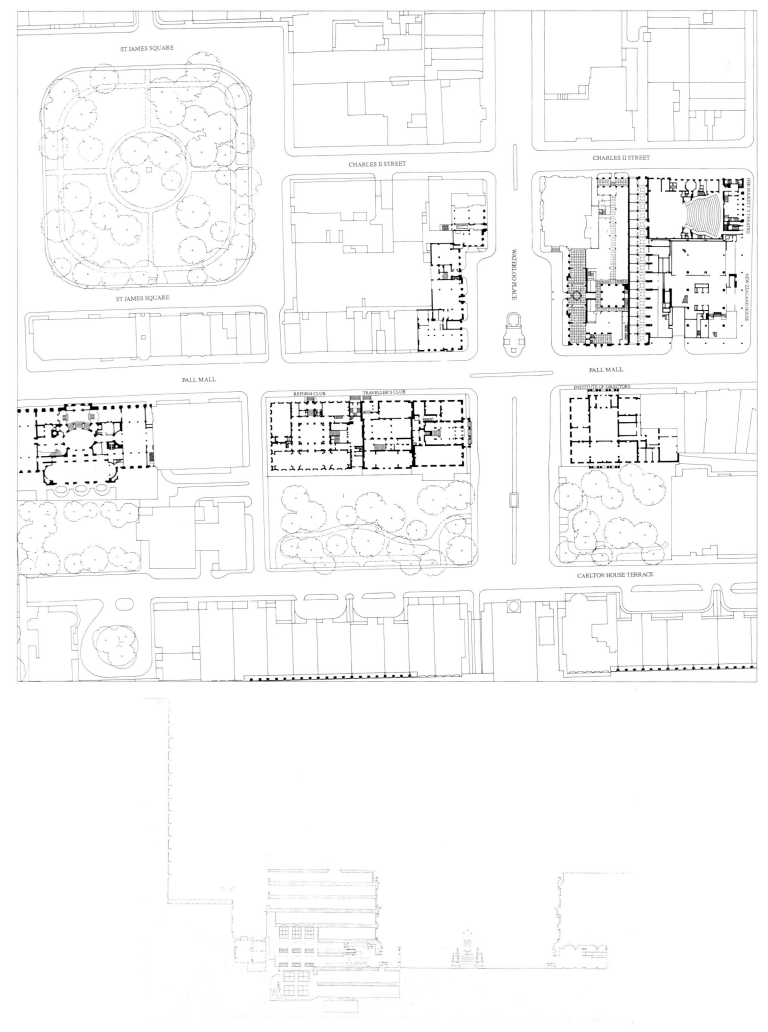

ST JAMES SQUARE

CHARLES II STREET

CHARLES II STREET

HER MAJESTY'S THEATRE

NEW ZEALAND HOUSE

WATERLOO PLACE

ST JAMES SQUARE

PALL MALL

PALL MALL

REFORM CLUB

TRAVELLER'S CLUB

INSTITUTE OF DIRECTORS

CARLTON HOUSE TERRACE

CROSS SECTION AND SITE PLAN WITH ADJOINING CLUBS

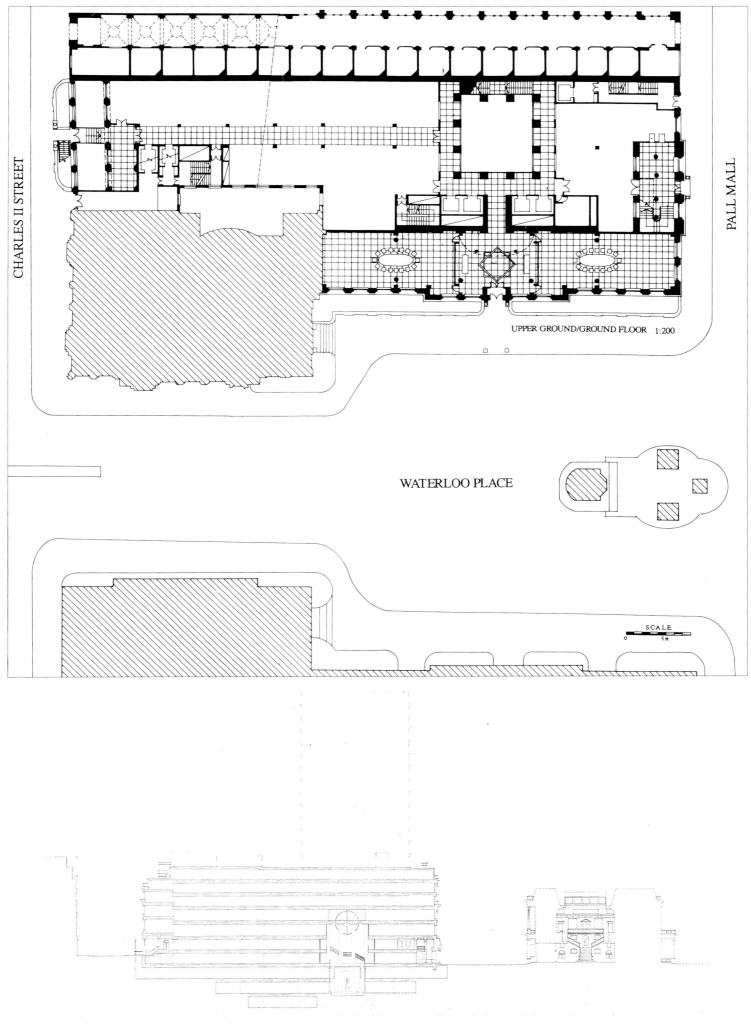

CHARLES II STREET

PALL MALL

UPPER GROUND/GROUND FLOOR 1:200

WATERLOO PLACE

SCALE
0      5 M

CROSS SECTION AND GROUND FLOOR PLAN

185

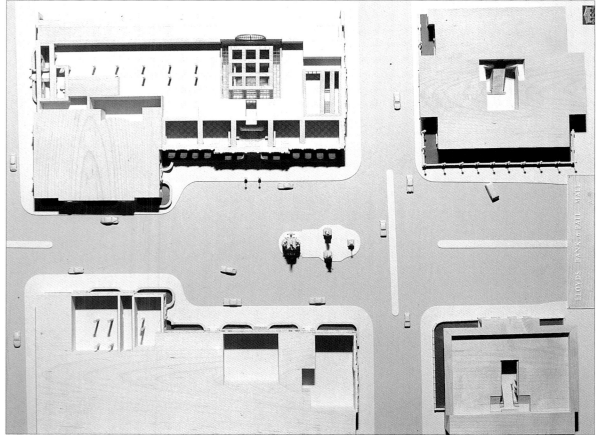

HISTORICAL PHOTOGRAPHS AND MODEL OF PROPOSALS

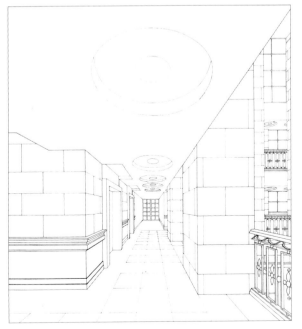

VIEWS OF PROPOSED INTERIOR

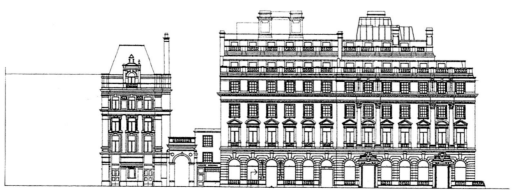

PROPOSED GRAND ROOM AND ELEVATION

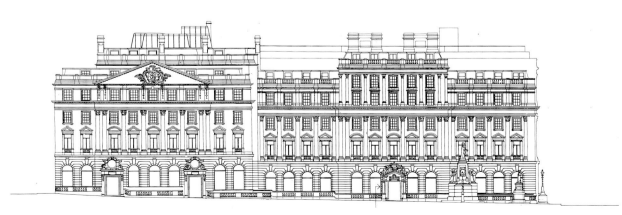

PROPOSED ELEVATIONS AND INTERIORS

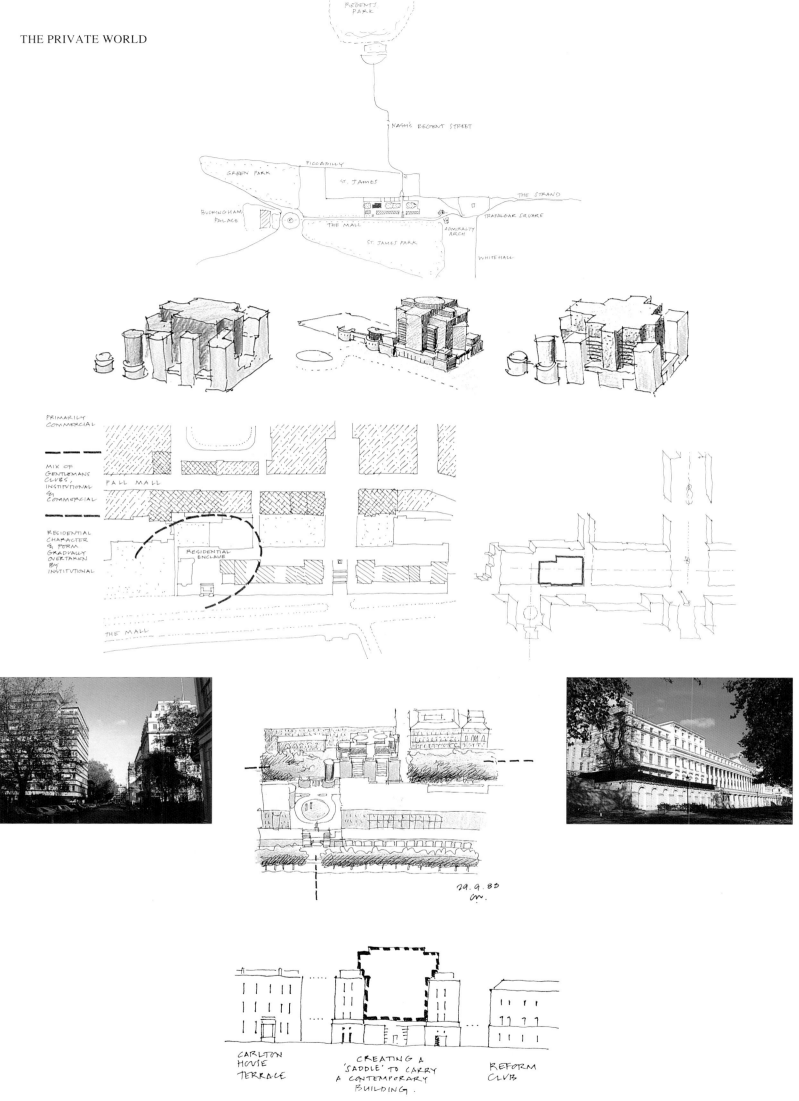

CONCEPT SKETCHES AND VIEWS OF THE SITE

# CARLTON GARDENS
## *CITY OF WESTMINSTER 1988*

The scheme for Carlton Gardens was a response to a competition enquiry to replace an existing 1960s building with luxury residences and some office accommodation. The site was located at the western end of Waterloo Gardens, in the heart of London's clubland. As with Farrell's other schemes in the area, the main interest in urban design terms was the traditional relationship developed between the external set pieces of Nash's urban design and the internal world of the club. Unlike the schemes for the Crafts Council and Lloyds, which were developed behind existing facades, here Farrell had the opportunity to design a new building that could respond to the different contexts it addressed and investigate more fully ways of linking the internal and external domains.

The formal concept of the building was a cruciform mass of seven storeys contained within a frame of four-storey towers, which defined the street edge and responded to the scale and character of Carlton House Terrace and the Reform Club. The eastern facade had a symmetrical elevation, with a central formal entrance to the offices above, which addressed and defined the western end of Waterloo Gardens, enclosing the public space.

In contrast to this facade, the scale and formality of the building to the west descended to the garden. Farrell placed the residential access at the south-east corner of the site and developed a series of spaces and elements that explored the relationship of internal and external. From the secure entrance lobby the route to the lift core, at the centre of the building, passed through a circular marble hall and rear hall, which contained staircases to apartments on the first floor.

This sequence of circulation spaces provided a series of long views into the garden to the west, which were crossed by a north-south axis which provided a view into a small sculpture courtyard. The building itself extended into the gardens by means of a garden terrace, accessed via the marble hall. From the entrance lobby, expressed as a tower, a colonnade formed the link to a garden alcove, which provided sheltered seating and access directly into the garden from first floor level. These elements both defined the southern edge of the gardens and extended Farrell's investigations into the wider urban context by addressing the axis running down to the Mall and beyond to St James's Park.

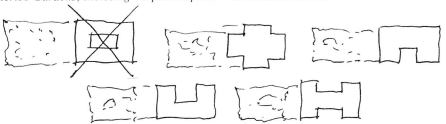

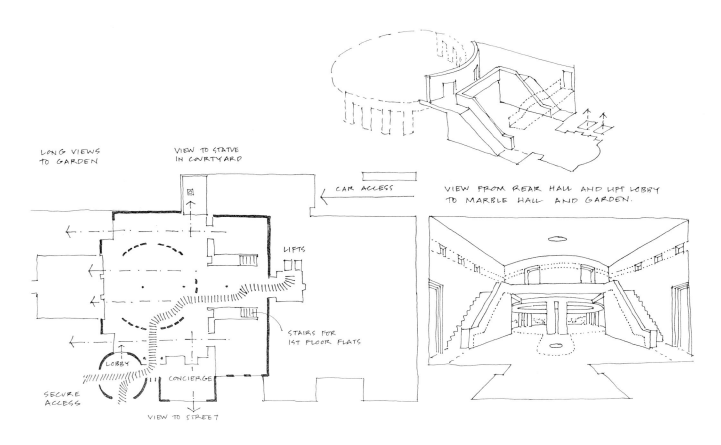

LONG VIEWS
TO GARDEN

VIEW TO STATUE
IN COURTYARD

CAR ACCESS

VIEW FROM REAR HALL AND LIFT LOBBY
TO MARBLE HALL AND GARDEN.

LIFTS

STAIRS FOR
1ST FLOOR FLATS

LOBBY

CONCIERGE

SECURE
ACCESS

VIEW TO STREET

RESIDENTIAL ACCESS AND VIEW OF THE MODEL

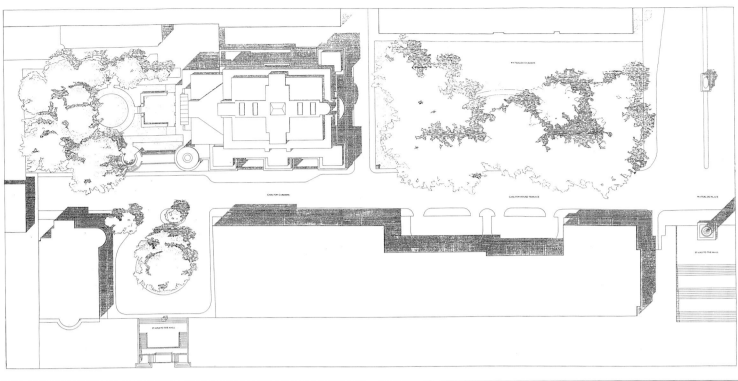

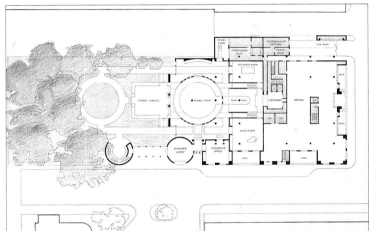

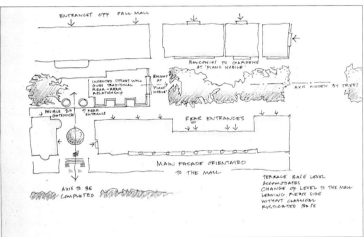

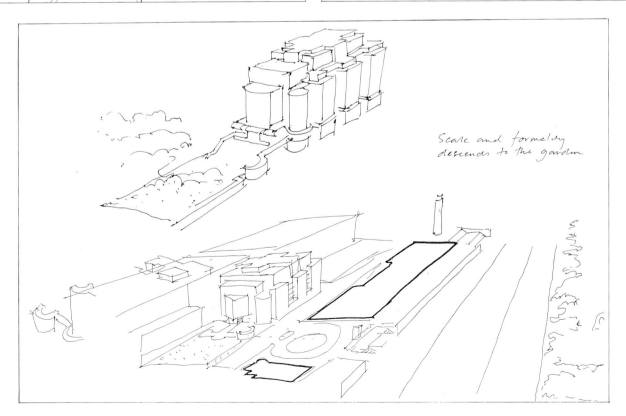

CONTEXT AND GROUND FLOOR PLANS, AND CONCEPT SKETCHES

NORTH, EAST, SOUTH AND WEST ELEVATIONS

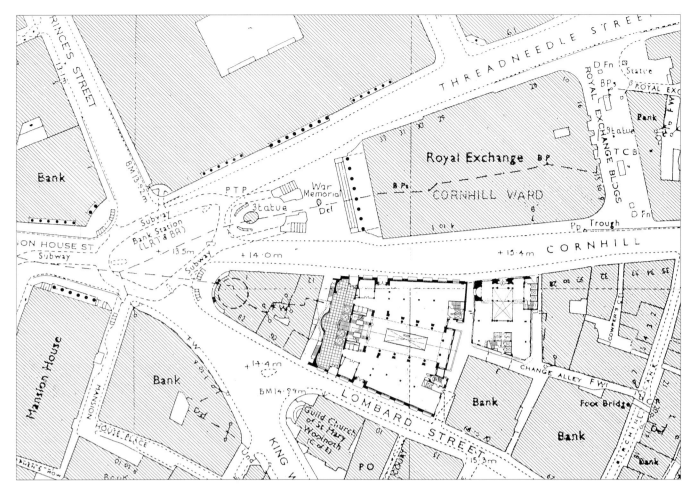

*ABOVE*: SITE PLAN PROPOSAL AND HISTORICAL VIEWS
*OPPOSITE*: HISTORICAL PLANS

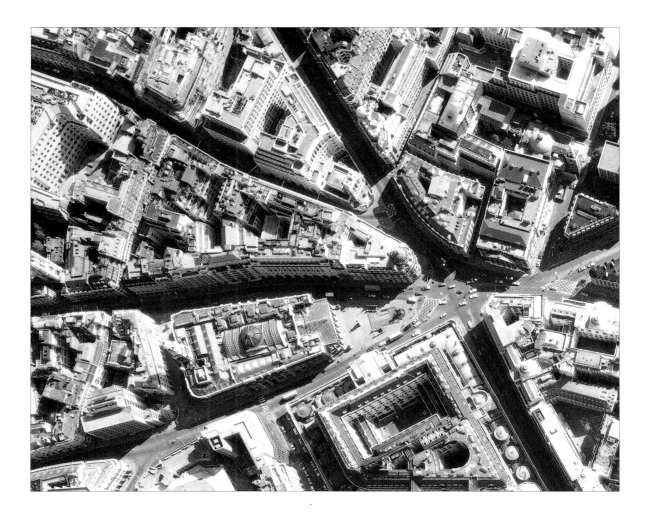

# LOMBARD STREET
## *CITY OF LONDON 1991-1992*

*Farrell's schemes in the City - Britannic House and Lombard Street - respond to the tradition of internal public spaces which form a unique part of the business network within the City. At Lombard Street, Farrell was involved in redeveloping the existing banking building designed by Sir John Burnet for Lloyds Bank. For Farrell, such buildings, designed by some of this century's major architects in the tradition of modern classicism, contain qualities that are often underrated today. The aim of the scheme was to recognize the changes in requirements of modern business, and adapt and convert existing spaces to suit modern needs, whilst retaining the inherent quality of the building. For Farrell this approach is a major theme of urban design - the interior spaces of buildings, just like areas of the city, are adapted to new uses and criteria.*

*The Lombard Street building contained a grand staircase that connected the great internal entrance hall to the major boardrooms and directors' offices on the upper floors, in a grand procession. Between these spaces were*

*the mass of offices, expressed externally in the tripartite hierarchy of the elevation. By moving Popes Head Alley westwards, Farrell created a new entrance hall which linked Cornhill to Lombard Street, with a main reception area adjacent to the grand staircase. A new reception area for the ground and lower floors was placed at the opposite end of the hall to enable visitors to enjoy the space in its entirety. The scheme was also dictated by the great history of pedestrian routes through the site. Popes Head Alley was developed into a shopping street, in the tradition of Nash's Royal Opera Arcade, providing an enhanced short-cut to major buildings on either side of the site. This concern for the activity at ground level was matched by concern at roof level, allowing for distant views of the building from the surrounding streets. Farrell designed a new seventh floor and roofscape, influenced by a number of Burnet and Tait's designs, which enhanced the composition of the building, particularly when viewed from a distance along Cheapside.*

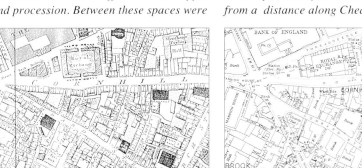

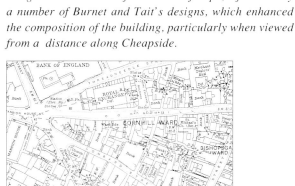

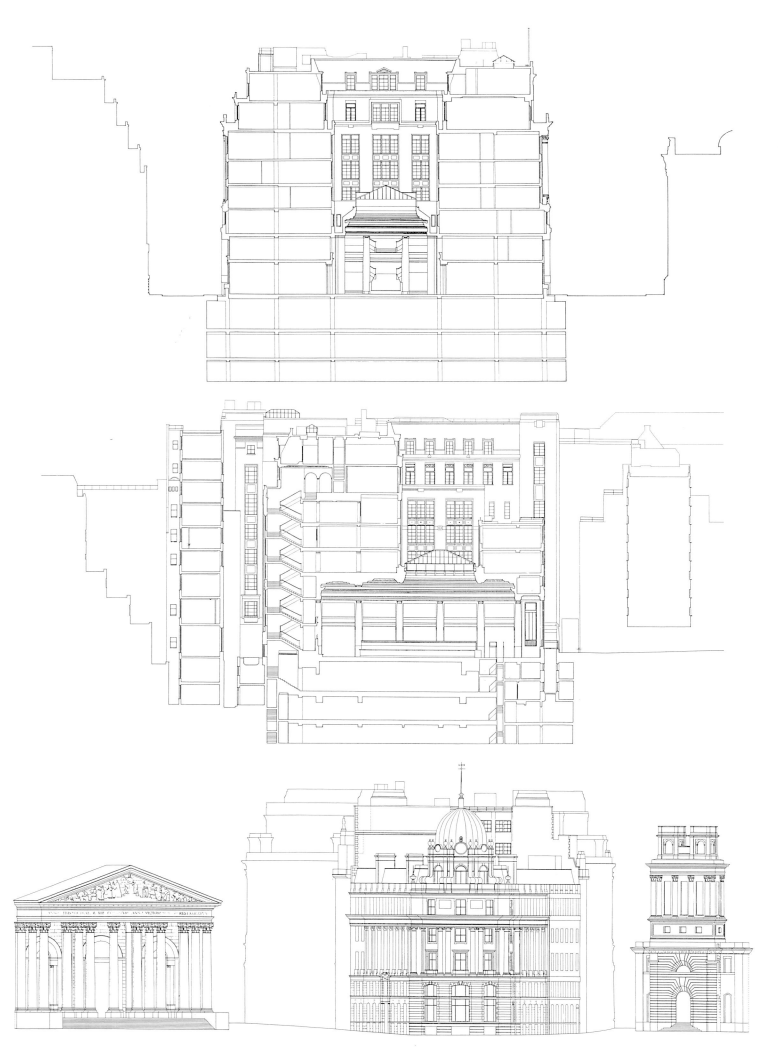

EXISTING CROSS AND LONGITUDINAL SECTIONS, AND SITE ELEVATION

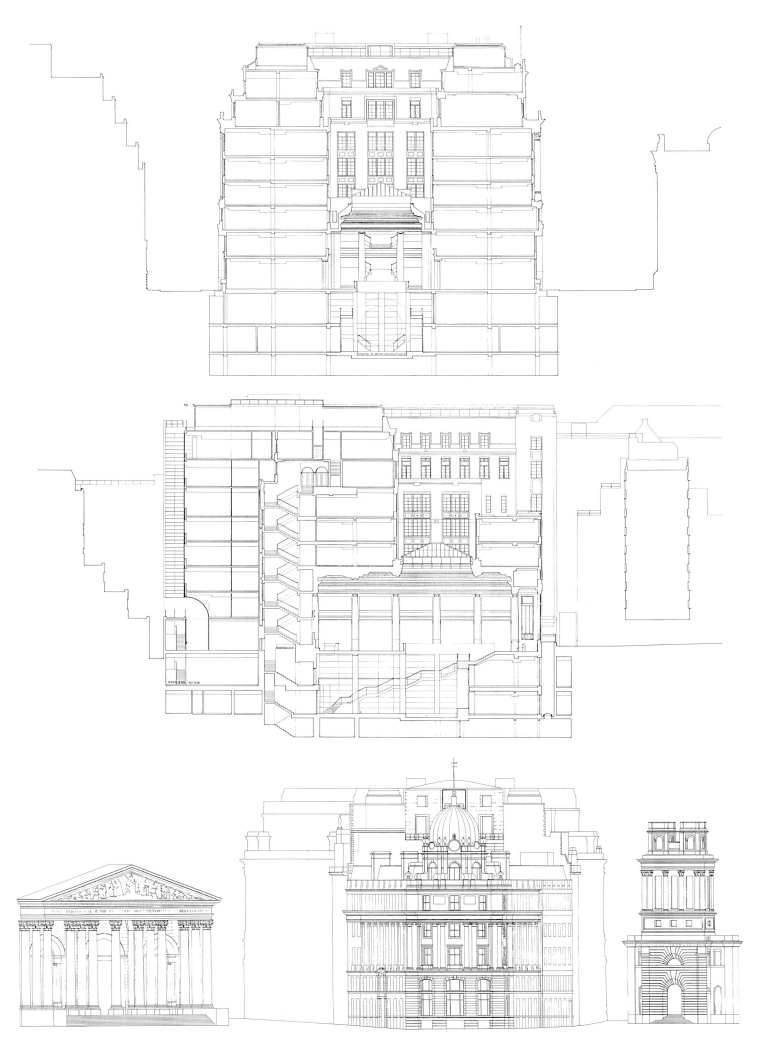

PROPOSED CROSS AND LONGITUDINAL SECTIONS, AND SITE ELEVATION

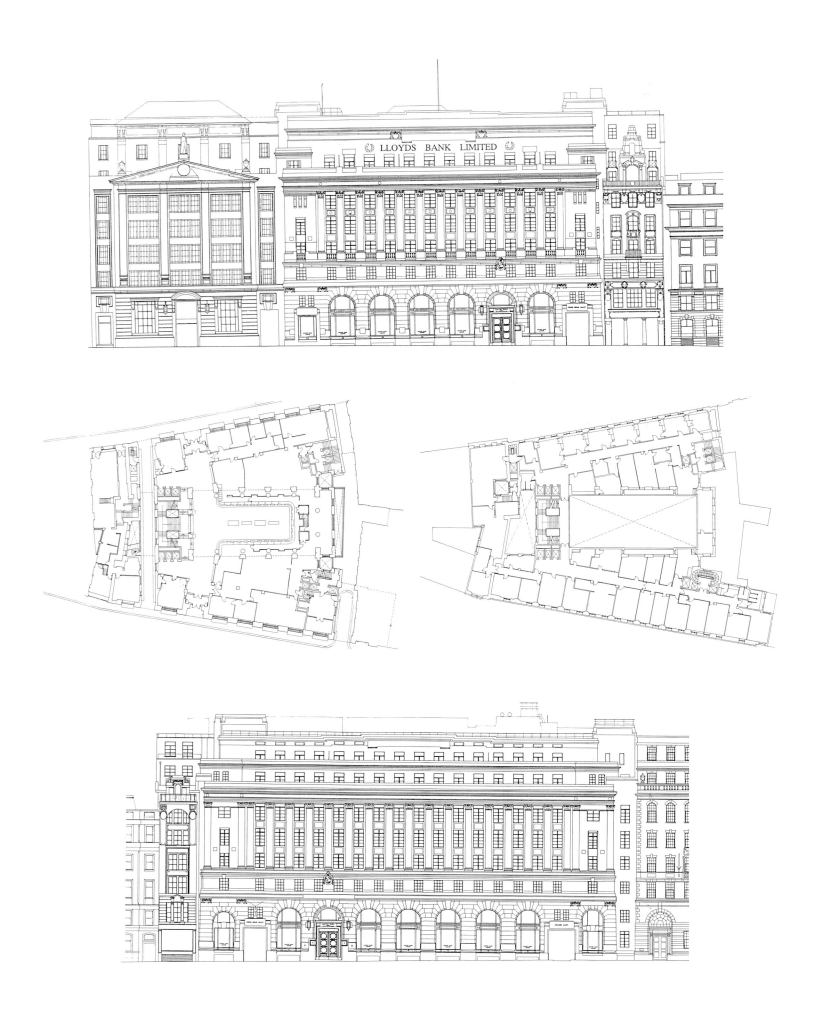

EXISTING CORNHILL ELEVATION, GROUND AND FIRST FLOOR PLANS, AND LOMBARD STREET ELEVATION

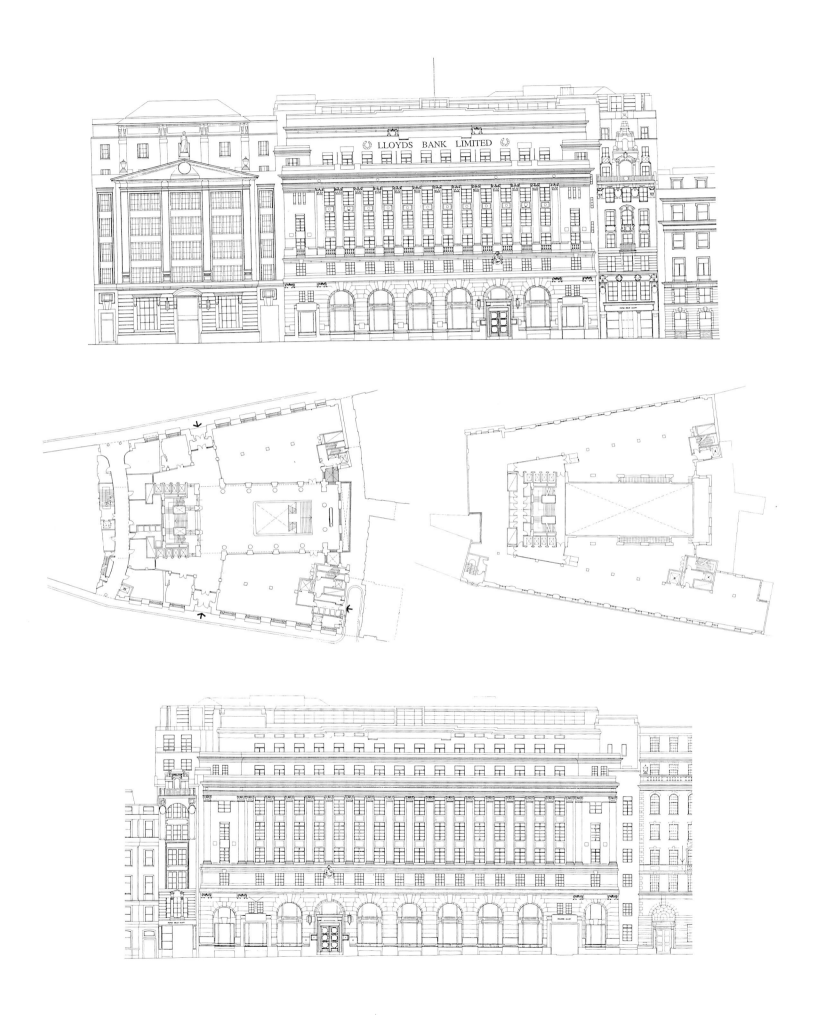

LLOYDS BANK LIMITED

PROPOSED CORNHILL ELEVATION, GROUND AND FIRST FLOOR PLANS, AND LOMBARD STREET ELEVATION

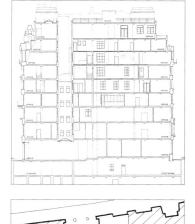

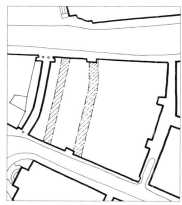

EXISTING AND PROPOSED VIEWS AND PLANS OF POPES HEAD ALLEY, AND CROSS SECTIONS

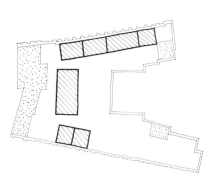

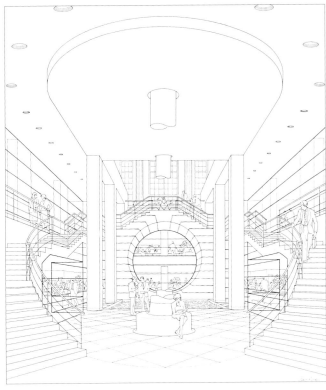

EXISTING AND PROPOSED INTERIOR VIEWS, AND FLOOR PLANS

# OUTER VILLAGES

The description of London as a collection of villages is a familiar one. London is a continuum, spreading from the two cities of Westminster and the City, rather than a formal centre such as the defended cores of other European cities. Many of the villages absorbed into London maintained a semi-rural nature: Highgate and Hampstead to the north, Putney and Wimbledon to the south. Village centres in themselves, they were usually located with some rationale, positioned by landownership, or a strategic point on a hill, next to a stream, or on a communication route. Many of these 'villages' contained a number of features, such as a village green, parish church, town hall or 'High Street' that defined the centre for the area. For Farrell, it is this piecemeal evolution, the accretion of village centres, each with its own specific character, that makes London a unique place to live.

As well as the established village that became part of the city, London's expansion resulted from the development of the suburban estate, built around the city from the 19th century onwards. The British vision of the suburb resulted from a desire to create a world that would provide the best of both countryside and city. St John's Wood was the earliest of London's suburbs attracting residents by its proximity to the entrapped countryside of Regent's Park but also by its easy access to the city. It offered an escape for the upper classes from the unhealthy life in the congested, over-populated city. The detached and semi-detached villas with gardens of the Eyre Estate in St John's Wood, designed by the architect John Shaw, were the origin, after much debasement and alteration, of all suburban houses. With the development of an efficient public transport system, great numbers left the city to live in the suburbs. Many of the estates lacked the qualities of the earlier upper-class suburb, and today the suburb is often viewed disparagingly. But generally, for the masses, the suburb offered a more satisfactory environment to live in than the inner city or new town or village away from the city.

Farrell has been involved in a number of schemes in London's suburbs and outer villages, which were based upon an understanding of the particular characteristics - of density, scale and spatial organization - of the suburban or mid-urban

*Opposite*: Henley Royal Regatta Headquarters; *Left*: Wood Green and Maunsel Housing

CHISWICK PARK

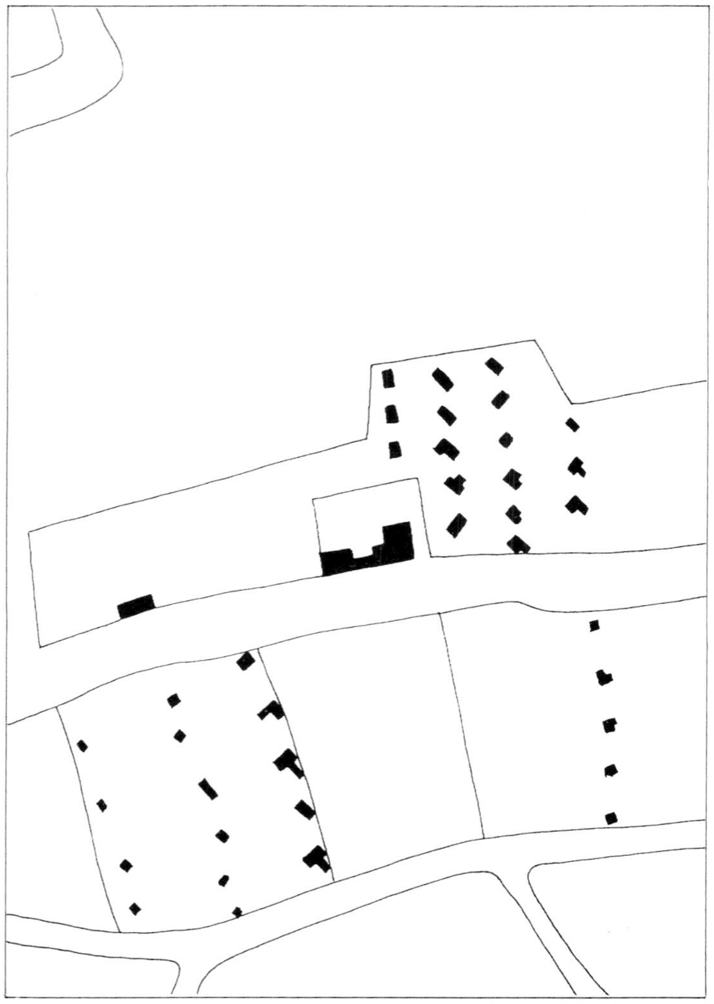

1822

1871

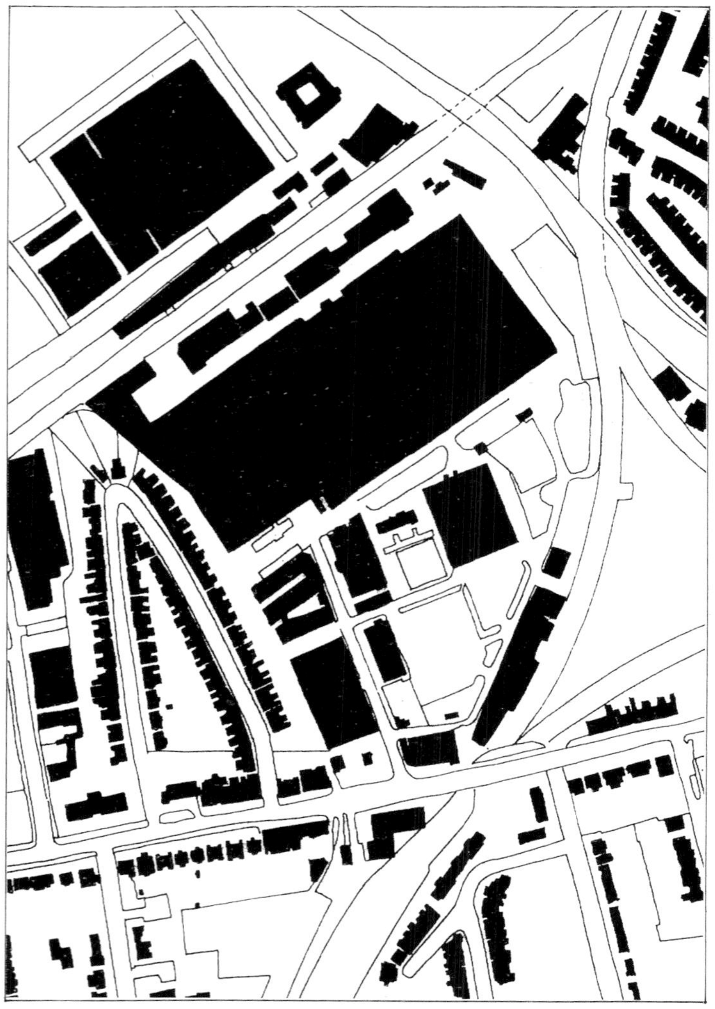

EXISTING 1990

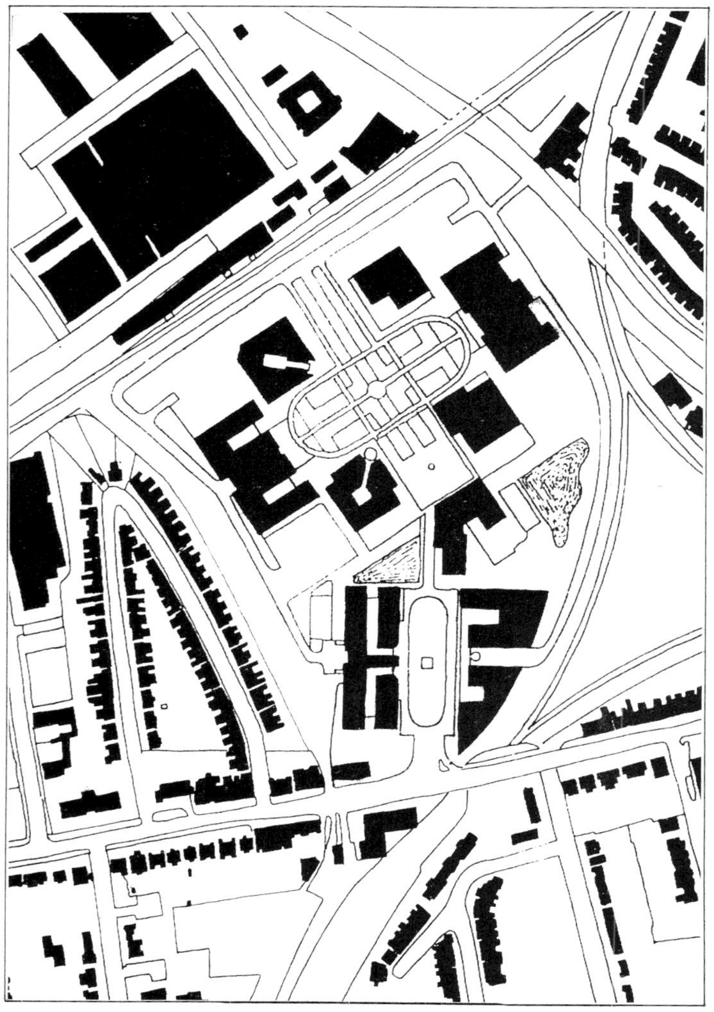

FARRELL 1991

development. One of Farrell's earliest projects, in the mid-seventies, involved the design of housing complexes for a number of outer villages dispersed around the periphery of London, from Luton to Romford to Croydon. Commissioned by a housing association, the houses were all constructed from a standardized timber frame, with adaptations designed to relate each individual complex to the local neighbourhood. In order to integrate the schemes into the suburban context of low-rise housing, the original planning consents for blocks of flats from four to seven storeys were translated into applications for low-rise schemes with a maximum of four storeys, and wherever possible the new scheme was for houses rather than flats. Replicating the suburban pattern of development, each dwelling had its own front door accessible from the street, and an area of private open space, in the form of a terrace, patio or garden. Much time was spent in persuading the authorities to have the address of each dwelling numbered as a normal continuation of the surrounding streets. The schemes were dictated by a desire to integrate into and repair gaps in the existing fabric.

The development of London, absorbing a number of villages, created areas or villages outside the city which provided a particular service for London, such as that offered by the airports, Heathrow and Stansted. Henley-upon-Thames has evolved as a sporting extension of London, primarily connected with the annual Regatta. Farrell was commissioned to design the Henley Royal Regatta Headquarters, on a site at the entrance to the town adjacent to the listed 18th-century bridge. Farrell's scheme, accommodating the disparate functions of the organization within one building, was conceived as a civic building, emphasizing the importance of the Regatta in the life of Henley, and the relationship and role of the area to London. The building was designed in the tradition of the Thames boathouse, but other features, including the heraldic emblems of the Regatta organization and architectural references to the Roman ideals of the sport, reinforced the civic role of the building within the area.

For Farrell, one of the greatest problems for the urban designer dealing with sites around central London, is posed by the inner suburbs, where there is considerable decay and a conflict between a diversity of uses. Farrell was involved with such an area, Wood Green, a residential area that had become progressively industrialized in the last part of the 19th century. Cheap land attracted industry into these areas which became mixed use - and Farrell was fascinated by the patchwork of sites and uses that created the specific character of the inner suburb. As industries closed, a surfeit of land in the suburb resulted in areas of dereliction that undermined the quality and density of the built fabric. At Wood Green, the sites for redevelopment

*Left*: Temple Island, Henley; and Oakwood

HAMMERSMITH ISLAND

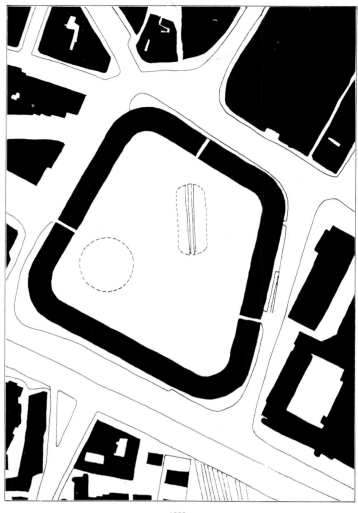

1980s

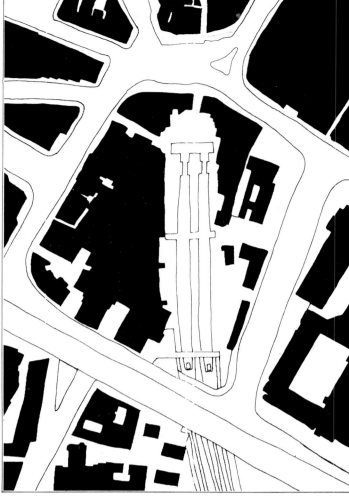

FOSTERS 1977

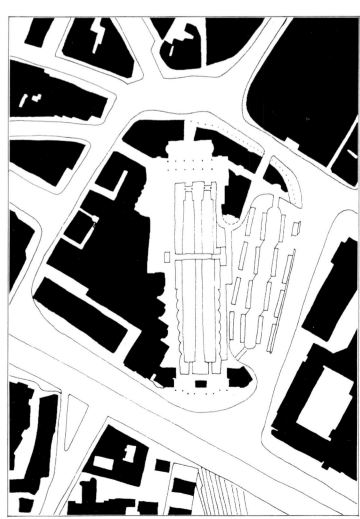

FARRELL GLC 1984

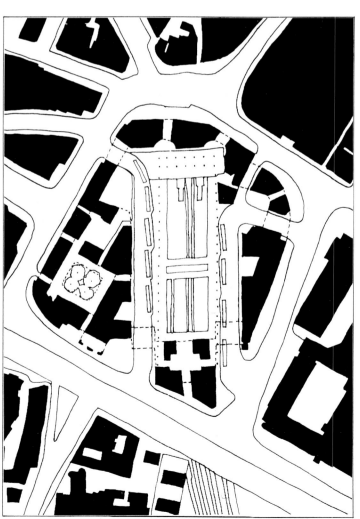

FARRELL SPLIT BUS STATION 1987

were defined by strips of terraced housing, light industry, a gasometer and a railway line. In view of the low rental potential of any new developments, Farrell developed a solution similar to that of the housing projects - a standardized factory unit that was adapted for five sites. Relating to the main characteristic of the suburb with its repetitious manufacture of the standardized house type, pubs and shops, a typology of introverted industrial buildings was developed around a courtyard as an internally-organized nucleus. The main strategy of these industrial projects was to separate the activity of industry from the residential areas around. The internal spaces were planned around the turning circle of large vehicles, and provided car-parking and access for all vehicles and pedestrians. The edges of each site were defined by walls of banded brickwork to relate to the surrounding fabric, while the walls facing the courtyards were built of a proprietary wall system with reflective glazing. For Farrell the design of the buildings was less critical than the space between them or the spaces and streets they defined, and as a whole the buildings sought to reverse the fragmentation of the area and reconcile its various functions.

Another important feature of the suburb or village is the concern of the residents about their environment. Unlike the resignation of the inner city dweller to the problems of urban life, the suburban resident has moved to escape the mêlée of the city, and as part of a small community, public concern can more easily be galvanised into opposition against specific developments and changes. At both Hammersmith and Wimbledon Farrell was brought in by local residents to oppose vast new monolithic developments which threatened to destroy the existing town centres and civic hearts of these outer villages. The scheme for Hammersmith, on the site of the original village broadway, replaced all the existing buildings with a new bus and underground station and a vast office complex. Farrell's alternative proposal advocated the conservation and conversion of the existing buildings as the basis for a re-established mixed use civic centre for the area. Similarly at Wimbledon, local residents opposed a scheme that demolished a collection of civic buildings to make way for a huge shopping centre. For Farrell such opposition was generated by the conflict of scale between the traditional suburban fabric and the vast scale of the proposed new developments. The issue of scale is an essential factor in the redevelopment of the suburban environment, and the business park at Chiswick, for which Farrell acted as master planner, was formed from a collection of lower rise buildings. As such, the scheme sought to repair the interplay between different uses in these suburban areas, avoiding the need for zoning by relating to the characteristics of the suburban or mid-urban environment.

For the urban designer, communication remains another major issue for these 'in-between' areas, which are often situated on one of the transport lines radiating from the hub of the city centre. In simplistic terms, in the countryside the reliance on the car is almost total, whereas in the city the good public transport system and short distances that can be covered on foot, reduce the necessity for travel by car. In the suburbs, neither inner city nor countryside, reliance is divided between public transport and use of the car, with its easy access to motorways and greater distances to travel due to the lower density environment. The suburb presents a particular problem of reconciling the need for traffic access and parking with a concern for the pedestrian domain integrated into an efficient public transport network.

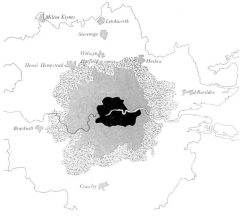

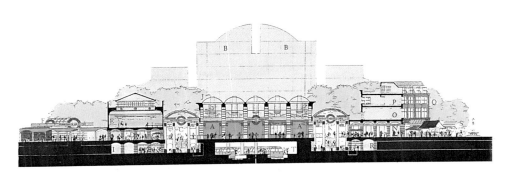

*Left*: Hammersmith cross section; *Above*: London's green belt

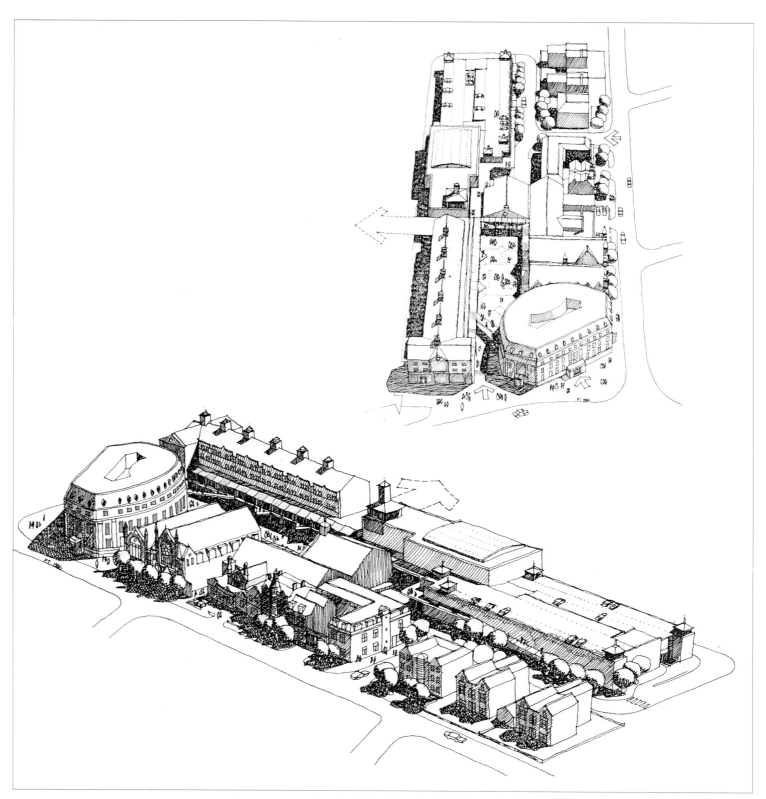

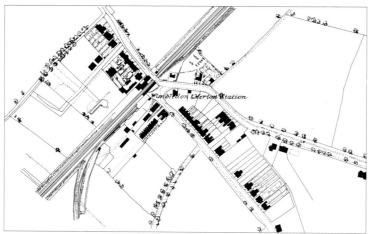

AERIAL PERSPECTIVES BY FRANCIS TIBBALDS AND MAPS OF WIMBLEDON DATING FROM THE 1860S AND 1911

# WIMBLEDON TOWN CENTRE
*LONDON BOROUGH OF MERTON 1987-1988*

Wimbledon developed like many outer London suburbs - an old village centre which was expanded by new suburban growth. The new centre of Wimbledon developed outside the original village centre, near to the railway station which provided the main transport link to central London. A number of civic buildings - the Town Hall, the Fire Station and the Police Station, all examples of late 19th or early 20th century architecture - made up the identity of the centre of Wimbledon. For Farrell this collection of buildings created a set piece within the urban fabric that gave the area its own distinctive spatial and visual qualities.

Farrell's scheme was essentially one of advocacy against the large-scale redevelopment of the town centre, and contained a number of common themes which run through Farrell's approach to urban design in such areas: the notion of a physical and historic centre to a town; the provision of open and enclosed public spaces linked by pedestrian routes; and the scale of town-centre buildings.

Farrell proposed to retain the existing buildings on the site to maintain a continuity with the recent past, using the resource of these buildings, which for Farrell had a collective vitality and quality. For Farrell the town centre depended upon the diversity of uses and amenities available, and development of the appropriate scale. Proposals were based on a number of separate but related buildings, as opposed to the single massive complex, and were grafted into the existing fabric.

Farrell's scheme for the Town Hall/Queen's Road site reinforced the area's civic role as a town centre. The retained Town Hall, part of the Civic Hall and the Queen's Road buildings formed the basis of the conservation-based scheme, which provided a variety of new uses on the site to generate activity throughout the day.

Wimbledon contained no large-scale public space and a new town square was created which acted as a focus for the town, and connected to a quieter garden square behind the Fire Station. The new square was edged with arcades and pavilions, to provide shelter for cafés, bars, shops and other activities, and provision was made for an auditorium at the rear of the Courthouse for events to engage with the square. By placing parking beneath the square, Farrell created a totally pedestrian area articulated by a variety of entrances and spaces which linked to a number of public spaces and circulation and transport networks in the area.

The site at Hartfield Road was designed by Ardin & Brookes & Partners, as a modern shopping development integrated into the existing town pattern. The scheme created an all-weather, traffic-free shopping centre without destroying the heart of the Town Hall/Queen's Road site. Together the schemes provided Wimbledon with a series of improved civic amenities, whilst reinforcing the existing character of the town centre.

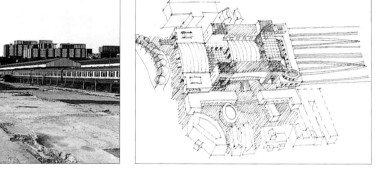

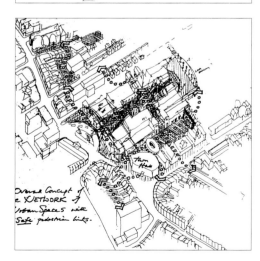

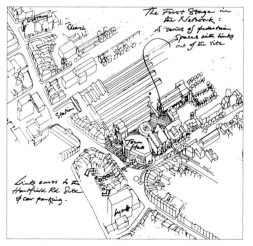

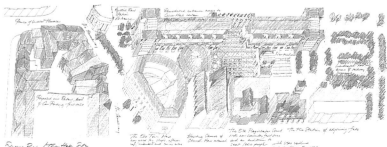

CONCEPT STUDIES AND PHOTOGRAPHS OF EXISTING SITE

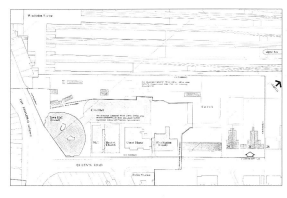

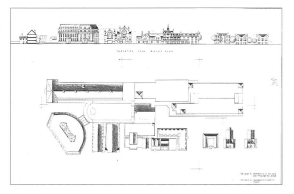

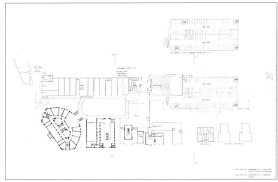

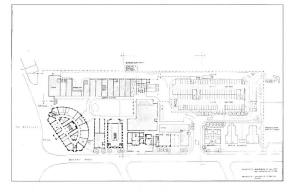

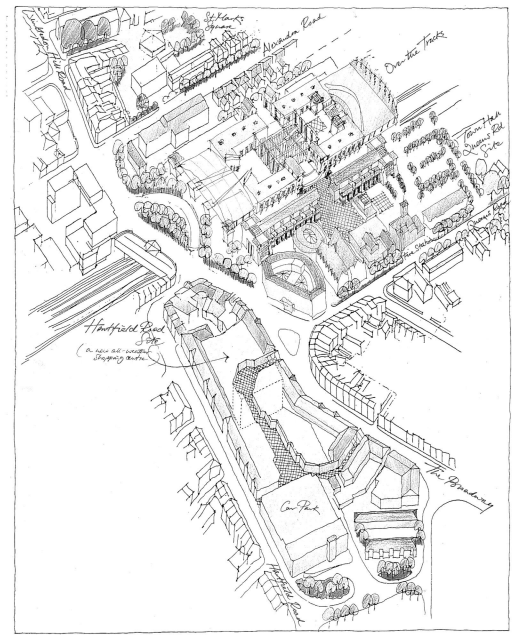

PLANS OF PROPOSALS AND COMBINED PROPOSALS FOR THE TOWN HALL SITE BY TERRY FARRELL AND THE HARTFIELD ROAD SITE

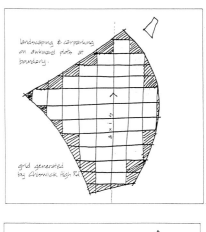

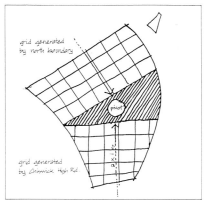

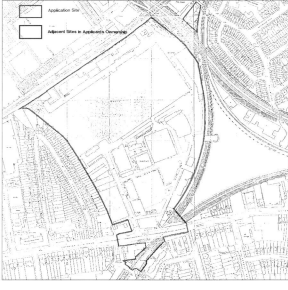

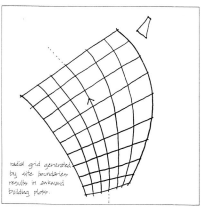

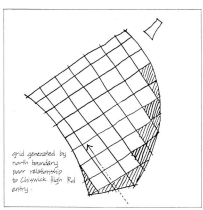

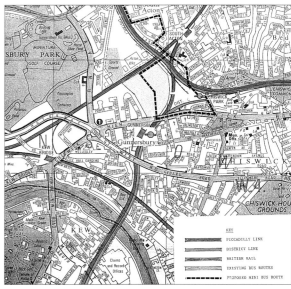

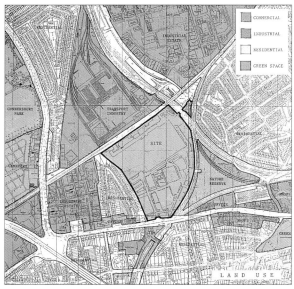

EXISTING SITE, EARLY STUDIES AND HISTORICAL PLANS

# CHISWICK PARK
*LONDON BOROUGH OF HOUNSLOW 1989-1992*

Chiswick Business Park was located in a typical area of suburban development, on a site previously occupied by a bus works. The surrounding fabric, primarily low-rise housing and gardens dictated the nature of the new buildings and site landscaping. For Farrell the most interesting aspect of the scheme was the development of the suburban or mid-urban business park that united the qualities of town and country, similar to the advantages outlined in Ebenezer Howard's famous magnet diagram of garden cities. This intention influenced the masterplan in ways dictated by the concept of the mid-urban in which the landscaping becomes the dominant unifying element.

From an empty site, Farrell had to create new infrastructure, concentrating on the landscape and patterns of spaces within which buildings were placed. The triangular park area, generated by the irregular boundary geometries, drew the natural landscape of the adjacent nature reserve into the site in contrast to the more formal squares on the site. These public spaces drew on the spatial planning and scale of other London squares - the main square is similar in size to Berkeley Square, the Orchard, spatially similar to Montagu Square - which offered the advantages of enclosure and a good micro-climate.

Another important factor in the masterplan was the creation of transport infrastructure, which raised the issue of public transport and the pedestrian domain versus the car. Pedestrian routes followed the shortest links between destinations, and wherever possible were segregated from vehicle routes, which were based upon the formal arrangement of the service and main entrances of the London square. Within the site, vehicular routes connected to drop-off points at an upper ground level relating to the main entrances of the buildings; the routes then descended to a lower existing ground level at the perimeter, connecting to car parking accessed from the rear of the buildings. For Farrell the quality of the ground-level public domain depended on the reduction of car parking and vehicular activity at this level. Priority was given to improving the quality of pedestrian routes which provided access from existing transport facilities to the centre of the site, and provision was made for a local mini-bus service from the site to surrounding stations.

At Chiswick Park, Farrell's masterplan provided a framework within which a number of different architects could respond. Unlike the Paternoster scheme in which the buildings formed a densely packed group enclosing the spaces between, the lower density at Chiswick Park meant that the buildings were objects in themselves, standing in open space, which was filled with movement systems. But the massing responded to both the new public spaces on the site and the surrounding context. A focal high point provided a buffer between the site and Chiswick High Road, with buildings of five to six storeys fronting on the main square, diminishing in height towards the boundary, relating in scale to the surrounding residential fabric.

Farrell developed the masterplan working closely with landscape architect Laurie Olin.

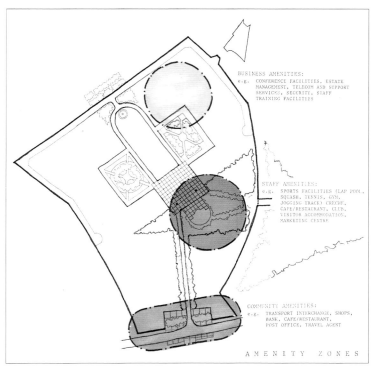

BUSINESS AMENITIES:
e.g.   CONFERENCE FACILITIES, ESTATE
       MANAGEMENT, TELECOM AND SUPPORT
       SERVICES, SECURITY, STAFF
       TRAINING FACILITIES

STAFF AMENITIES:
e.g.   SPORTS FACILITIES (LAP POOL,
       SQUASH, TENNIS, GYM,
       JOGGING TRACK) CRECHE,
       CAFE/RESTAURANT, CLUB,
       VISITOR ACCOMMODATION,
       MARKETING CENTRE

COMMUNITY AMENITIES:
e.g.   TRANSPORT INTERCHANGE, SHOPS,
       BANK, CAFE/RESTAURANT,
       POST OFFICE, TRAVEL AGENT

A M E N I T Y   Z O N E S

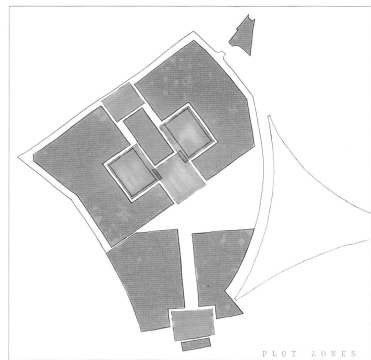

P L O T   Z O N E S

P L O T S   -   O P T I O N   A

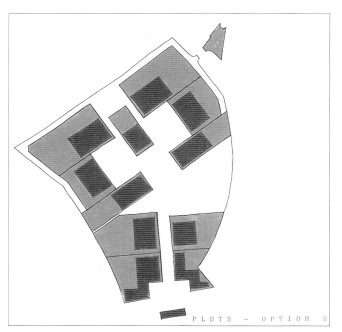

P L O T S   -   O P T I O N   B

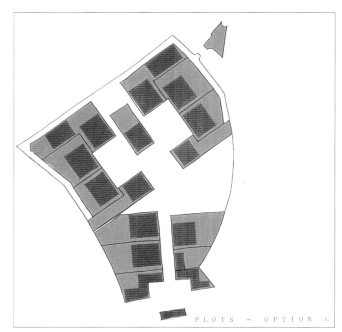

P L O T S   -   O P T I O N   C

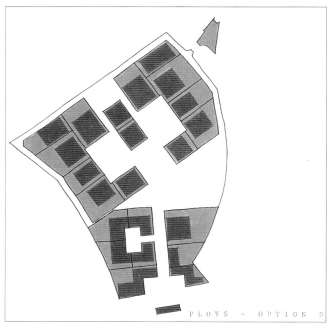

P L O T S   -   O P T I O N   D

EARLY STUDIES OF BUILDING PLOTS, AMENITY AND OPEN SPACE

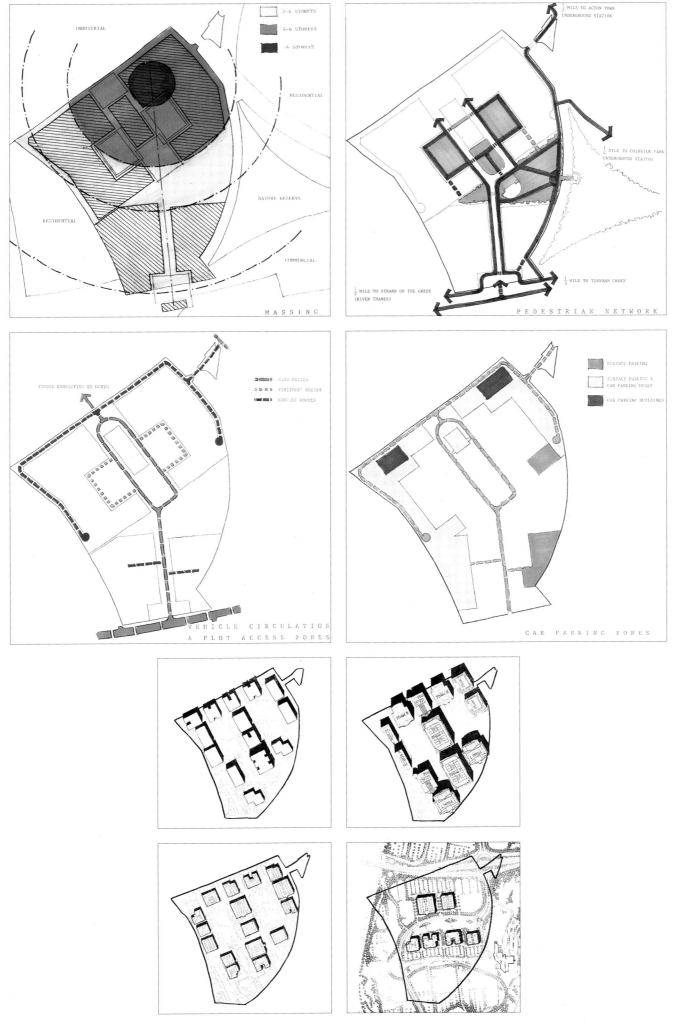

STUDIES FOR MASSING, PEDESTRIAN AND VEHICLE CIRCULATION, AND BUILDING FLOOR; PLATE OPTIONS

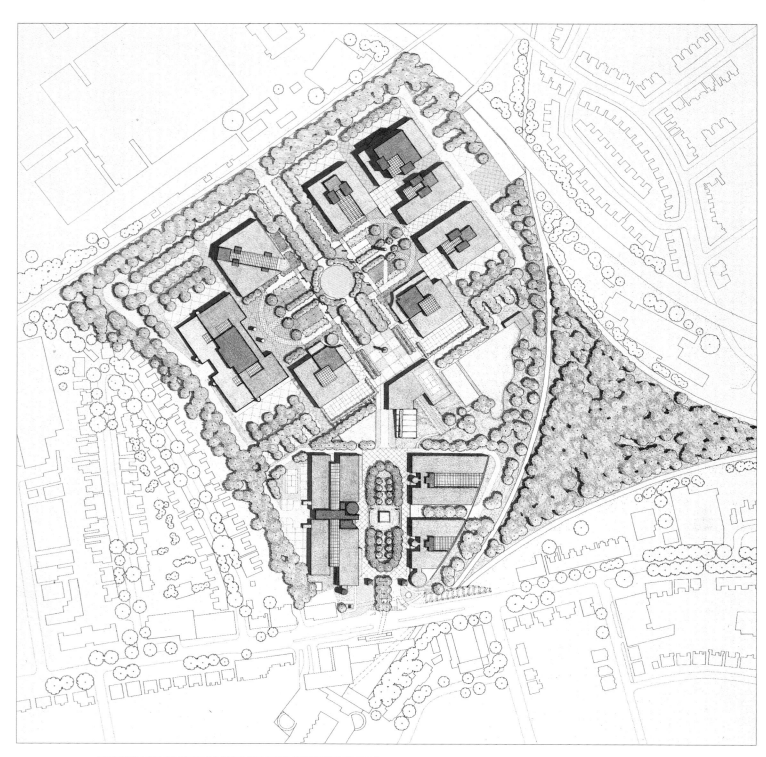

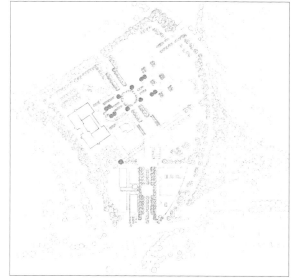
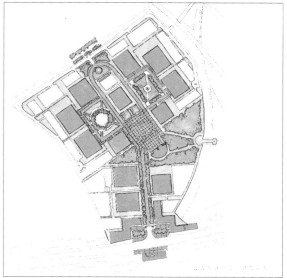

EVOLUTION OF THE MASTERPLAN

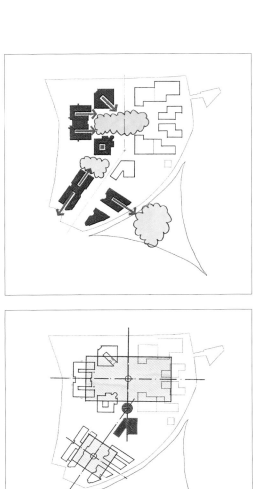
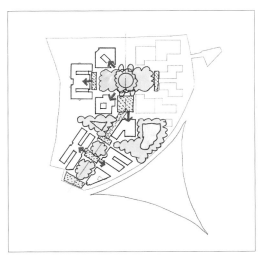
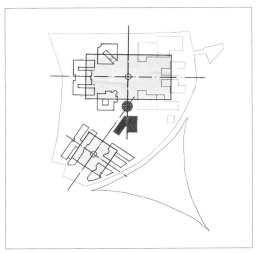
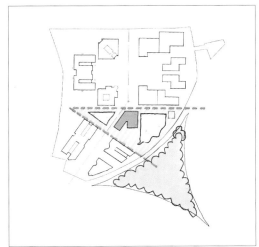
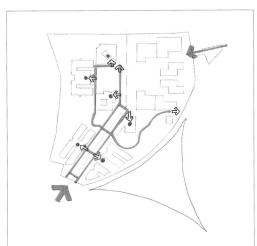
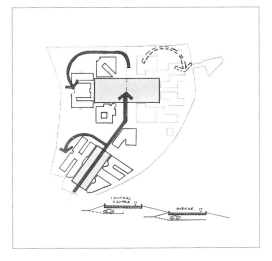
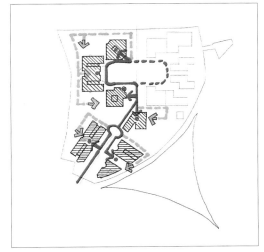
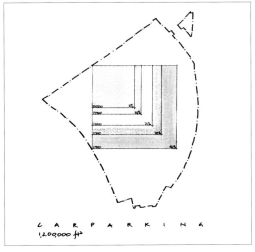

PRINCIPLE CONCEPTS FOR LANDSCAPING, VEHICULAR MOVEMENT AND CAR PARKING

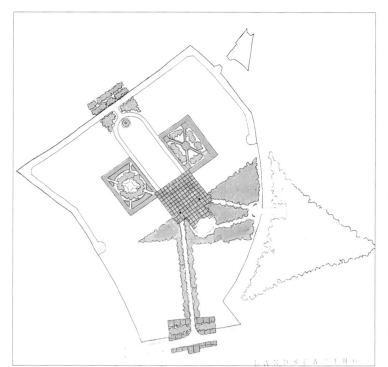

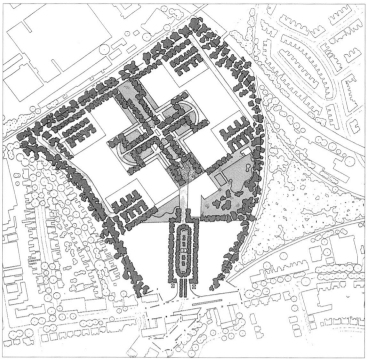

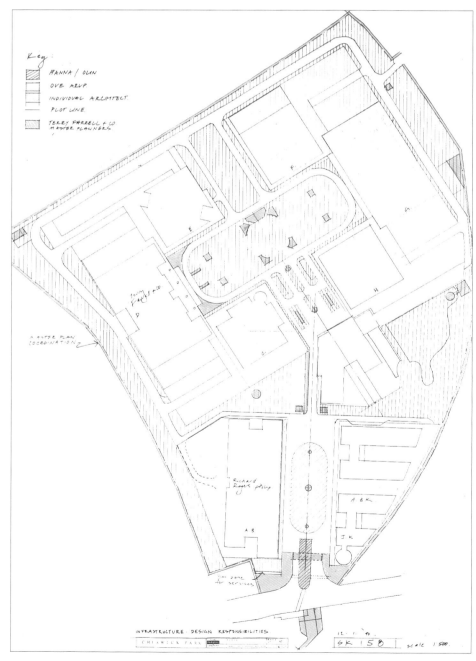

LANDSCAPE MASTERPLAN OPTIONS AND KEY PLAN SHOWING ZONES OF RESPONSIBILITY FOR INFRASTRUCTURE DESIGN

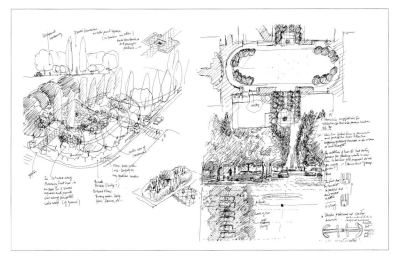
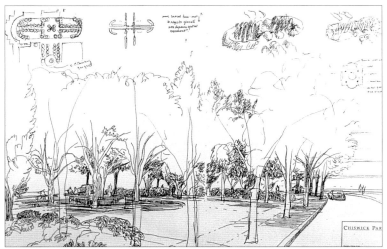

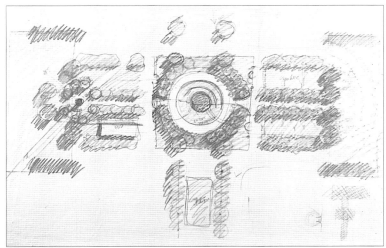
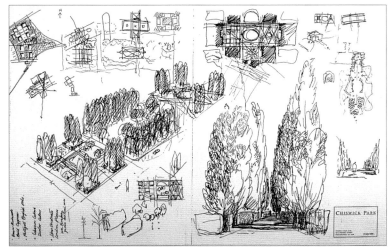

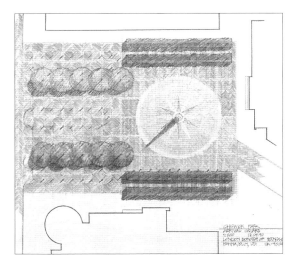
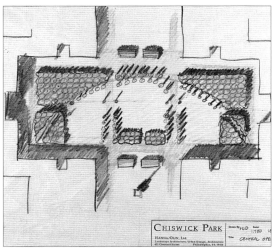

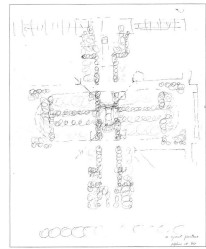

LAURIE OLIN'S AND TERRY FARREL'S LANDSCAPE SKETCHES

221

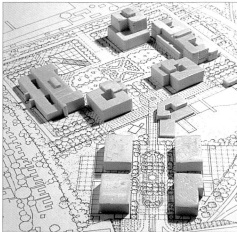

MASTERPLAN MODELS

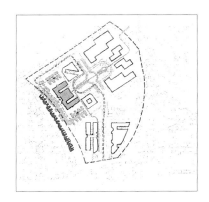
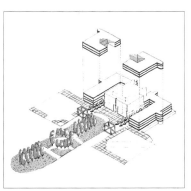

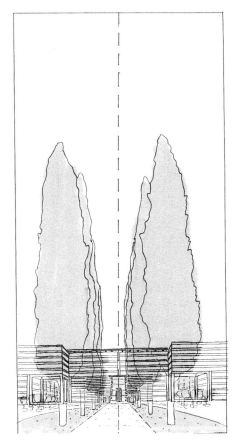
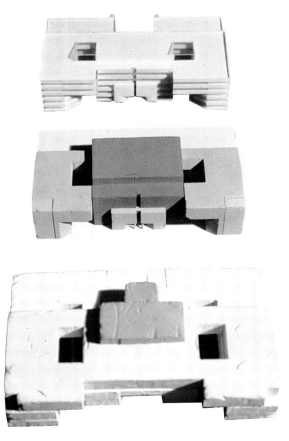

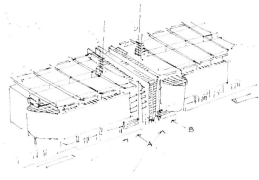

*ABOVE AND CENTRE*: FARRELL'S DRAWINGS AND MODELS FOR SITE *D*; *BELOW*: RICHARD ROGERS' AND NORMAN FOSTER'S SKETCHES

# LEARNING FROM LONDON

For Farrell, the idea of learning from the in-depth study of one place and passing on lessons to another is an important one. Another didactic method involves the study of many examples around the world, Banister Fletcher style, and selecting what is relevant for a personal contemporary architecture. But by an intense and thorough study of an example of a general phenomenon one can have an understanding of the structure and organisation of other examples. This has been the route of the formulation of Farrell's urban design ideas since, for the past twenty years, nearly all of his work has been in London, with only two projects in Warrington in the 1970s. In the past three years, somewhat to the surprise of Farrell, this situation has been reversed, with virtually all projects outside London. But from his experience and in-depth interest in London, Farrell sees a great relevance to the general problems of cities around the world.

That Farrell can apply the lessons learnt from London is partly due to the unusual pattern of his career, but also to the unique character of London. The complexity and size of the city, and the problems it faces make it an extremely valuable source of inspiration and understanding for all other cities. Unlike most cities which have a highly dense centre, surrounded by suburbs, London has no real centre in the conventional sense. Instead it has two or three major centres, but also a whole constellation of satellite villages and nuclei. It is this unique structure that makes London a particularly rich learning centre, and is the reason why Farrell followed the tradition of leaving his home town to learn from and experience all that London had to offer.

London has provided lessons not only for Farrell's projects around the country, in Birmingham, Leeds, and Edinburgh, but also for his work in major cities abroad: in Germany, France and the Far East. What interests Farrell is how international communications and the growing universality of culture and technology make lessons from one city relevant and applicable to another. This does not signal the development of an international style of town planning, but an understanding of problems commonly experienced in all cities, as cultural, political and economic systems become more integrated and increasingly global. This means that it is far easier to translate the lessons learnt in-depth from one major phenomenon, such as London, to all other cities in the field of urban design, and this is paralleled in many other areas of activity, as a number of common beliefs and trends emerge.

One such trend is the relatively recent appreciation of the importance of the past: that in an age of such rapid change, the continuity of history and the lessons of the past provide clues to the direction for development, and form the basis for maintaining a sense of place in the face of loss of identity. This problem of identity is one of a number of problems common to all cities, as new buildings and new urban solutions are applied world-wide. Universal urban artefacts - the elevated motorway, the tower block, the office building, the pedestrian underpass - are found in every city, and the loss of identity such repetition presents is self-evident. Another universal and seemingly incontractible problem is the car, whether it is the historic city besieged by vehicles or the new town like Milton Keynes, designed for the car, and consequently lacking any sense of centrality and focus of energy.

As well as the growing importance of history there are other common threads emerging, one of which is trying to repair and to heal the damage that has recently been inflicted upon the city. The chaos resulting from recent development, and the speed of this change, is common to all cities. The traditional growth of the historic city was a slow process of change, so that each generation had a sense of holding    Singapore Radio Tower

NEW CONFERENCE/ EXHIBITION CENTRE: EDINBURGH

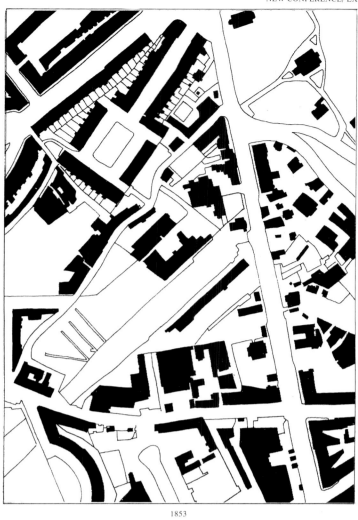

1853

EXISTING 1990

FARRELL 1989

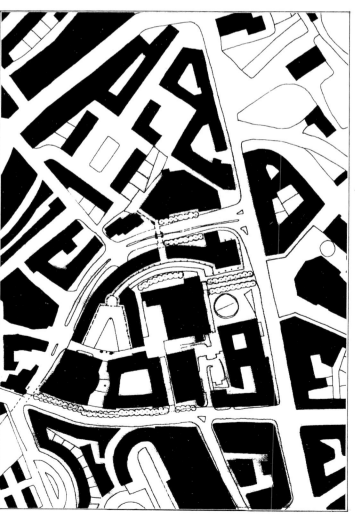

FARRELL 1992

their city or town in trust, of being custodians of the land and the buildings for the next generation, which invariably ensured that the past made a very positive contribution to the present. For Farrell it is the rapid and ill-considered change, with no reference to tradition, of the late 19th and 20th centuries that has left the city a depository of yesterday's chaos and mistakes. The railways were the first examples of this damaging development, followed by the intrusion of the road and motorway, the zoning theories of the middle of the century which segregated different uses into ghettos with a mono-cultural character. So at the end of the 20th century there is a growing belief that the chain of trust has been broken, and the city must be restored and repaired.

Another particular phenomenon throughout the world is the return to the city and a new-found respect for urban values. This is a reversal of the attitude, which began in the 19th century, that viewed the city as an unacceptable place to live. The flight to the suburbs, the theories of Ebenezer Howard and the garden city movement succeeded partly due to the convenience of transport, but primarily because of the chaos and deterioration of the city itself. Today the solution of the ever expanding transport line reaching out to the distant new suburb is being rejected in favour of the development of the city as a place to live. The role of the urban designer today is therefore of great importance owing to this rediscovery of urbanity, of town and city as great depositories of culture and identity for communities and nations. This positive attitude to the city, well-known throughout history, is re-emerging in cities throughout the world at present. This trend mirrors Farrell's own personal interest and fascination for the city, which has evolved into an urban design approach that utilises all that the city has to offer as a basis for facing the pressures of change today and meeting new demands that threaten the future of the city. This approach consists of a number of principles that Farrell's experience of working in the context of London over many years have generated, and which dictate his urban design process for schemes around the world.

**The pedestrian domain**
The first of these principles is the idea of the city as primarily a place of the pedestrian, where other modes of transport, the aeroplane, the railway and to some extent the car are abandoned. A good city is defined by the quality of the pedestrian domain, by the ability to walk from one's place of work or home to amenities such as shops, or a place of entertainment. This sense of place, defined by the ability to walk pleasurably and conveniently, relates to the whole psychology of walking. The pedestrian has been the focus of recent studies by Professor Hillier, at University College London, and Transmark, and these studies of the movement of the pedestrian - of the way people use there legs, what they perceive, what stimulates and interests them and what they see as convenient - are becoming increasingly important and are being recognised as the essence of repairing the city as a good place to be. One of the most important characteristics of the pedestrian domain is that it should occur at ground level, as it is the most convenient to the pedestrian. The other basic feature of the nature of pedestrian movement is the desire to travel by the shortest distance between origin and destination, that the pedestrian does not want to be diverted, thus expending personal energy.

Within the pedestrian domain, the visual mental map leading from one place to another, stimulus en route, and a sense of a pattern or order to the movement of the pedestrian are extremely important. This mental map provides clues and gives relationships between elements. Unlike the road signs that are followed by the car user, the pedestrian follows a personal set of clues - a church steeple, a tower block, a tube station entrance, a row of shops - to locate and move around the city. The pedestrian travels at a slow pace and can therefore absorb and take in much more of the surrounding environment, looking into shop windows, watching other people.

For Farrell the major problems of the city today, resulting from forces that have dictated urban development this century, such as the car, the discontinuity with the past and tradition, have had a detrimental effect upon the pedestrian domain. In

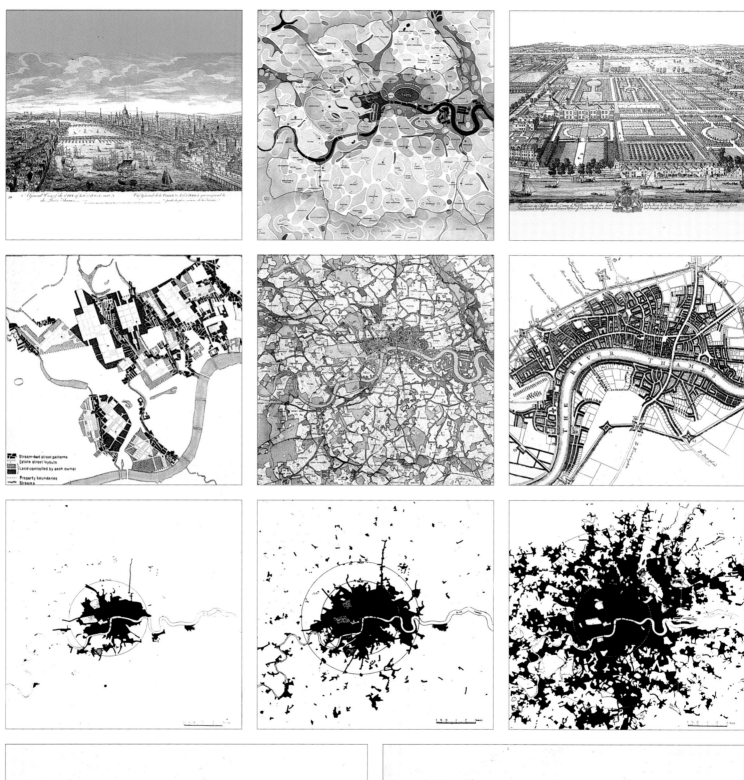

particular modern methods of transport created great pressure to segregate the pedestrian from other transport systems resulting in experiments, such as those at the Barbican and the South Bank, in split level pedestrian networks - versions of which can be found throughout the world. For example, a great deal of the pedestrian domain in Hong Kong is elevated, due to the intrusion of the car but also to the sheer density of people in the city. It is for the convenience of the traffic rather than concern for the pedestrian that sends them above or beneath roads. These situations provide possibilities for exciting and stimulating pedestrian movement, but for Farrell this cannot be a substitute for walking on the ground, and in the scheme for Hammersmith, Farrell went to great lengths to place pedestrian movement at ground level so that it did not damage the centre of the area by interfering with the natural pedestrian network of the town as a whole, whereas in Hong Kong, Farrell has been working on an urban design project where the existing ground plan is two storeys high. The project must therefore deal with the existing situation and become an exercise in damage limitation, with a set of new techniques to develop urban solutions that work and make the best of the existing.

The study of the pedestrian has fascinated Farrell for many years, and his final dissertation at the University of Pennsylvania was a study of pedestrian movement within the parks and squares of a number of cities, not as areas of landscape, but how they functioned as part of the pedestrian network. Farrell was fascinated by the way the grid in the American city provided an interesting compromise between the car and the pedestrian, as a system that is ideal for neither but can be made to work. This contrasts with a city like London, which is designed for the pedestrian, where the pedestrian domain is a complex radiating system generating triangular blocks and a triangulating movement system. Pedestrian movement systems are frequently on the diagonal as pedestrians naturally prefer the most direct route.

In urban design terms, one of the interesting aspects of designing for the pedestrian is the contrast between the small scale nature of pedestrian movement when compared to the great size of the modern city as an entity. Thus each individual project is a microcosm within the pedestrian scene and even small projects such as Comyn Ching and East Putney station can exert an influence on the pedestrian movement within an area. Larger schemes, Charing Cross and Paternoster Square, can totally alter the pedestrian scene. By restoring Paternoster Square to ground level, the nature and character of the whole area around is changed as it becomes a more accessible and permeable piece of the urban fabric. Within Farrell's office this notion of permeability is used frequently, as within the city today the urban designer is often confronted by a breakdown of permeability, with the great railway stations and goods yards and areas of private ownership that limit public access. Whilst such features are an important part of the urban fabric they invariably disrupt the pedestrian domain, resulting in longer walking distances and areas of limited interest. Solutions to such problems are all part of the work of the urban designer today. The City of London is, of course, a great example of traditional permeability with its complex network of pedestrian routes passing through the buildings, as within the traditional Mediterranean city where the main church or cathedral is passed through to reach other parts of the town. The quality of the pedestrian domain relies heavily upon the design and permeability of individual buildings - loggias, porticos and colonnades, the shape of buildings - which form a critical part of each element within the city fabric and are an important feature of urban design guidelines and any masterplan.

For Farrell one of the most interesting aspects today is the increasing complexity and three-dimensionality of the pedestrian domain within the city, with vertical layering of the underground transport system and pedestrian elevated walkways. The importance of London as a field of study is its position as primarily a pedestrian city. If it is considered as a vehicular-based city then the horse and carriage is theoretically still the most appropriate mode of transport, as the average speed of the car within the city has never exceeded that of the horse and carriage - 18 to 20 miles per hour. The key to the success of London, the West End and the

London historical views and plans; *From above left to right*: River Thames, 1943 social and functional analysis, aerial perspective, inter-relation of stream-beds and villages, community and urban space, historical map, maps of 1840, 1880 and 1929 built area; south-east view and the Tower of London

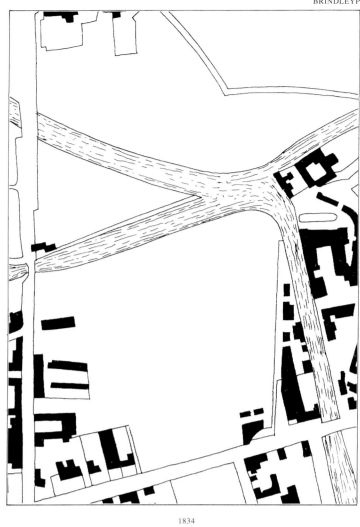

1834

1918

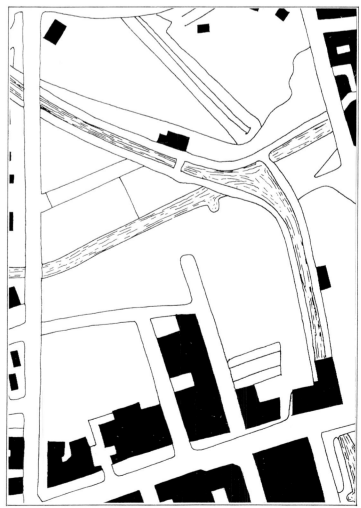

EXISTING 1990

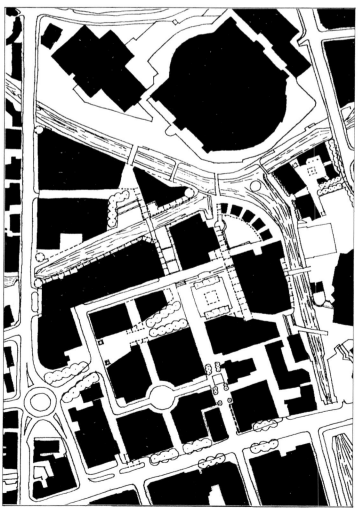

FARRELL 1992

villages around is the quality of the pedestrian realm within each of these centres, and how they relate to the transport system that links these areas. Tokyo has developed a complex network of pedestrian routes that completely destroys a sense of ground level, but replaces this with a new idea of how the pedestrian moves. These levels, below and above ground, connected to shopping arcades and areas of activity, replicate the role of the original ground plan, unlike the South Bank where the routes become isolated means of getting from A to B.

## Historical continuity

Another major principle of Farrell's urban design approach is historical continuity. This begins with a very basic appreciation of the existing artefacts, physical objects, and buildings that surround the city dweller. There is a growing awareness that such elements in themselves have a value that can transcend function and for Farrell the destruction of the original Euston arch in London was perhaps the last act of urban vandalism of a high order that occurred without much of a fight. Although the arch no longer served as the entrance to the station it was an important symbol of Victorian endeavour, giving the area a focal point of reference and meaning. If one scratches the surface of London, the historical continuity, the origins of much that exists today can be traced back to the days of Roman settlement. Roman routes and patterns of land occupation dominate and influence so much of what exists in Western Europe. It is the richness of the layers of history that lie below the surface of modern London and the manner in which they affect the city today which makes historical continuity so important.

What fascinates Farrell is that historical continuity can be of as much importance to a new town as to a historic area. A notion of tradition can be surprisingly new, and on a project in the new town of Harlow, the local residents defended the tradition of the existing original fabric, built in the 1950s, and maintained that any new development should be in the spirit of the town, and have a continuity with the tradition of Harlow. This attachment to tradition opposes the view that tradition must be destroyed for progress to be achieved. Farrell's defence of tradition is not a nostalgic attachment to the past, but a belief that the violence of the sheer pace of change today is such that tradition can be mistakenly seen as a minority interest in the urban scene and that to retain and conserve it merely maintains a balance and harmony. The destruction of the past has always existed - conquerors razing cities to the ground, Henry VIII's destruction of the monasteries - and has always been a very symbolic act to place emphasis on one's own contemporary existence and beliefs. For Farrell the universal and total destruction that is prevalent today has ecological parallels with the destruction of the rainforest; tradition, the oxygen of urban life in a cultural sense, is being extinguished and eliminated. The city is a conduit that passes on so much to future generations that its destruction can only leave the world a poorer place. Ultimately the urban designer and architect must remain contemporary but also adopt the role of custodian of the estate of man, passing on to future generations not only what has been achieved today but also what has been inherited. Farrell's attitude to tradition can be viewed as an act of self-preservation, for if there is no respect for what is inherited, then future generations will not respect what has been achieved by today's contemporary generation.

## Cities as a resource

As well as the cultural reasons of historical continuity, there is also the pragmatism of reusing the resource of what exists, instead of the often purely symbolic act of replacement - so widespread after the war. Farrell reacts strongly against any city that makes change for change's sake, and advocates that any scheme for city renewal must begin with a study of what already exists - roads, walls, trees, buildings - as an often enormous resource. Beyond this pragmatic argument is Farrell's belief that historical continuity is a spiritual thing, in that each place, town or city has a spirit, generated from a complex mix of religious, civic, domestic,

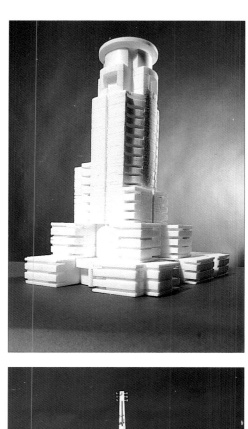

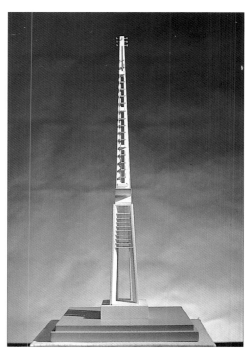

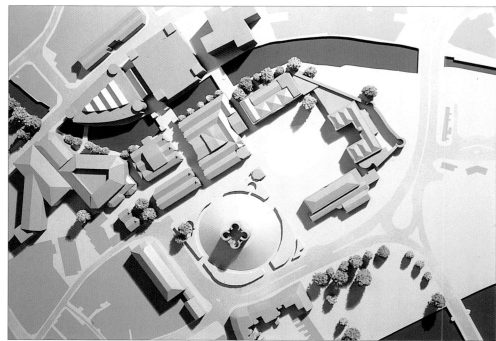

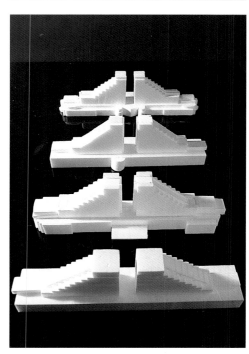

ethnic, and racial identity. In his projects in London, Farrell has always looked for ways to understand the deeper cultural value of what exists, to appreciate the essence and spiritual characteristic of a place, and this has also applied to the new projects around the world. For the Peak project in Hong Kong, Farrell was fascinated by the tradition of the Chinese temple, its use as a gathering place and the silhouette of the building which is a unique physical expression and presence in the city. The presence of certain buildings, the Eiffel Tower, the Houses of Parliament, exerts a strong influence on the pervading sense of place of an area, as can a general style - the art deco quality of New York from the 1920s and 1930s.

The pragmatic side of historical continuity means, of course, the conversion and adaptation of existing buildings. This has been an important thread and principle in Farrell's work since his first ever project, and is backed by a belief that re-use or conversion is a fascinating and creative mode of architectural expression in its own right. The adaptation and rearrangement of elements in a living room, or a house, or a city, is like the rotation of crops in a garden or on an estate - it is a sort of logical process which modifies the same stable system in different ways, in such a way that the inter-relationships between the elements do not alter, yet there is an appearance of change. There is great pressure today for the novelty of the new, perpetuated by architectural schools that function as fashion houses, intent on spawning the latest architectural mega-star. To argue for the creativity of the conversion requires the modesty of merely dealing with what exists, and an understanding how appreciation of the work is limited by the knowledge of what was before. History provides a great number of examples of impressive conversions, and part of Farrell's submission for the Mansion House enquiry consisted of a number of examples - Robert Adam's Chiswick House, Castel Vecchio by Carlo Scarpa, and the modernist classic, the Maison de Verre - with which Farrell argued that the architect's ingenuity and invention was increased by having to deal with what existed. The main thrust of the argument was to assert that the retention of buildings is no less a creative solution than building from a *tabula rasa*. This myth of the creative superiority of the new, that invention and creativity were synonymous, was perpetuated alongside the modernist rejection of the past. Farrell has argued many times that the urban designer who works with the existing city has the greatest chance of contributing to the city, and that urban design cannot help but be an exercise of adaptation simply because it involves working with the existing city, whereas the modernist vision of Le Corbusier's Plan Voisin, which involved the destruction of the traditional city, is not the work of an urban designer, but utopian and anti-urbanist.

The advocacy of conversion is a major theme that runs through Farrell's career from the student hostel to more recent schemes such as Comyn Ching and Tobacco Dock, schemes which are reliant and are based upon the resource of what exists. Farrell often uses another of his conversion schemes, the Crafts Council galleries, to illustrate the parallels between the elements within a building and those that make up the city - the central pedestrian route and hallway are like the street, the rooms are like squares or groups of buildings. Service and leisure areas, the relation of vertical circulation to horizontal, the hierarchical ordering of spaces all reoccur in urban design, and so conversion and adaptation is as important a feature of urban design as of building. For Farrell, as for Alberti, the house can be seen as a small city and the city as a large house.

In the past Farrell has also made certain parallels between urban adaptation and agricultural or ecological adaptation, and in this respect the work of Repton fascinated him. The before and after illustrations, used in the Red Book, show Repton's use of features of the landscape to create a more natural integration of what existed with his proposed vision. Farrell believes Nash became one of the greatest urbanists by adapting Repton's ideas to the urban realm, by applying to the city the ideas of English landscape design, of adaptation and conversion. For Farrell the tradition of garden design, and the great gardens of Jekyll and Lutyens, have relevance for urban design with the continuous rotation of use and upgrading

*From above left to right*: Orchard Boulevard, Singapore; The Peak, Hong Kong; Radio Tower, Singapore; Castle Piccadilly development, York; Hilton Hotel, Birmingham

GREY STREET: NEWCASTLE

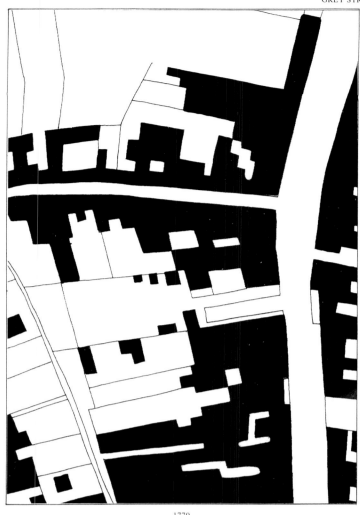

1770

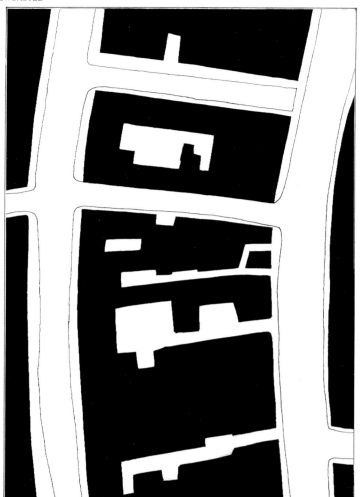

1838

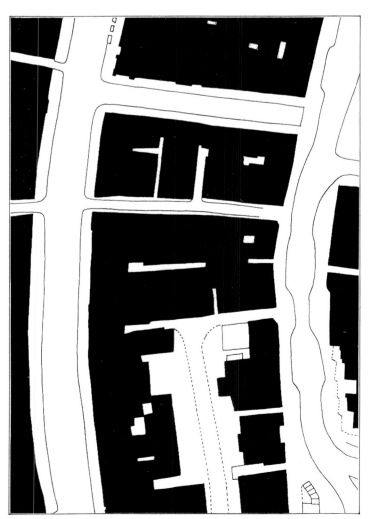

EXISTING 1991

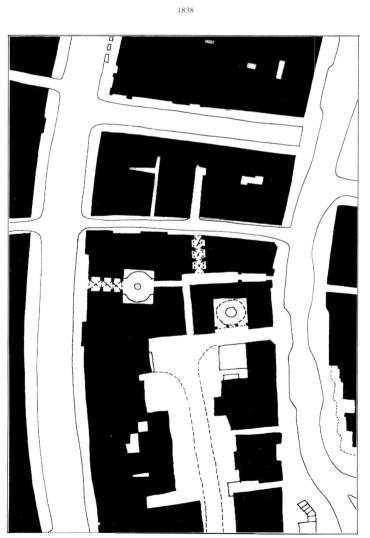

FARRELL 1992

of elements, the relationship of spaces, of openness and enclosure, but also in terms of time, with a short and a long term plan, a mixture of tradition and new growth.

The Greeks and Romans had to invent generic types - the temple, the street, and the market place - and orders for architectural expression from which to construct the new phenomenon of the city. Such invention is not a primary requirement today, as the process of urban design begins with the great mass of artefacts, culture and traditions, and can never be a process of pure invention. The same is true in scientific terms, that the greatness of the inventor comes not from the initial moment of innovation, but the on-going process of harnessing and re-using the invention to serve mankind. The role of the urban designer is similar - the working with and improving upon what previous generations have built.

## Variety and pluralism

Variety and pluralism is another feature of the city which Farrell views as essential, but the sheer pace of change in the 20th century and the great number of new buildings that have been added to existing stock have reduced the ability to create a variety of architectural expression, and differences between building types. For Farrell this desire is made all the more difficult by the tradition of modernism which rejected the difference between building type and any national or regional tradition in favour of a universal aesthetic. Today the legacy of modernism poses the problems of how to create variety not only in architectural expression but within the urban scene. Farrell feels strongly that the importance of variety must now be accepted by architects and urban designers, and rejects the belief that architects should produce their own recognisable style from a limited palette as much as the belief that what he does is the correct solution. Instead he believes that the architect or urban designer should be able to respond to different thematic ideas, to different contexts, and develop the possibilities of expressing buildings in different ways. In the 1980s much of the work of the post-modernists began with an exploration of the pluralistic potential of architecture, and an investigation into the notion of different tastes. Farrell finds the notion of taste a very rewarding one to explore - the belief that there is an ideal and correct taste, there is the taste of the middle and upper classes, there is the taste of the architectural school and profession. Farrell rejects this élitist view, and considers it possible to have different ideas about what might constitute good taste, that the Odeon cinema has as much relevance to the history of architecture as the Corbusian house, or St Paul's Cathedral. This idea of other people's taste, of what others want to be built is one that Prince Charles has strongly supported. Why should the architectural profession solely determine the built environment, particularly when as a profession it has such a narrow view of what constitutes good taste? The age of pluralism, whether one approves of it or not, has been hammering at the door of architectural taste for a long time, and during the 1980s the door was opened. For Farrell the battle over Mansion House was fought over a group of buildings which was more representative of the taste of the general public than the Mies tower, which appealed only to a very specialized and rarefied taste.

The designer therefore requires not only a broad view, but must look at ways that variety can be introduced, through the involvement of different architects, and therefore develop an ability to respond to varied expression. At Paternoster Square the group involved were classicist, at Chiswick Park they are modernist, but Farrell believes there should be an even greater natural mix than this. Variety is increased by retaining buildings from an earlier age, as they naturally provide contrast to new additions. If newer buildings respond to the past, this adds a new dimension to contemporary architecture, beyond the bland, by generating an individual, and local character. Thus the role of the urban designer is to create a masterplan or framework which enables a broad response, and offer guidelines, rather than rules, which allow for the expression of what a completely new vision of urban design might be. What interests Farrell are the after-effects of post-modernism, which have affected the architectural scene as a whole. There is now a self-consciousness

QUAYSIDE: NEWCASTLE

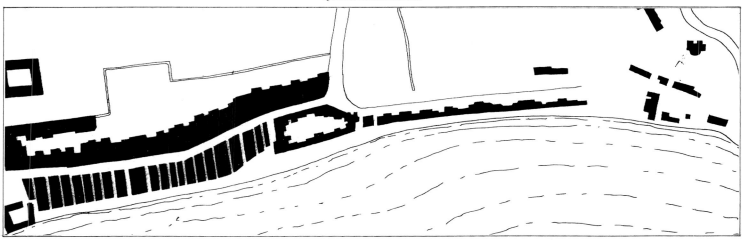

1727

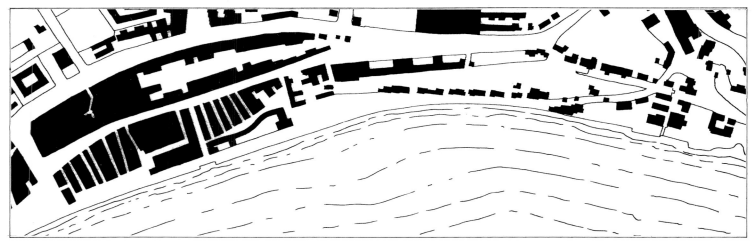

1851

EXISTING 1990

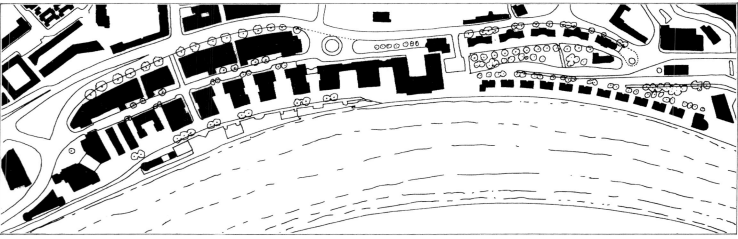

FARRELL 1992

with respect to how one deals with the past and a rejection of the doctrinaire and dogmatic. There is recognition that there are no utopian, holistic solutions to the problems of architecture and urban design. The absorption of the lessons of post-modernism has heralded a new era of greater variety, and an acceptance of a more pluralistic and varied architecture in the city.

**Integrating the new**
For the urban designer today many of the greatest problems to overcome have been the result of recent intervention. These problems of the new are a theme that runs through many of Farrell's projects in London - how to absorb the office buildings of the London Wall and the elevated walkways of the Barbican back into the City, how to integrate railway and underground stations with the city fabric - and have provided useful lessons for Farrell's work in other cities in providing solutions to the damage suffered by northern cities such as Newcastle, Birmingham and Liverpool. Birmingham, in particular, has suffered from the legacy of ideas of the 1950s and 1960s, which were dictated by the needs of the car. For Farrell this has created an interesting exercise in working with the existing landscape of the vehicle and with Birmingham's ring road which is tied like a noose around the city. This pattern of development, repeated around the world, was defeated in London, but the respect for London was one not enjoyed by many provincial cities.

Dealing with the effects of the recent theories of zoning and mono-culturality is another area in which Farrell's experience in London has been important in the formation of his urban design approach. The projects for the South Bank Arts Centre, the BBC, the great hospitals, and the Polytechnic of Central London, have taught Farrell that the success of these mono-cultural estates depends upon how well they are integrated into the city. The key to this lesson is recognising that each represents a mini-city in itself, and that they contain all the diverse uses that make up a traditional piece of the urban fabric. The cafés, public and private spaces, the recreation and leisure areas, the street lighting, are parallel to the common functions and elements of the city, and by breaking down the mono-cultural estate into its urban components it can be integrated into the city in a natural way.

By viewing the mono-cultural estate in this way, the problems suffered by examples such as the South Bank can be a process of understanding what is missing. Farrell compared the South Bank with other traditional parts of the city such as the West End, where galleries and theatres are mixed with a great variety of other uses, so that after a performance one can hail a taxi, go to a restaurant, stroll along the pavement, and enjoy the normal vitality of the urban scene. By contrast, the South Bank today is an isolated cultural ghetto, where people do identical things - arrive and depart - at exactly the same time. It is an area of the city that suffers from the worst aspects of zoning, which is being increasingly recognised as a great planning mistake. The great housing estates, such as the Quarry Hill estate in Leeds, are examples of an excessive zeal for zoning. At Quarry Hill, Farrell is involved in overcoming the problems of zoning, to bring back balance and variety of uses to this residential complex. The project has therefore been an extension of Farrell's work in London, and involves creating solutions to the planning theories of modernism, which were dictated by a desire to separate the different functions, and translate the rational processes of mass production into simplistic planning theories, which for Farrell have no relevance in the traditional, varied city.

**Public and private realms**
Another important theme of Farrell's approach is one which Leon Krier propounds - how the city is made up of essentially two building types. There is the public building, such as the church, the town hall, the institutional building, and there is street architecture, the ordinary buildings. It is the latter which Farrell finds the most fascinating within the urban scene as they form the backdrop and the great mass of fabric within the city. Whereas the great public buildings provide the landmarks and focal points, the ordinary buildings enclose external public spaces,

1890s

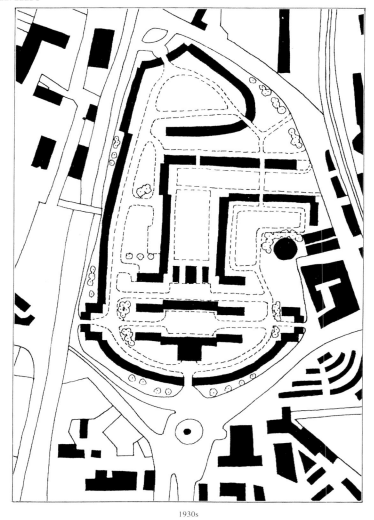

1930s

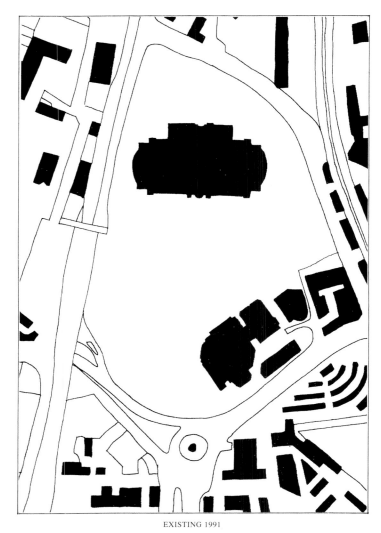

EXISTING 1991

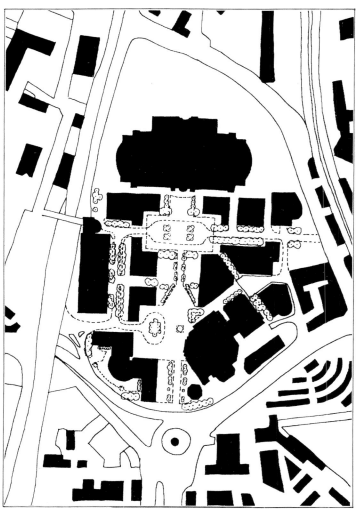

FARRELL 1992

streets and squares. It is the notion that such buildings create an enclosing wall, that each building is a component within this wall, which Farrell believes is a simple rule which is ignored in much urban design. Each element in the wall is composed of a tripartite hierarchy, with the ground floor consisting of shops and public entrances, and related to pavements, signage and lighting. At the very top is the roof element, often not visible from the street, but an opportunity to give an expression and an interesting profile giving definition to the building when viewed across the wider urban landscape. Within the interior of the building it offers the potential for scenic views, good daylight and unusual spaces. Finally there is the element between, the sandwich filling, which houses the majority of the accommo-dation of the building - the repetitive floors of housing or offices - and which forms the very stuff of the enclosing wall. These simple rules are for Farrell too frequently overlooked in urban architecture and are therefore essential to the formation of urban guidelines.

The major buildings, the great institutions, face problems as their relationship with society changes through time. Increasingly it is cultural buildings, art galleries and museums that have become the major institutions. Nevertheless, the unique architectural qualities of churches, town halls and other public buildings create an important role as counterpoints to the great mass of ordinary fabric. Within an area of major redevelopment such buildings provide a continuity and a sense of place that new buildings do not provide.

## Land ownership and development

For Farrell another interesting feature of urban design today is the role of the land or building owner in the process of development. Farrell traces the problems of early twentieth century planning to a desire to make a comprehensive plan, which invariably necessitated some degree of monopoly of land ownership and control. Early developments, such as Letchworth and Welwyn, even Hampstead Garden Suburb, relied upon some level of control over land ownership. A twentieth century tradition developed which perpetuated the belief that comprehensive development and State ownership went hand in hand with good planning, leading to the elimination of the ability of the private sector to respond to the public sector's level of investment in infrastructure.

In contrast to this tradition Farrell was particularly impressed with the American urban design and town planning theories of the 1960s, which rejected the monopolisation of development by the State in favour of a balance between the public and private sector. When Farrell returned from America this approach was viewed in Britain as a statement of failure and compromise. There was still a belief that Milton Keynes and the new expanded towns of Peterborough and Warrington were better because of their development as State monopolies. The desire for comprehensive development, massive housing estates, zoning and new towns, has today been tempered by a reassessment of the variety and mixed development of the traditional urban scene. For Farrell this has been an important lesson that has been learnt in the last fifty years - that despite the seductive idea that an urban design, as a complete statement, can be brought about by coercion or monopoly, this does not necessarily produce a problem-free product. The involvement in urban design of many individuals and groups in the community is an idea that is still viewed with some degree of suspicion in Britain. An interesting development in recent years has been the emergence of the private sector as the monopoliser, as State involvement has disappeared, but Farrell believes that any large-scale development should have as great a variety as possible in different methods of ownership and participation in building ownership.

Another feature of urban planning in Britain about which Farrell feels strongly is the misconception that the commercial developer is an inferior animal to the building owner/occupier. The building owner is primarily concerned with the plot of land his building will occupy, with invariably little concern for the domain outside his own land and building. This can, of course, result in outstanding

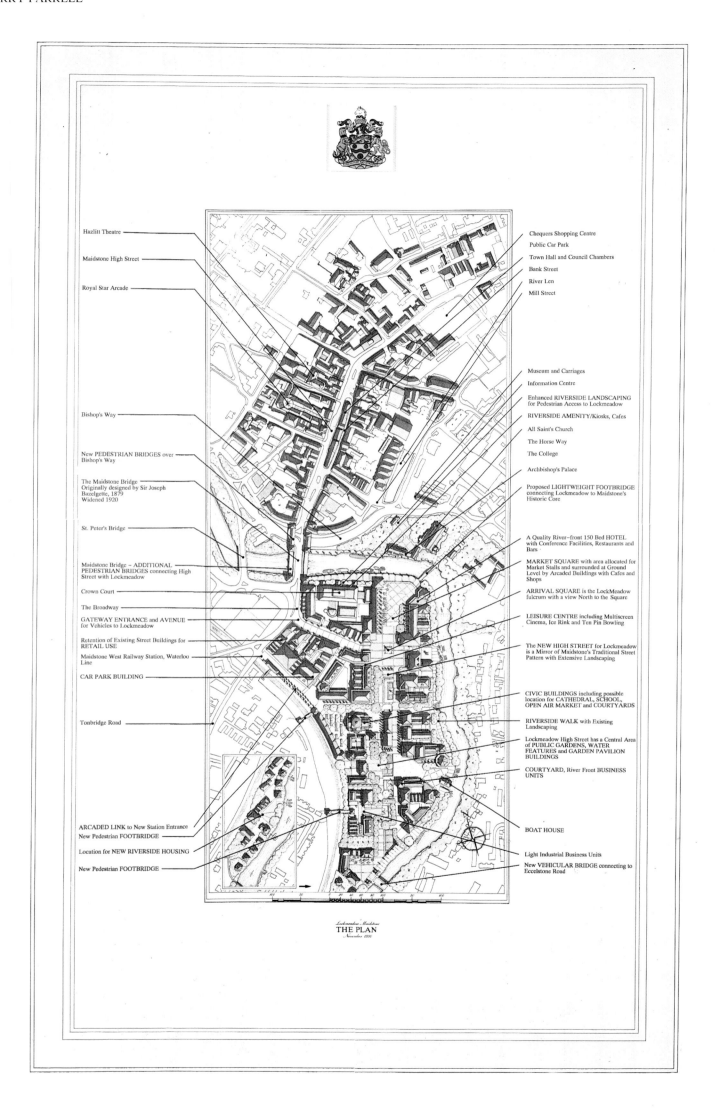

Hazlitt Theatre

Maidstone High Street

Royal Star Arcade

Bishop's Way

New PEDESTRIAN BRIDGES over Bishop's Way

The Maidstone Bridge
Originally designed by Sir Joseph
Bazelgette, 1879
Widened 1920

St. Peter's Bridge

Maidstone Bridge – ADDITIONAL
PEDESTRIAN BRIDGES connecting High
Street with Lockmeadow

Crown Court

The Broadway

GATEWAY ENTRANCE and AVENUE
for Vehicles to Lockmeadow

Retention of Existing Street Buildings for
RETAIL USE

Maidstone West Railway Station, Waterloo
Line

CAR PARK BUILDING

Tonbridge Road

ARCADED LINK to New Station Entrance
New Pedestrian FOOTBRIDGE

Location for NEW RIVERSIDE HOUSING

New Pedestrian FOOTBRIDGE

Chequers Shopping Centre

Public Car Park

Town Hall and Council Chambers

Bank Street

River Len

Mill Street

Museum and Carriages

Information Centre

Enhanced RIVERSIDE LANDSCAPING
for Pedestrian Access to Lockmeadow

RIVERSIDE AMENITY/Kiosks, Cafes

All Saint's Church

The Horse Way

The College

Archbishop's Palace

Proposed LIGHTWEIGHT FOOTBRIDGE
connecting Lockmeadow to Maidstone's
Historic Core

A Quality River-front 150 Bed HOTEL
with Conference Facilities, Restaurants and
Bars

MARKET SQUARE with area allocated for
Market Stalls and surrounded at Ground
Level by Arcaded Buildings with Cafes and
Shops

ARRIVAL SQUARE is the LockMeadow
fulcrum with a view North to the Square

LEISURE CENTRE including Multiscreen
Cinema, Ice Rink and Ten Pin Bowling

The NEW HIGH STREET for Lockmeadow
is a Mirror of Maidstone's Traditional Street
Pattern with Extensive Landscaping

CIVIC BUILDINGS including possible
location for CATHEDRAL, SCHOOL,
OPEN AIR MARKET and COURTYARDS

RIVERSIDE WALK with Existing
Landscaping

Lockmeadow High Street has a Central Area
of PUBLIC GARDENS, WATER
FEATURES and GARDEN PAVILION
BUILDINGS

COURTYARD, River Front BUSINESS
UNITS

BOAT HOUSE

Light Industrial Business Units

New VEHICULAR BRIDGE connecting to
Eccelstone Road

Lockmeadow - Maidstone
THE PLAN
November 1996

individual buildings, but lacks the greater contribution that more widespread land ownership of the developer can create - as at Charing Cross or Paternoster, or earlier developments, such as the Bedford Estate. These earlier examples of urban development were concerned with the total environment, with the land between the buildings designed with squares and trees, lights and the bric-à-brac that goes to make up the urban scene, and contributes to it in a way that endures and extends beyond the value of the individual building and its use. This is a point Farrell makes great issue of when producing a masterplan, against the belief invariably held by clients, private or public, that the starting point for such a development should be "use". This is one of the major misconceptions widely held in town planning in Britain. For Farrell a good plan does not begin with use or zoning, but with infrastructure - roads, transport network, squares, trees and spaces between buildings - and a desire to create the right level of density and the appropriate relationship between buildings in height, mass and architectural character. In this process the individual building owner and the use for the building come some way down the list of priorities. In the architectural world it is considered that the owner/ occupier provides the architect with a more desirable client. This is disputed by Farrell, as in modern times the requirements of the client can change, so that the original building can be detrimentally altered, as has been proposed even for recent buildings such as the Willis Faber Dumas building in Ipswich. Charing Cross, Paternoster Square, Chiswick Park, and indeed all of Farrell's masterplans outside London demonstrate clearly that the involvement of a developer with a wider interest permits the urban designer to generate schemes which make a  much greater contribution to the city.

The Charing Cross scheme began with the a series of questions. What does the site want to be? What does the land want to be? What is the natural thing to happen to this part of the city? Thus the clues and the origins of the scheme came from the site itself, the land, the building and the area around, not from outside pressures and uses imposed on the site. The problems of designing from the latter are self evident in schemes such as Canary Wharf, where a mini-city of offices has been developed on an area of land which lacked the transport infrastructure, population infrastructure and support amenities that such development required. These failings were overlooked by a scheme driven primarily by economic advantage.

An idea which appealed to Farrell and which connected the involvement of both the public and private sector in urban development, was developed by an architect and planner, David Crane, in the 1960s. Crane suggested that the on-going public investment in the urban infrastructure of roads, traffic lights, pavements, etc. generated a network across the city - a "capital web". By planning this web, one could influence the response of the private sector. Farrell still refers to this idea when planning schemes today, and considers how to generate private sector involvement when investing public money. In the design of any large scheme, whether the major investment comes from a developer or the State, there is always the need to attract a variety of involvement with small scale enterprises, such as shops and cafés, which provide a diversity of scale and of use.

**The process of masterplanning and urban designing**

The lessons and principles that Farrell has learnt from his work in London have developed into a process which can be applied to urban design and masterplanning elsewhere. The process of urban planning and design for Farrell is a specific discipline that lies somewhere between planning and architecture. The planner tends to concentrate on uses and control, on two-dimensional generalities, whereas the architect tends to focus on specific design solutions which can suppress variety and flexibility, and  provide a three-dimensional vision which can be too defined. The urban designer's role is to create a three-dimensional framework within the city, which has a very specific investment in the public realm, and which allows for a variety of response and expression to occur in the private realm. Farrell has distinguished three particular areas of activity within urban design.

Masterplan for Lockmeadow, Maidstone

241

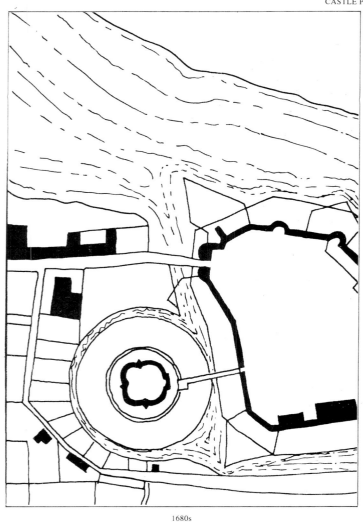

1680s

1850s

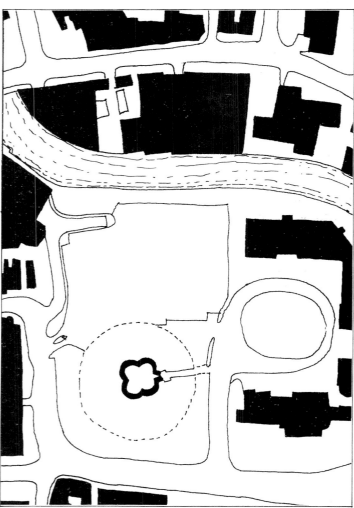

EXISTING 1990

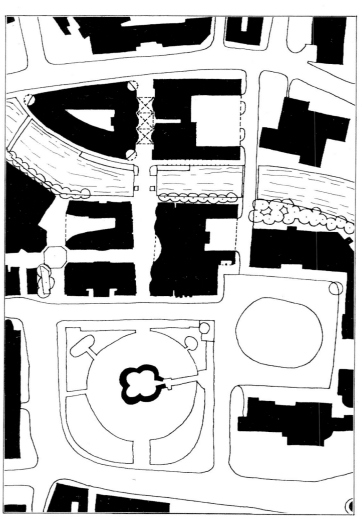

FARRELL 1992

The first area is the actual process of developing an urban design scheme which itself can be divided into three distinct phases - masterplanning, infrastructure and architecture. Masterplanning is perhaps the most two-dimensional phase of the exercise during which the layout, the distribution and the plan are generated. This is the inevitable initial process when the broad layout of transport, densities and usage and the legal framework are defined. This stage usually ends with the approval process, and leads to the second and more complex phase, during which the urban designer actually designs the public realm, the space between the buildings. As at Chiswick Park this public domain, the roads and landscaping, can be completed in advance of all the buildings, and for Farrell's projects in Edinburgh, Leeds and Birmingham the infrastructure already exists. The complexity of this activity is heightened in the projects for Hong Kong where a three-dimensional solution is needed, and this requires a very complex organisational diagram. At this stage design guidelines relating to the extent of control over other building elements are established. The third and final phase is the design of the individual buildings, the architectural phase which can be carried out by the masterplanner architect or involve a number of architects. For the Chiswick Park project Farrell developed a diagram showing the influence of the various parties on the different pieces of land, and the timing of these various roles.

The second area of activity is advocacy of certain beliefs, inherent in any design process, but which can take various, more blatant, forms. For example, as a response to existing proposals, acting on behalf of the local community, as Farrell did at Wimbledon and Hammersmith, or acting for preservation groups, as at Mansion House. There is also great potential for the urban designer to work in an interventionist way, with schemes and ideas put forward to stimulate response and interest, as in the Thames Study and the Polytechnic of Central London project. Both of these initiatives involved the ideas of a number of architects, and through publicity generated debate about the issues and areas involved.

The final role of the urban designer is as advocate of his own scheme. Farrell's starting point for any urban project is a consultation with all bodies affected and involved, to assimilate views and then generate a number of possible solutions to which the bodies involved can respond. At the South Bank, Paternoster, Chiswick Park, Birmingham and Edinburgh, public exhibition and public explanation were an important part of the whole design process. For Farrell, the ability to explain clearly is an integral part of urban design because one is dealing with the public domain, unlike architecture where one is creating a private world for a client. In the public realm, in a democracy, it is necessary to involve interested parties, as is happening in Berlin and Farrell's project in Montpelier. The need to have an interactive design process, beyond the involvement of client and designer, is an inherent part of the skill of the urban designer today. This requires the urban designer to act as a coordinator, as with the involvement of different architects, one must be able to work with different creative cogs, and allow for a creative contribution from a number of parties. There is also the coordination of a great number of other professionals, such as economists, politicians, and various specialists whose expertise forms part of the response of the urban designer today.

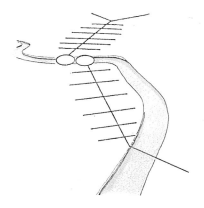

*Left*: Plan concept for Lockmeadow, Maidstone

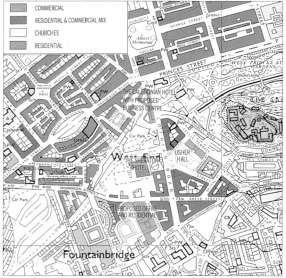

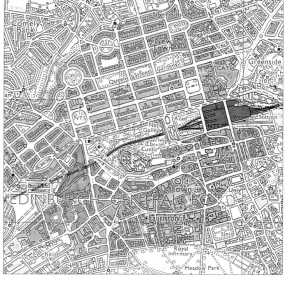

AERIAL VIEW OF EARLY SITE AND LOCATION PLANS

LANDMARK BUILDING

CALEDONIAN HOTEL
EXTENSION

# MASTERPLAN AND NEW CONFERENCE/EXHIBITION CENTRE
## *LOTHIAN ROAD, EDINBURGH 1989-1992*

*Farrell's scheme for an International Conference Centre formed the focal point of a masterplan for the redevelopment of a vacant site to the west of centre of Edinburgh, as part of a new business quarter for the city.*

*As the site had formerly been a railway station, Farrell's response drew from his work in London, at King's Cross. Once again Farrell had to overcome the problems of mono-culturality: the area around the station had turned away from the station, and had been detrimentally affected by its neighbour. Another primary task of the scheme, in urban design terms, was to form a connection between the old town and the new. The nature of the existing site was a result of the history of Edinburgh as a northern fortified city which replicated the European city, its form concentrated within a defended centre with a medieval street pattern. The site was located at the critical point were the old town met the new.*

*The main aim of the masterplan was therefore to break down the site as a barrier and establish pedestrian permeability to integrate it with the old town to the east and the new to the west. Extensive pedestrian and cycle routes formed connections with the existing streets beyond the site. The public domain was dictated by the concept of space positive, and also the notion of historical continuity, by drawing on Edinburgh's tradition of terraces enclosing urban spaces and gardens. The Crescent provided a defined entrance to the scheme from the north, enclosing*

*an urban space which led pedestrians into the main Conference Square, a triangular pedestrian space which formed the heart of the masterplan. The northern edge of Festival Square was enclosed with a new building, which enhanced the relationship between the space and Usher Hall. The change in level across the site was exploited to provide separate vehicular servicing from the pedestrian network of routes and spaces.*

*The majority of built elements in the scheme were examples of street architecture. Shops and access points were placed at ground level, with office and residential accommodation above, with an articulated roof line at the top. In northern cities, such as Edinburgh, the lack of sunlight means the contrast between the sky and the solid mass of building is emphasised, and as a result the roofline silhouette is a major feature of the city - a tradition which Farrell exploited. The conference centre, as a major public building, was designed as a set piece within the urban mass. The importance of the building was emphasised by its positioning as the focal point for a number of key views - from Princes Street and as a frontdoor landmark for the new business area from the primary western approach. The relocation of the conference centre to this position was the result of a number of changes to the original competition scheme which resulted from consultation and ideas from a range of official bodies and the public.*

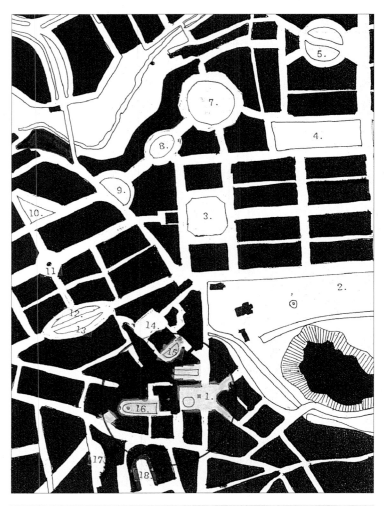

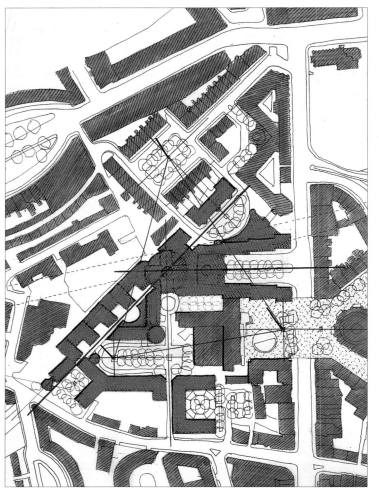

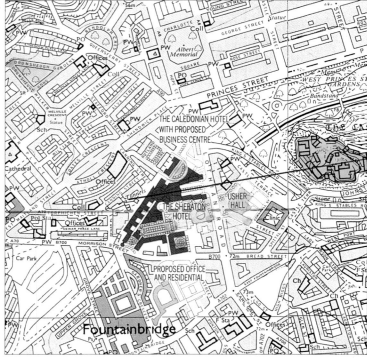

PLANS SHOWING THE FIRST COMPETITION SCHEME

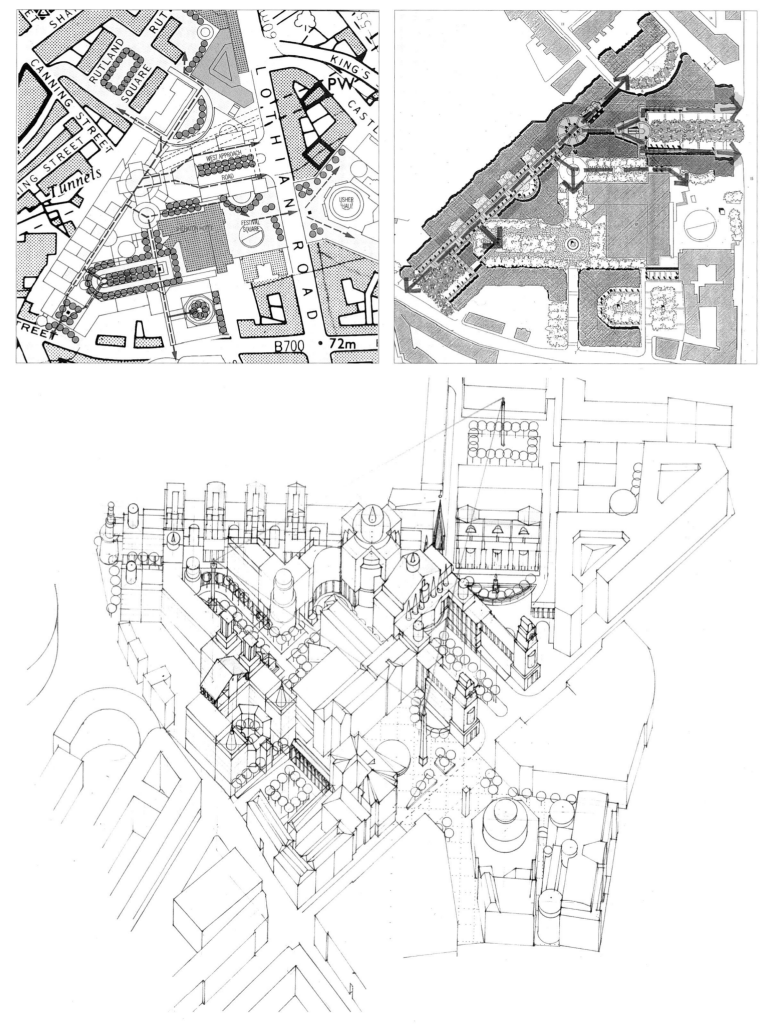

DRAWINGS OF THE FIRST COMPETITION SCHEME

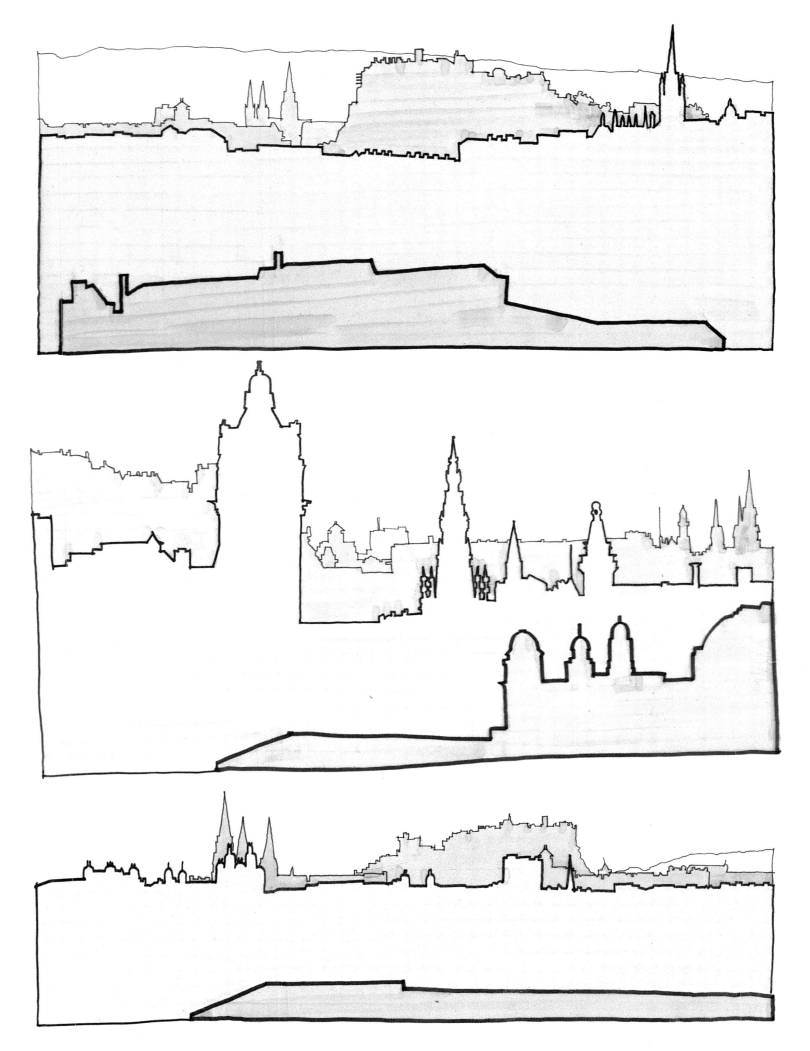

SKYLINE STUDIES

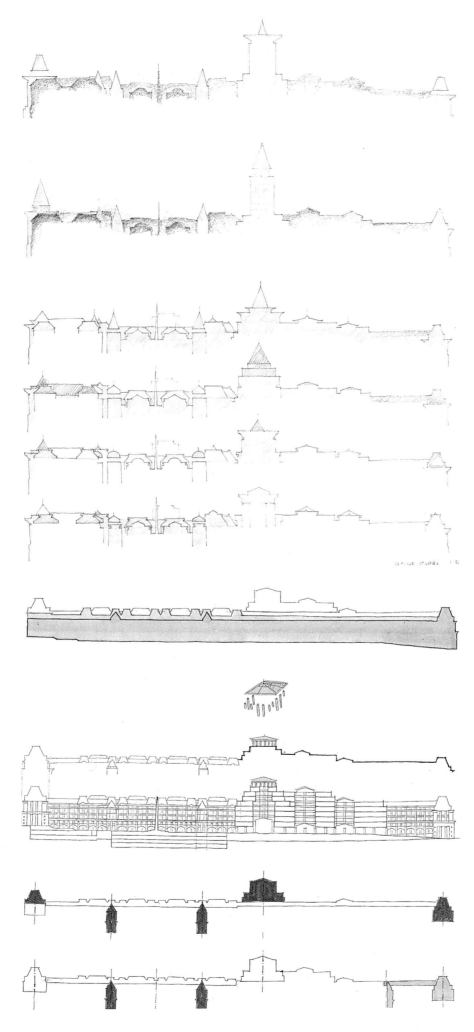

SKYLINE AND SILHOUETTE STUDIES

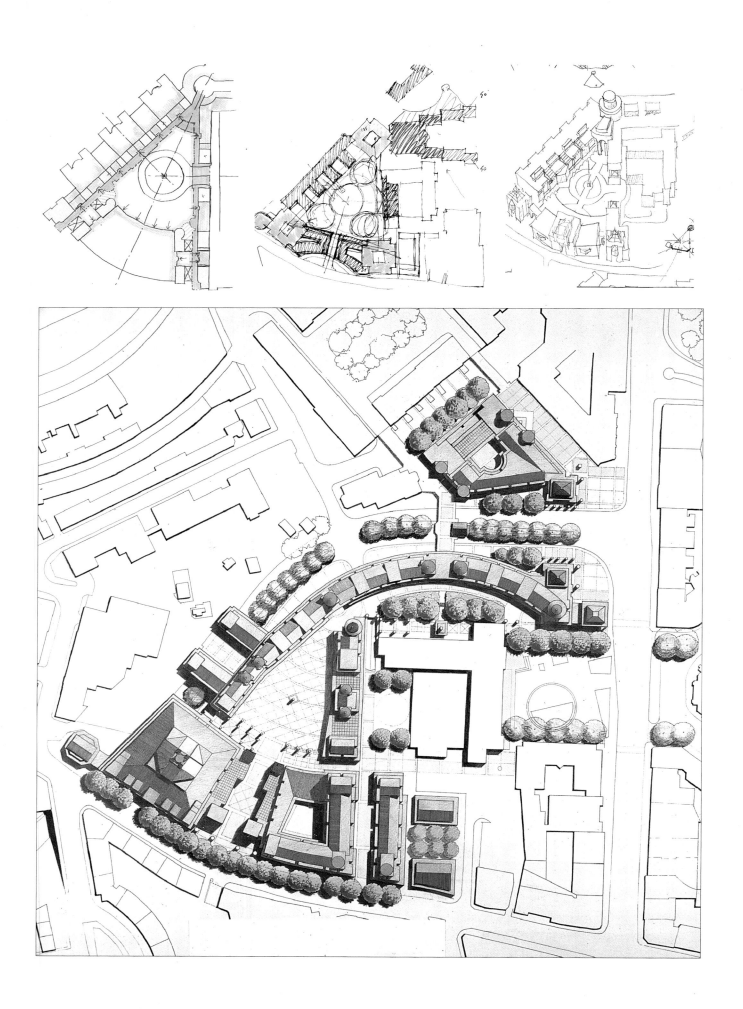

THE SECOND MASTERPLAN

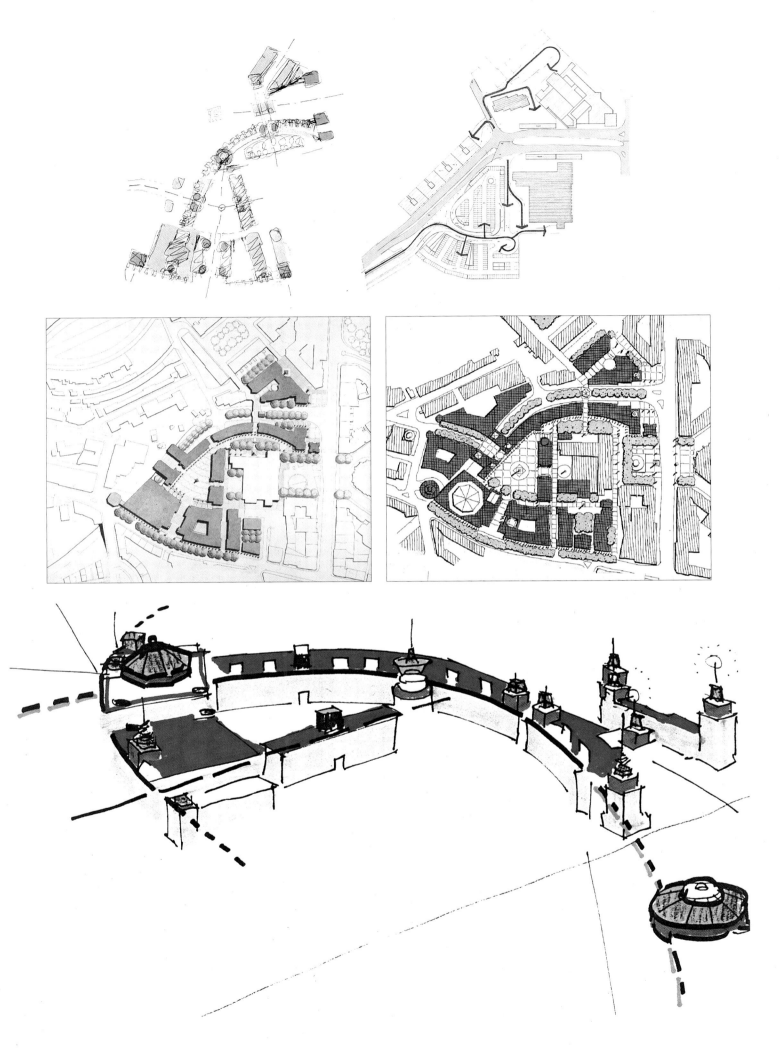

STUDIES FOR THE SECOND MASTERPLAN

251

PERSPECTIVE DRAWINGS FOR THE SECOND MASTERPLAN

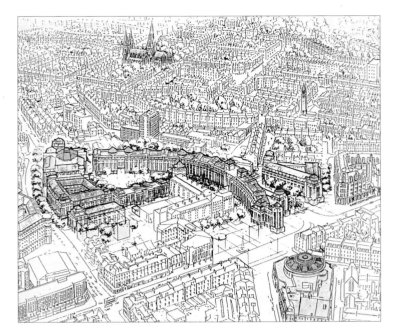

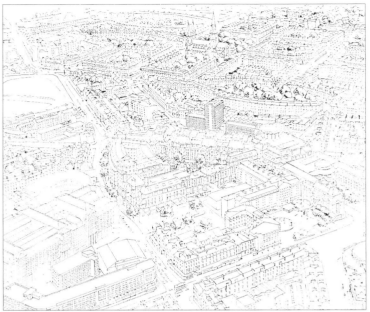

AERIAL VIEW AND MODEL FOR THE SECOND MASTERPLAN

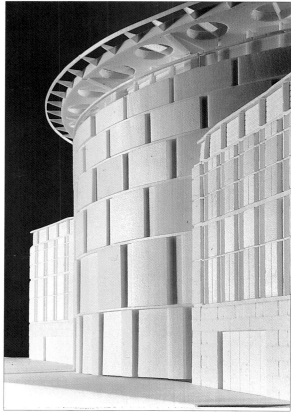

STUDIES MODEL OF THE CONFERENCE AND EXHIBITION CENTRE

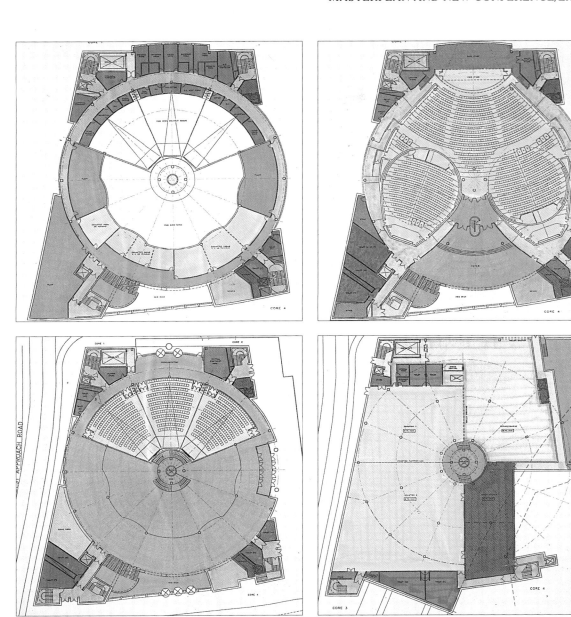

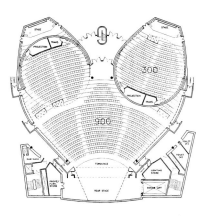

PLANS AND INTERIOR STUDIES OF THE CONFERENCE AND EXHIBITION CENTRE

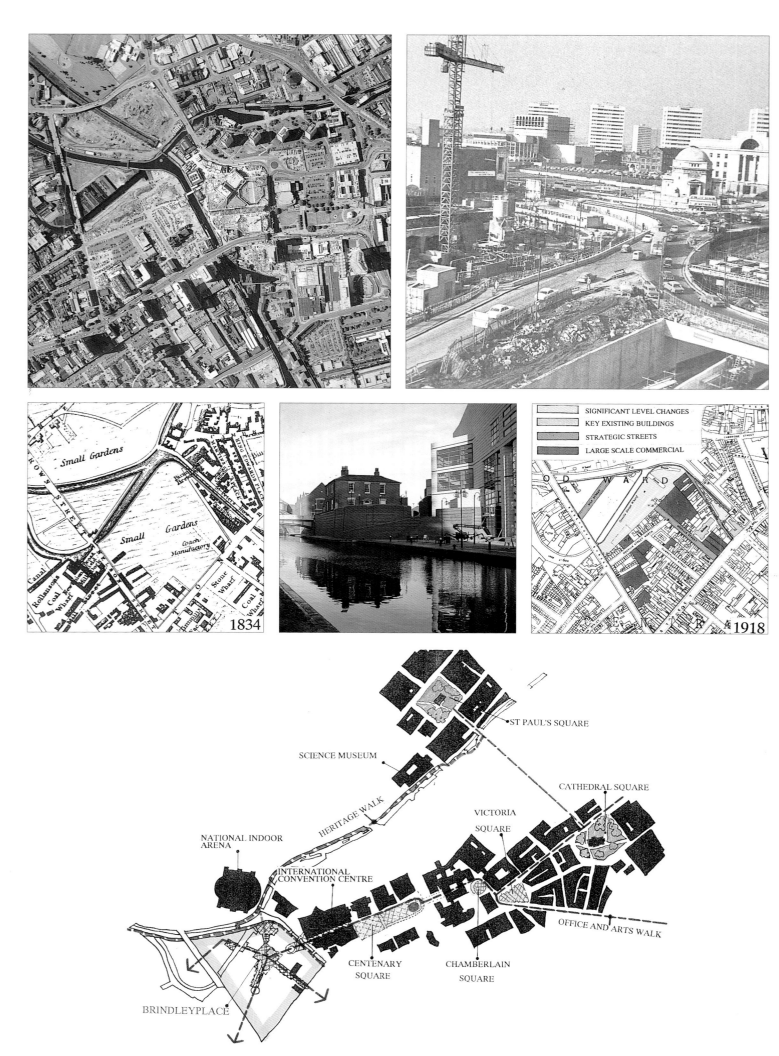

SIGNIFICANT LEVEL CHANGES
KEY EXISTING BUILDINGS
STRATEGIC STREETS
LARGE SCALE COMMERCIAL

1834

1918

ST PAUL'S SQUARE

SCIENCE MUSEUM

CATHEDRAL SQUARE

VICTORIA SQUARE

HERITAGE WALK

NATIONAL INDOOR ARENA

INTERNATIONAL CONVENTION CENTRE

OFFICE AND ARTS WALK

CENTENARY SQUARE

CHAMBERLAIN SQUARE

BRINDLEYPLACE

HISTORICAL AND CONTEMPORARY SITE ILLUSTRATIONS

## MASTERPLAN FOR MIXED USES
### *BRINDLEY PLACE, BIRMINGHAM 1990-1992*

*The primary relevance of Farrell's experience of working in London applied to Birmingham is the role of the urban designer today as one of mending and healing the city. Birmingham, in particular, has suffered from the over-simplistic solutions of town planning of the 1950s and 1960s, with theories of zoning and vehicular priority. The inner ring road has acted like a noose around the city centre, restricting natural expansion and severely affecting the pedestrian domain.*

*The scheme had particular importance as the first piece of Birmingham, beyond the confines of the ring road, that had been deliberately planned to create a good pedestrian realm since the second world war. The site had been reconnected to the city by the lowering and bridging of the ring road at Paradise Circus. Within the site the planning of the pedestrian routes, articulated by a series of urban spaces, has been dictated by three existing axes on the site - the axis of the main mall of the International Convention Centre which was projected, by the creation of new canalside spaces, into the centre of the site; the axis along the existing Oozells Street; and an axis from the new roundabout on Sheepcote Street which provided vehicle access to the site. The pedestrian access points around the site were plotted and connected across the site to form a complete pedestrian network integrated with the urban fabric beyond.*

*A new square provided a heart for the scheme and formed a termination to the sequence of urban spaces along the city's main pedestrian spine, from Colmore Row*

*through Chamberlain and Centenary Square. This new square provided the focal point for the high level route connections to offices, shops and, via a bridge, to the leisure area. This movement system was connected to a secondary system based on the canal edge at lower towpath level which provided connections to the wider city by existing and proposed pedestrian bridges.*

*In terms of historical continuity, Farrell had to work with the recent developments, but also with those of the 19th century. The site was developed as an industrial area, located at the junction between the Birmingham and Worcester canals. The industrial relics of the canal system, the bridges and towpaths were all integrated to provide a source of character and amenity and to create a part of the city with a strong sense of identity, which so much of Birmingham lacks. Farrell retained three listed buildings - an industrial building, Oozells Street school by Chamberlain and a Presbyterian church - on the site as focal points within the scheme.*

*The process of development of the masterplan was primarily through models which generated a number of design guidelines for the buildings on the site, covering height, massing, floorplate, and servicing locations, to be designed by other architects. The process also involved negotiation, exhibition, and presentation, as at Edinburgh, and the involvement of a number of parties, including residents and workers in the area, the city council and other bodies.*

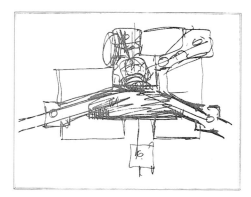
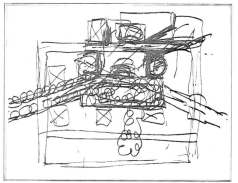

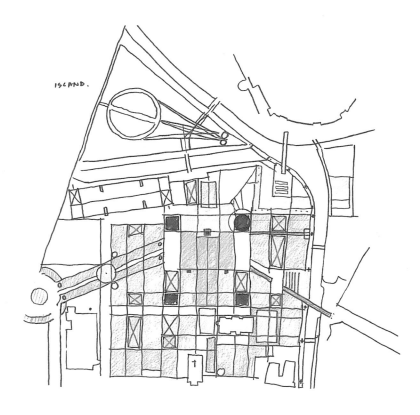

CONCEPT DRAWINGS

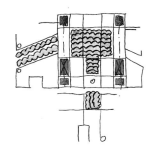

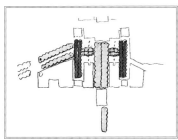

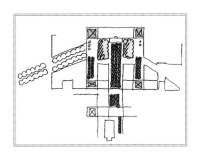

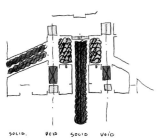

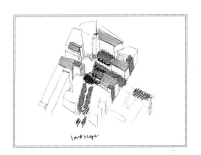

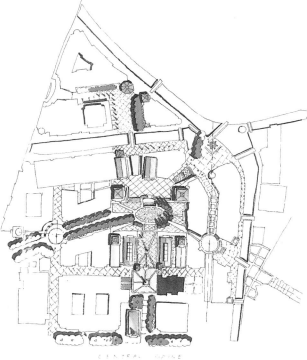

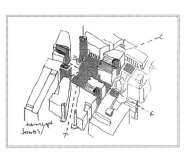

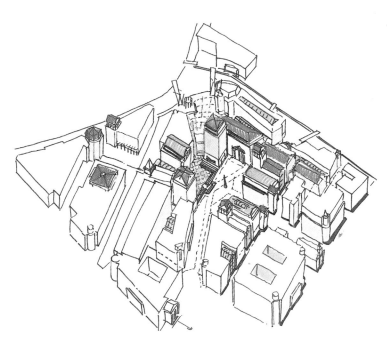

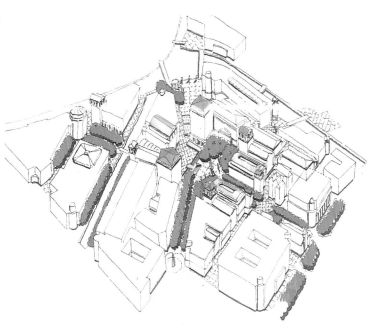

CONCEPT DRAWINGS

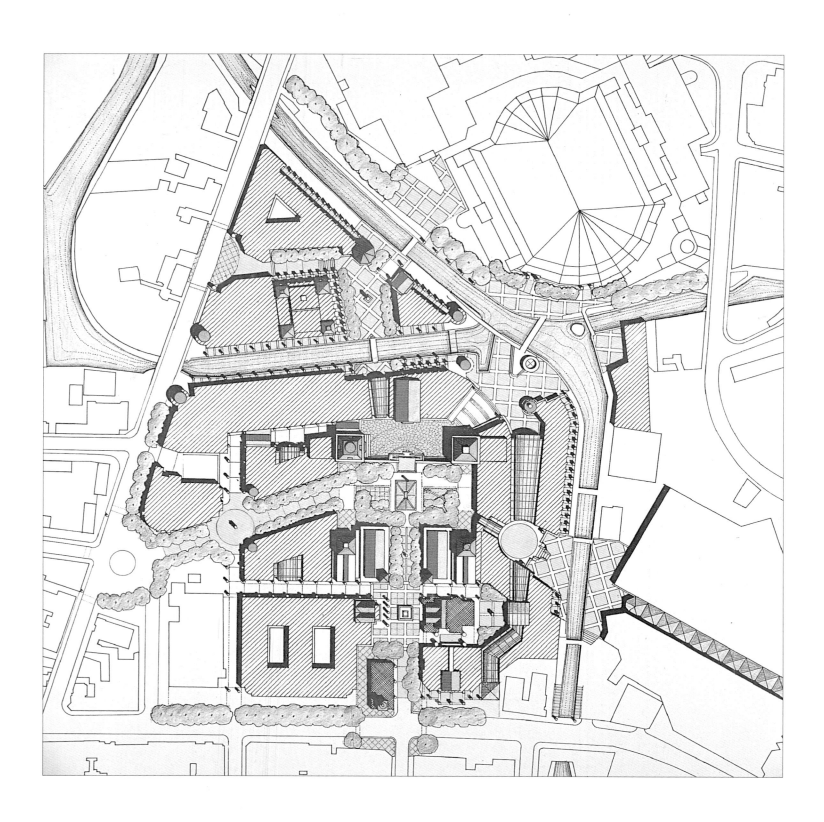

THE MASTERPLAN

SEPTEMBER 1989

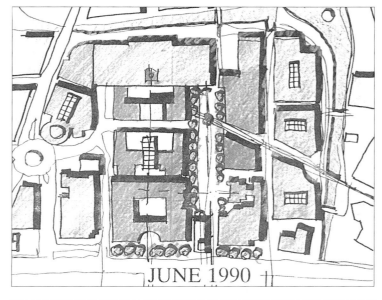

JUNE 1990

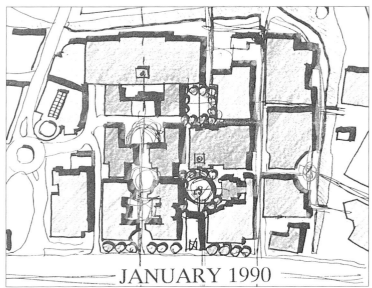

JANUARY 1990

NOVEMBER 1990

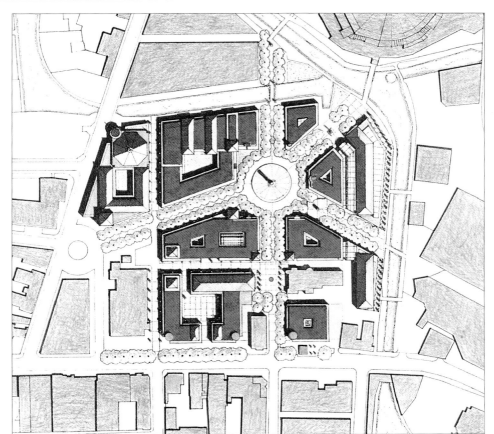

EVOLUTION OF THE MASTERPLAN

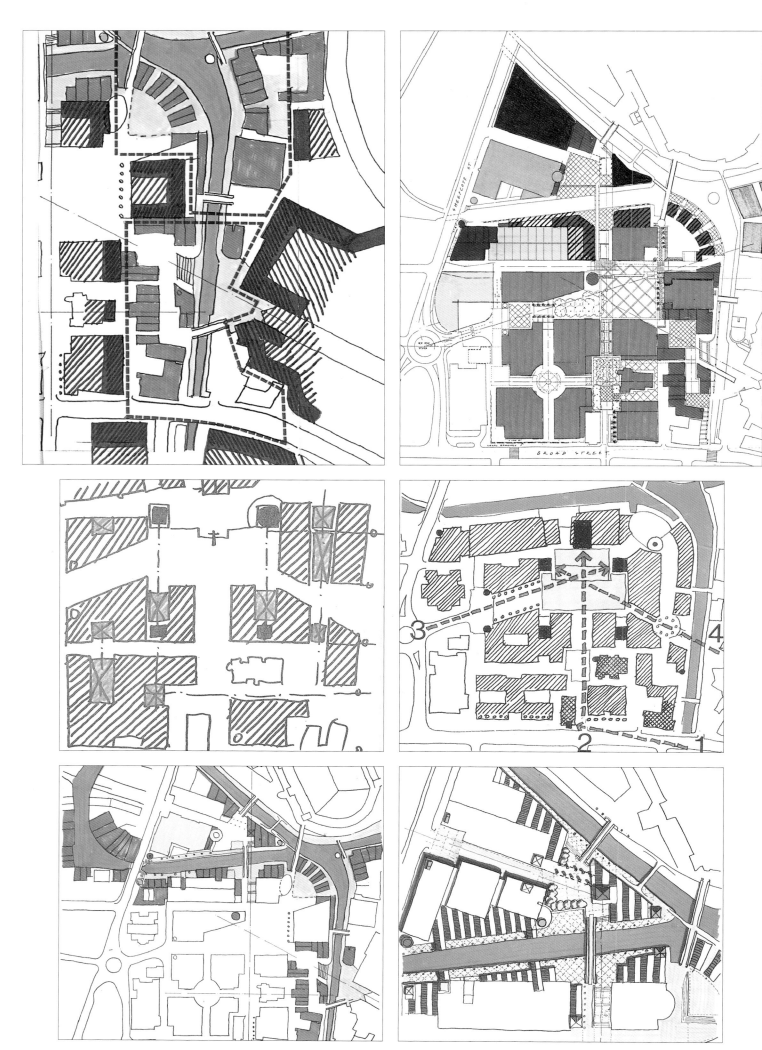

STUDIES OF LAND USE, MASSING AND BUILDING FORM

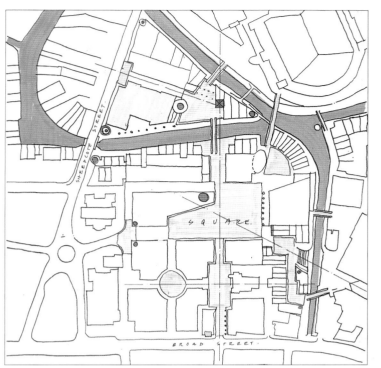

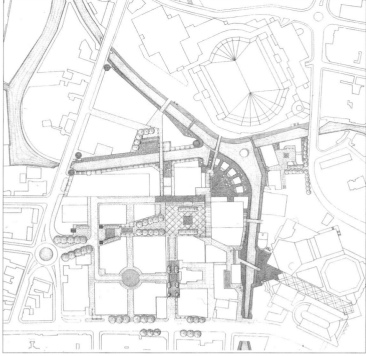

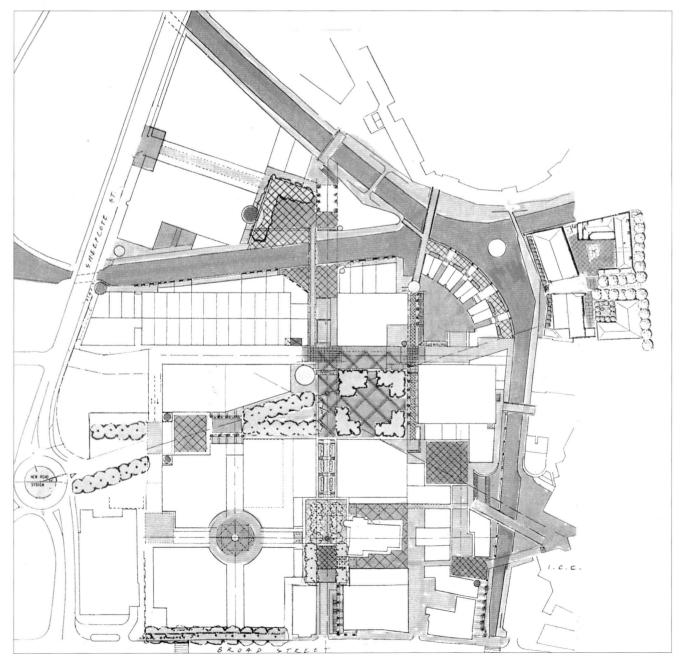

STUDIES FOR PUBLIC OPEN SPACES

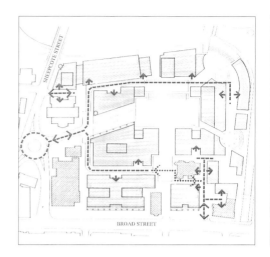

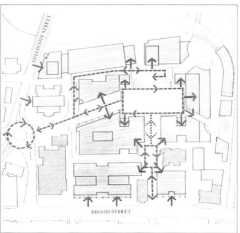

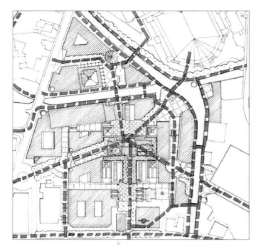

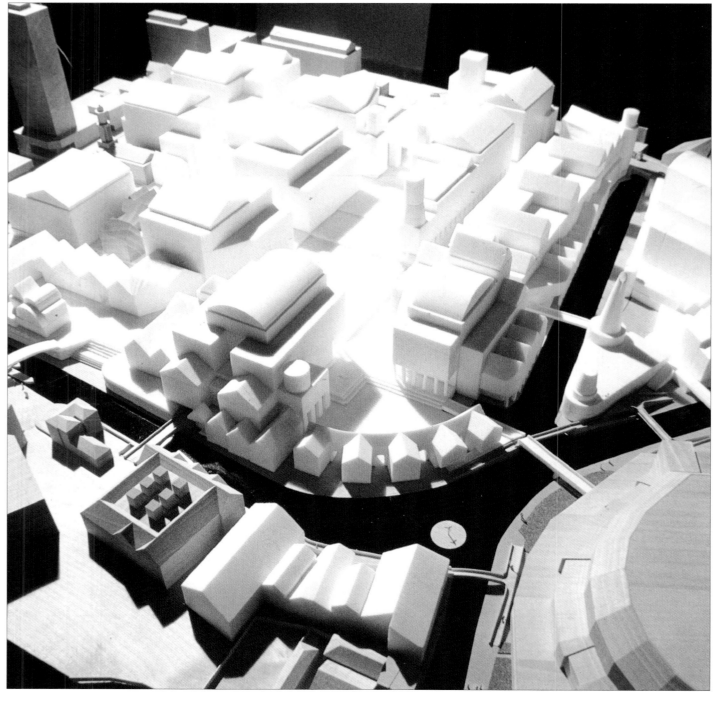

TRAFFIC MOVEMENT AND MODEL VIEW OF THE MASTERPLAN

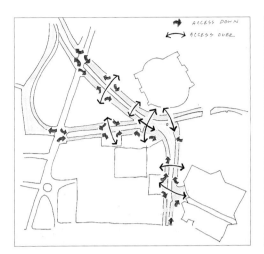

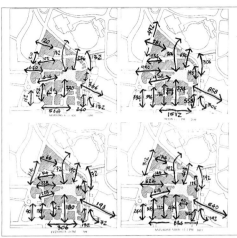

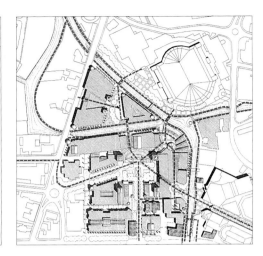

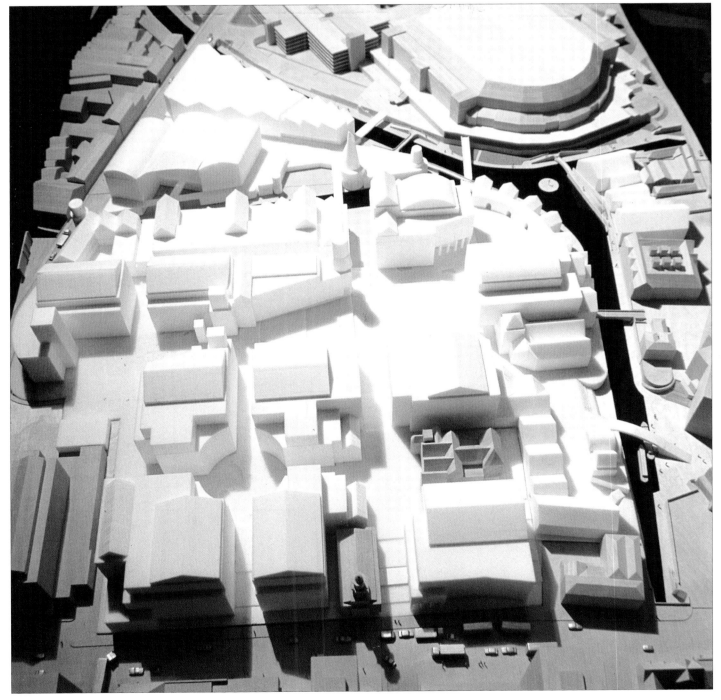

PEDESTRIAN MOVEMENT AND MODEL VIEW OF THE MASTERPLAN

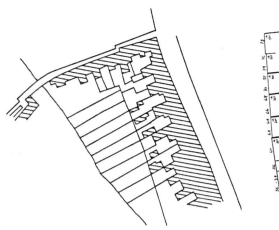

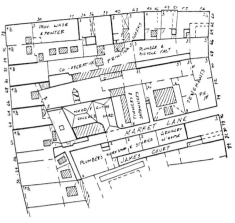

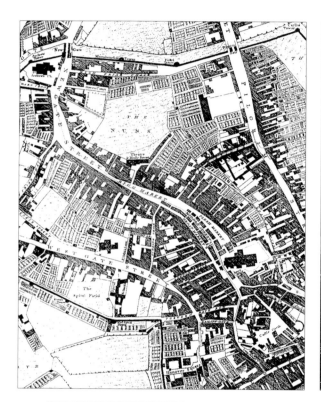

HISTORICAL PLANS AND PHOTOGRAPHS

# MIXED USE RENOVATION AND REDEVELOPMENT SCHEME
## *GREY STREET, NEWCASTLE 1991-1992*

*This project offers the opportunity to take lessons learnt from Comyn Ching and similar London projects, back to Terry Farrell's home town of Newcastle. Grey Street is the city's finest street and runs, like Regent Street in London, from one strata of the urban fabric across the grain of the city to a contrasting one - a journey of great drama which reveals so many sections of the surrounding neighbourhoods. In Newcastle, Grey Street runs uphill from the river to its crescendo at the monument and the site sits right at the top of this route.*

*The site has a fascinating medieval history, particularly expressed in old maps, where plot boundaries and changing street patterns record so much of the changing life of the community. Much of Farrell's study of the site has been to reflect and expose these boundaries and routes.The massing of the new building reflects the variety of scale appropriate to the site's position in amongst a collection of disparate properties.*

*The Grand Room roof rises above the centre of the site,* *with the surrounding area of roof pitched towards it. The zone established by this embracing roof pitch carries through to the first major subdivisions of the High Bridge elevation.*

*The roof above 52-60 Grey Street again relates to the subdivision of the facade on Grey Street itself, with a central zone projecting back towards Market Lane. The remaining new roofscape is developed as a series of linked pavilions. Whilst representing a unifying form, the fragmentation relates to the scale of the roofscape on the retained Pilgrim Street properties and addresses the new Garden Court. By setting back at third floor level, the apparent building height above Lloyd's Court is reduced, and balcony roof terrace areas are created for the benefit of the building's occupants.*

*Unlike other redevelopments along Grey Street, the proposed roofscape avoids extensive areas of flat roof or mansards on the Grey Street elevation, both of which are uncharacteristic of the area.*

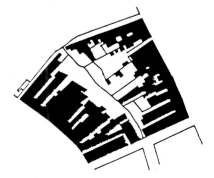

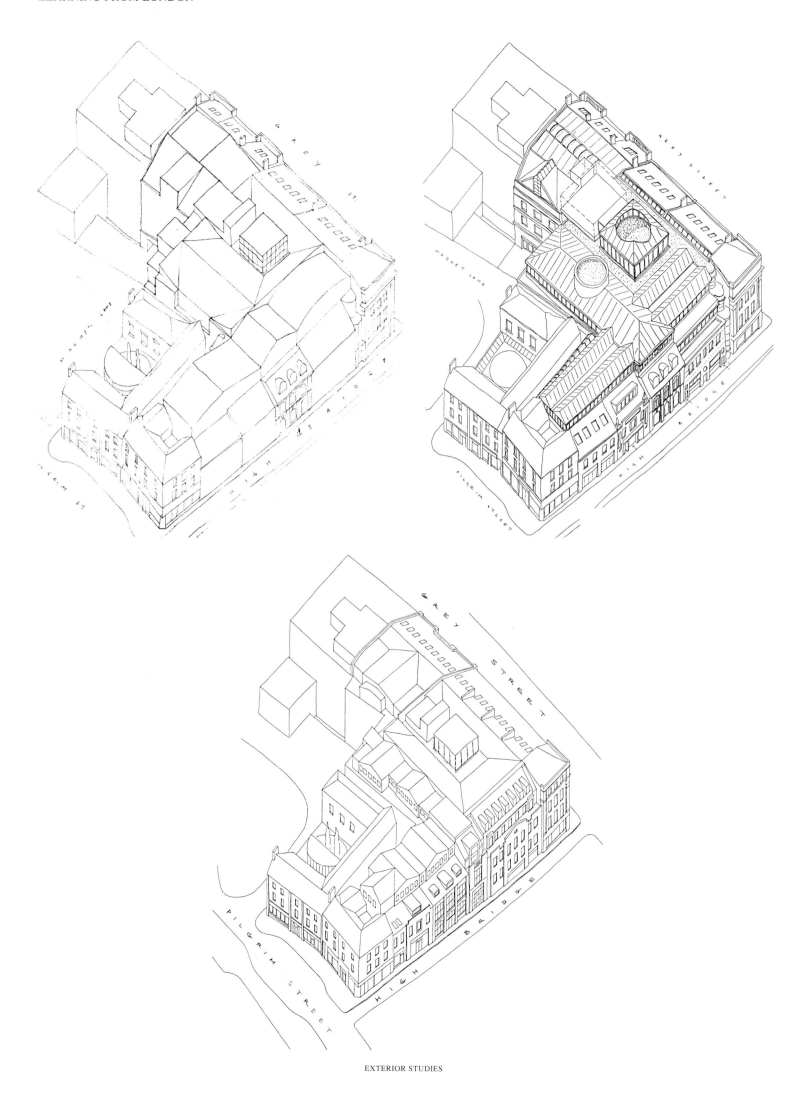

EXTERIOR STUDIES

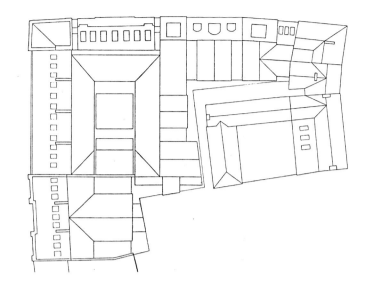

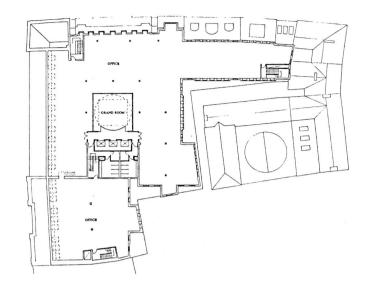

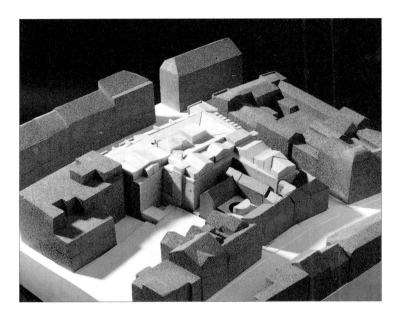

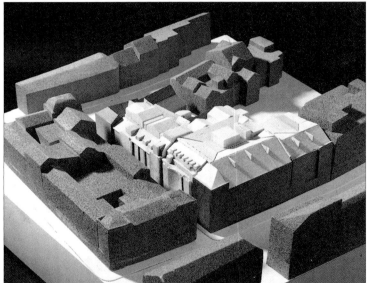

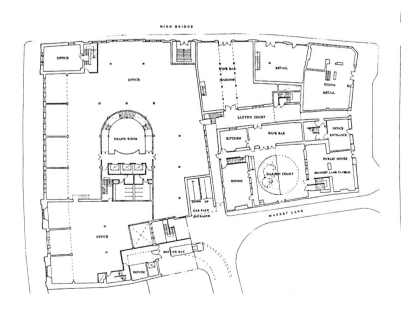

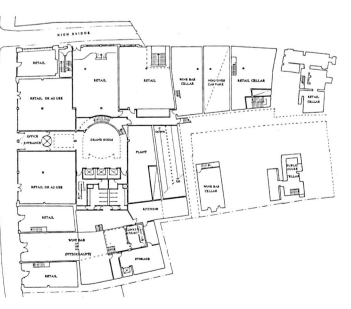

PLANS AND MODEL OF THE PROPOSALS

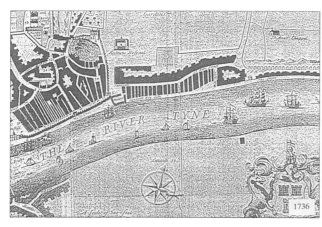

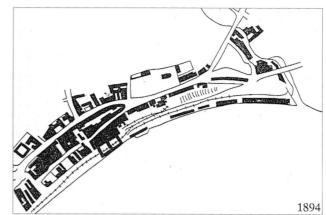

1894

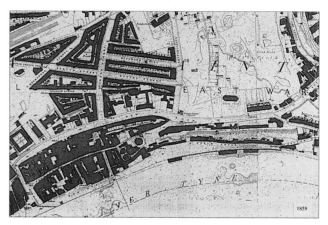

1858

EXISTING AND HISTORICAL PICTURES OF THE SITE

# MASTERPLAN FOR MIXED USES
## QUAYSIDE, NEWCASTLE 1991-1992

*The masterplan for the Quayside development in Newcastle gave Farrell the opportunity to work in his home town. The site, now derelict, was historically the heart of Newcastle's commercial dockland. The topography of the site had similarities with that of London - positioned on the steep north bank of the river, enjoying a south-facing aspect, and developed with a number of roads running down to the quayside. As in the port area in London, industry had moved downstream towards the estuary.*

*Another aspect of the Newcastle scheme, which was influenced by Farrell's work in London and originated from studies made in his student days, was the nature of riverside development as a linear situation in which the high street was often placed one block in from the river, away from the exposure and environment of the river edge. The scheme was very much based on this idea of the double-sided building plot with major river frontages addressing the river but the main access from the street set one block back. A quayside route ran the length of the site, and was divided into two parts. The uninterrupted pedestrian promenade along the river was a continuation of the existing route along the Tyne, with the higher part, next to the building edge, providing vehicular and public transit routes. The pedestrian network emanated from crossing points on surrounding streets, and a number of routes perpendicular to the river supplemented the major linear routes, increasing permeability and views to the river from within the site.*

*The trend of a return to the cities has led to many cities, including London and Liverpool, rediscovering the neglected areas of river front. In Newcastle, 19th century bridges began to by-pass the quayside and the original heart of the city. An interesting aspect of neglect for Farrell is how it serves as a great conserver. Here he used existing buildings on the site to create a sense of place and identity for the development, and to generate the geometry and form of the overall scheme. The existing Co-operative Wholesale Society warehouse defined the building line on the river front as a hard edge along the river, and formed part of the built enclosure for the main public square in the scheme. This space formed the focus for the leisure and retail portion of the scheme, located at the west end of the site, nearer to the city centre. The Sailors Bethel church defined a focus for the residential development at the east end of the site.*

*Once again the scheme established a set of guidelines to direct the future input of architects. The basis of Farrell's urban design approach was that each plot had great potential, and within the masterplan each was thoroughly designed with respect to access, aspect and servicing, and integrated within the whole scheme. Height limits and preferred building materials were established, the former with reference to views and massing dictated by the topography of the site, the latter with reference to the historical precedents in the area.*

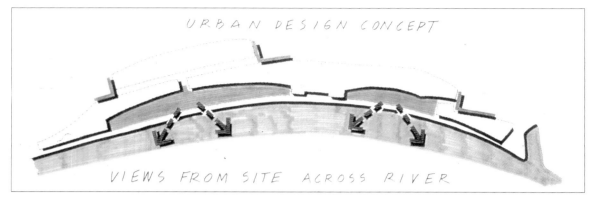

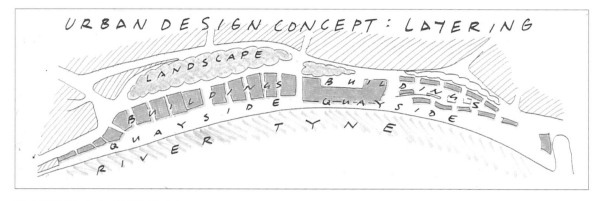

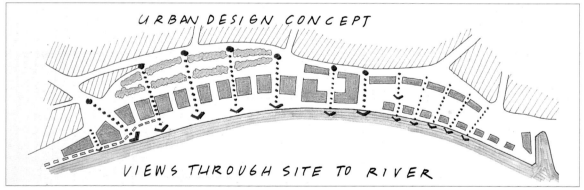

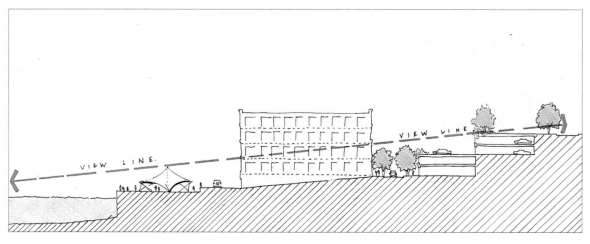

CONCEPT DRAWINGS

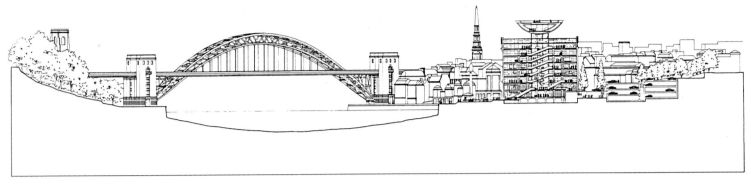

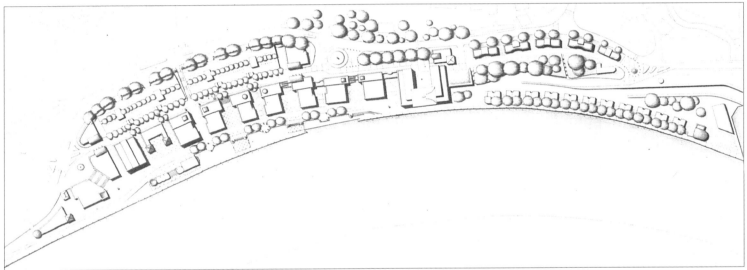

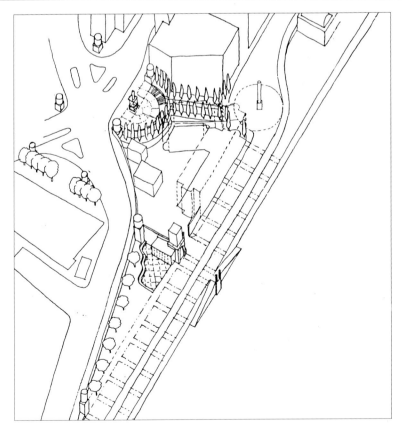

THE MASTERPLAN AND DETAILED STUDIES

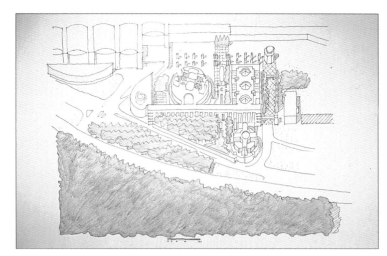
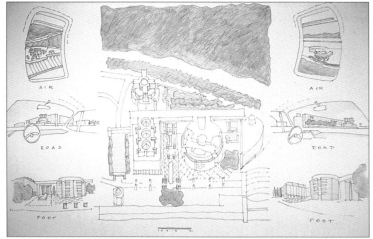

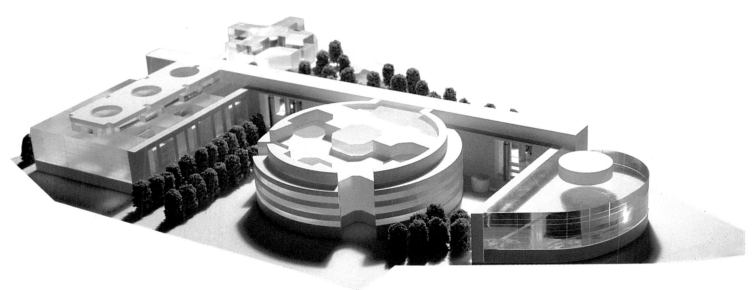

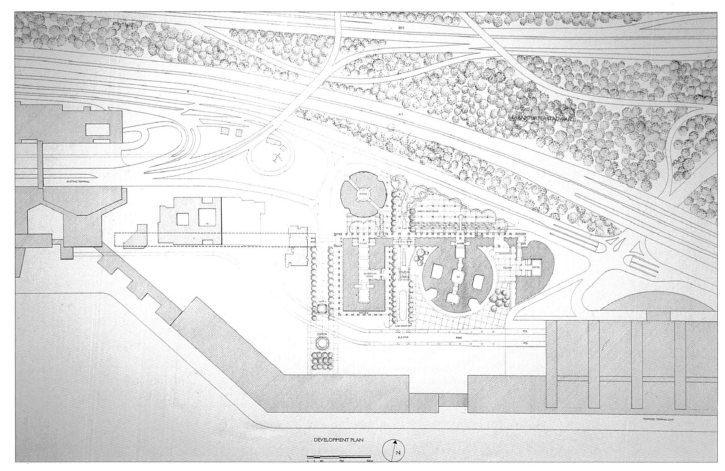

MODEL AND DRAWINGS OF THE PROPOSALS

# AIRPORT STAFF AND ADMINISTRATION CENTRE
## FRANKFURT AIRPORT, GERMANY 1989

The proposals for a new headquarters and administration centre for Frankfurt Airport provided Farrell with the opportunity to explore contextuality in a new and completely 20th century setting, and as such had certain parallels with Farrell's schemes for the modern developments at the Barbican and the South Bank. In urban design terms, the most interesting aspect of the competition entry was the airport as monocultural estate. During studies of Heathrow, Farrell was fascinated by the notion of airport as mini-city, with a chapel, medical centre, leisure facilities, restaurants and other amenities for travellers and airport staff. Frankfurt also contained all these elements, but the competition was to design facilities for the staff.

The interest for Farrell was the design of a building that encompassed an extraordinary range of scales. From a world scale that used topography and wind direction to establish the orientation of the runways, to a local scale that related to access routes from motorways. Then there is the micro-scale of the geometry of the building itself which must respond to the larger movement systems. At Frankfurt, certain buildings had ignored these overriding geometries, and Farrell was interested in restoring a contextual framework that came from the very essence of the place based upon wind, air, and car access, that had begun to be neglected. Farrell therefore created a spine route, 300 metres long, as the essential organising axis in alignment with the principal terminal building. Within this

ordered framework he located the new built elements that responded to this geometry, and integrated an existing rectangular building, that had rejected the orthogonal arrangement, by transforming it into a circular building with no directional geometry. This spine acted as the planning sector boundary that divided the public areas from the private operational security zone. This concept for future site development established a public zone of large scale spaces and vehicular movement systems. A landscaped roof top over the principal car parking building responded to the adjacent natural forest edge. This zone contrasted with the man-made environment of the security zone, the smaller, private spaces and pedestrian movement.

What fascinated Farrell was that the normal rules within the city are, within the airport, exaggerated to a new dimension and the great degree to which these powerful rules dictate the structure, buildings and movement system of the mini-city. As the organisational framework of the original Roman military camps was used as the principle for the planning of the city fabric, similarly the runways are the first act of colonisation that dictates all other movement systems. But the original monofunctional character of the airport, like the military base, becomes subsumed to the more complex and diverse activities with the result that the airport contains all the great diversity of human activity that exists in the normal urban scene.

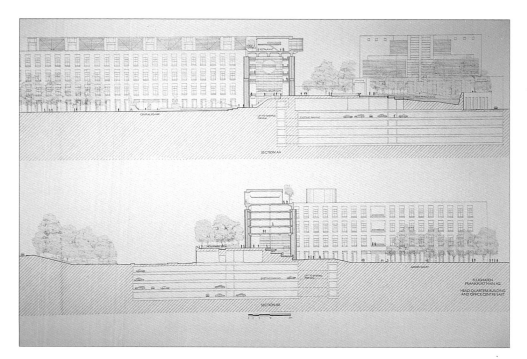

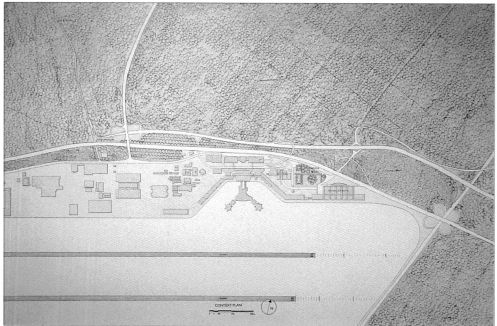

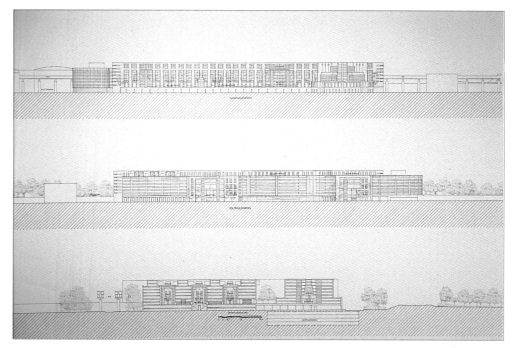

SECTIONS, ELEVATIONS AND SITE PLAN OF THE PROPOSALS

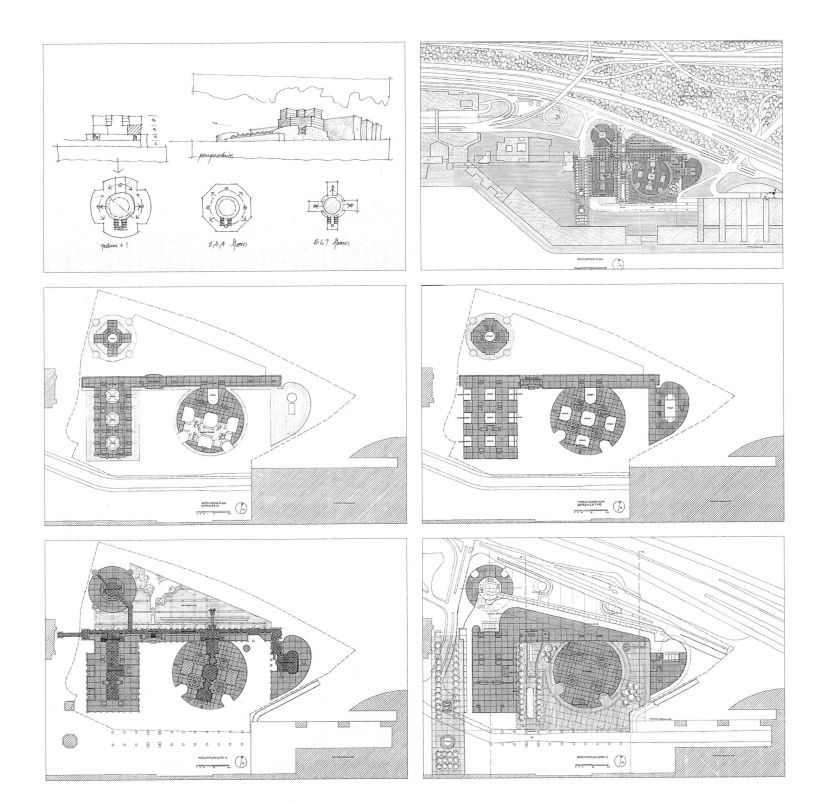

DETAILED PLANS

277

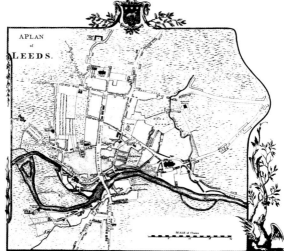

HISTORICAL VIEWS AND TOWN PLAN AND FIGURE GROUND STUDIES OF CENTRAL LEEDS

# MASTERPLAN FOR MIXED USES
## *QUARRY HILL, LEEDS 1989-1992*

*The Quarry Hill site in Leeds, historically integrated with the city, was developed in the 1930s as a massive mono-cultural housing estate. For Farrell, the 20th century solutions to problems of architecture and planning often exaggerated the problems they were meant to solve. Such was the desire for radical change, that the developments which replaced the slum housing on the site in time themselves became unacceptable. The Quarry Hill housing estate was based upon continental experiments rather than indigenous traditions. The massive scheme contained the seeds of its own obsolescence simply because it was so mono-cultural and totalitarian - it was demolished in the late 1970s. Farrell's main task was to develop an area of mixed use that overcame the mono-cultural history and isolated nature of the site, and transformed it into an integrated and active part of the city.*

*A result of such major urban clearance in recent years was that a hiatus in planning attracted elements such as traffic intersections that were located on these empty urban sites because of their availability. As in Edinburgh where the Sheridan Hotel was placed on the old railway site, at Leeds the West Yorkshire Playhouse was located on the site with little urban design forethought. Such developments limited the possibilities of the masterplan and presented problems of how they could be related to a wider urban design scheme.*

*In terms of historical continuity there was little upon which to build, but Farrell was interested in the relation-ship between the axial arrangement through Leeds, created by Blomfield in the 1930s, of a wide formal avenue, Headrow, that runs up to the town hall and the traditional warren of arcades and alleys. The Quarry Hill site had a very strong axial relationship to Headrow and Farrell projected this axis onto the site to relate it to the city centre. This axis was transformed into a sequence of wide formal public spaces, which exploited the sloping nature of the site to create a procession of steps and terraces.*

*At the Eastgate end of the site, Gateway Court formed the principal pedestrian gateway to the scheme, with stairs and ramps up to Playhouse Square. The pedestrian routes from around the site converged on this space, which was the cultural heart of the scheme, articulated by the entrance to the hotel, offices, cafés and the Playhouse, with an outdoor performance space served by the eastern edge of the square which was stepped to form an amphitheatre.*

*The Main Square, at the most elevated point of the site, terminated the Headrow axis and was enclosed by new built elements and the new DHS Headquarters. This main pedestrian route was crossed by a series of subsidiary routes that provided permeability through the site from north to south, and were linked to existing surface and bridge crossings. Vehicular access was also from the north and south edges of the site, at the rear of the buildings at a lower ground level, taking advantage of the sloping site conditions.*

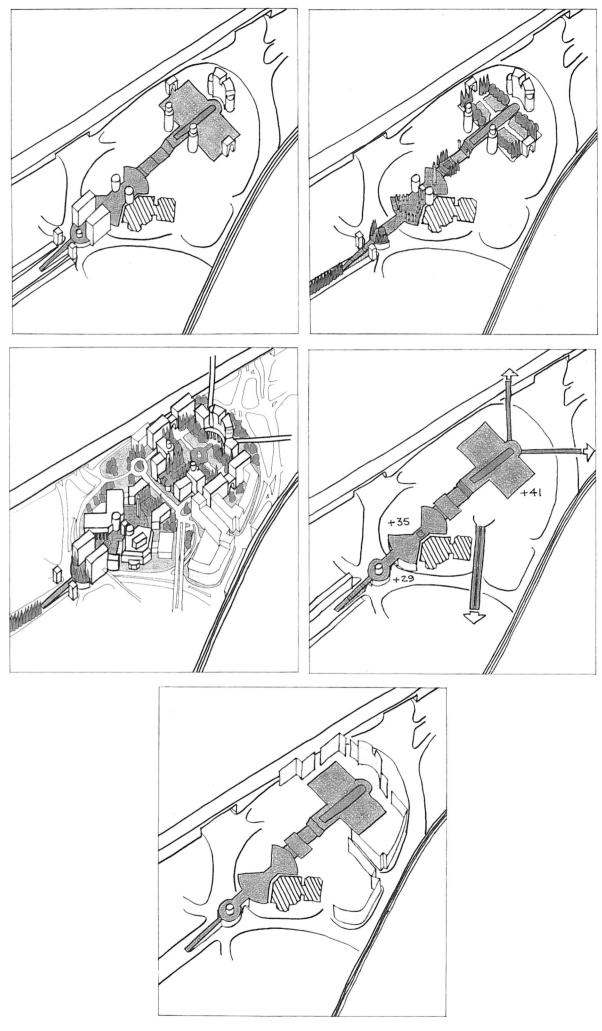

CONCEPT STUDIES

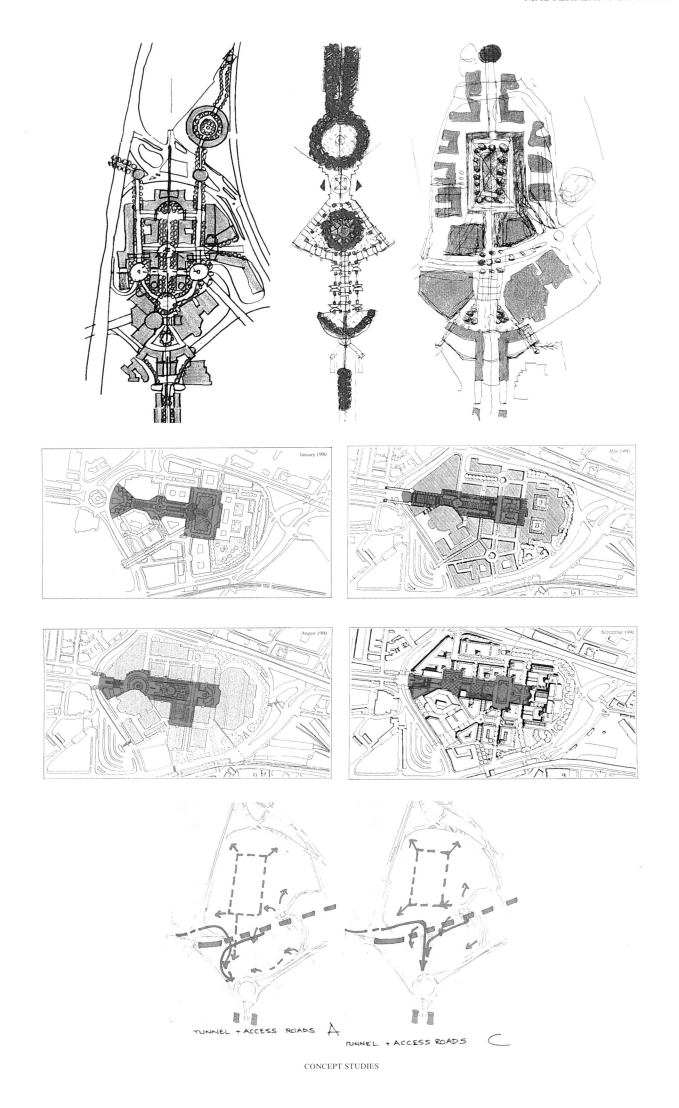

January 1990

May 1990

August 1990

September 1990

TUNNEL + ACCESS ROADS A

TUNNEL + ACCESS ROADS C

CONCEPT STUDIES

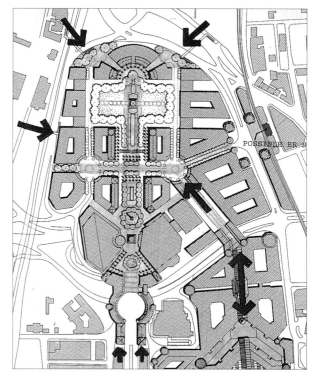

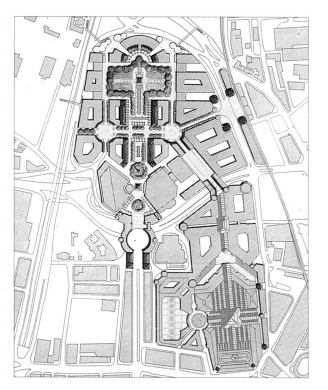

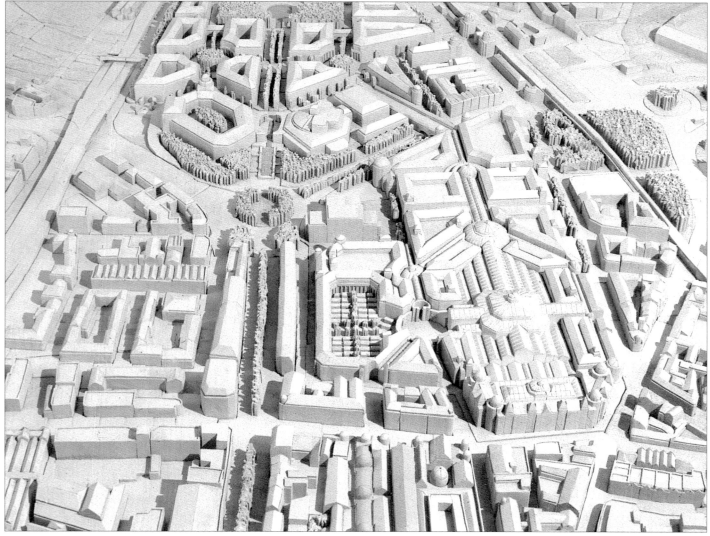

EARLY MASTERPLAN STUDIES AND MODEL OF COMBINED ROB KRIER AND TERRY FARRELL PROJECTS

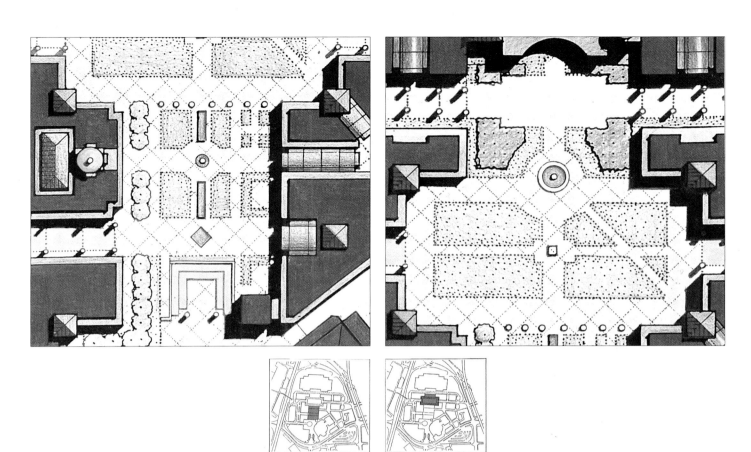

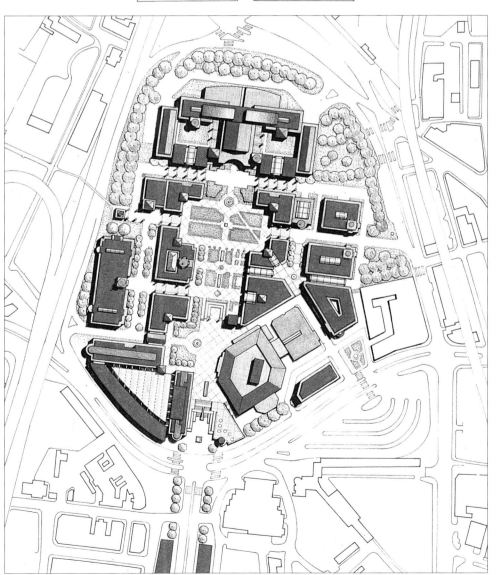

THE MASTERPLAN

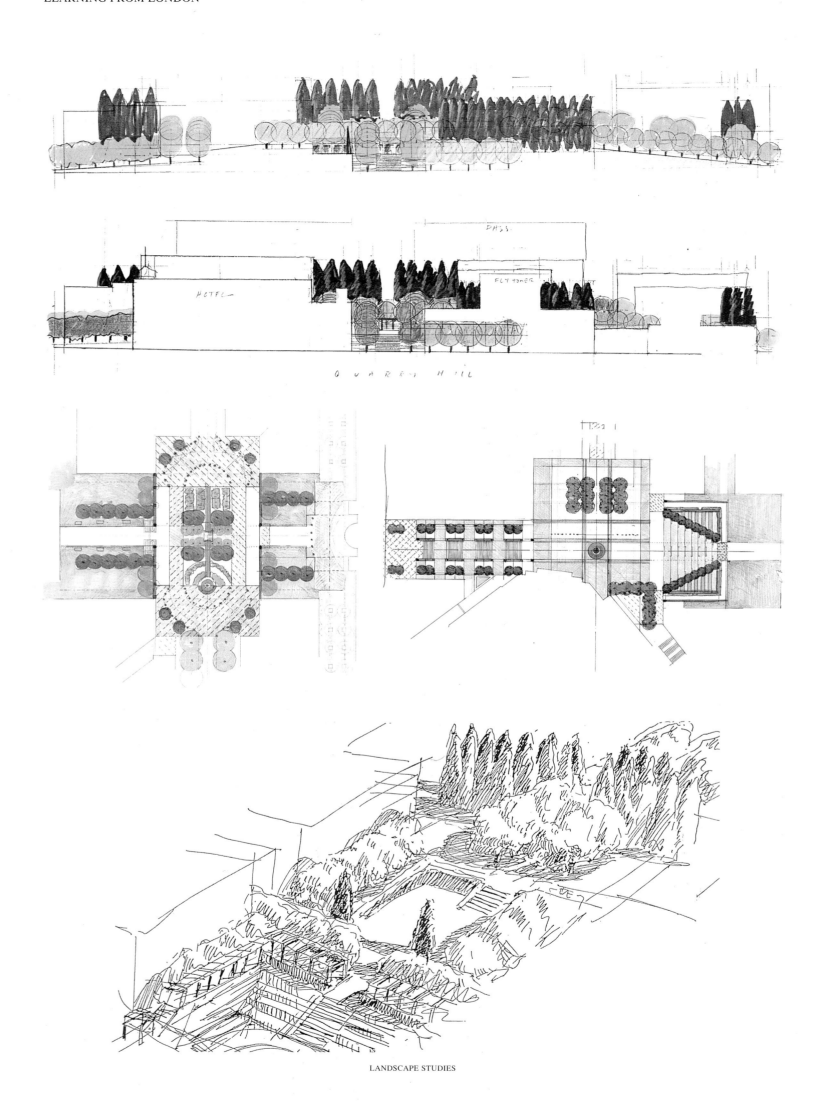

LANDSCAPE STUDIES

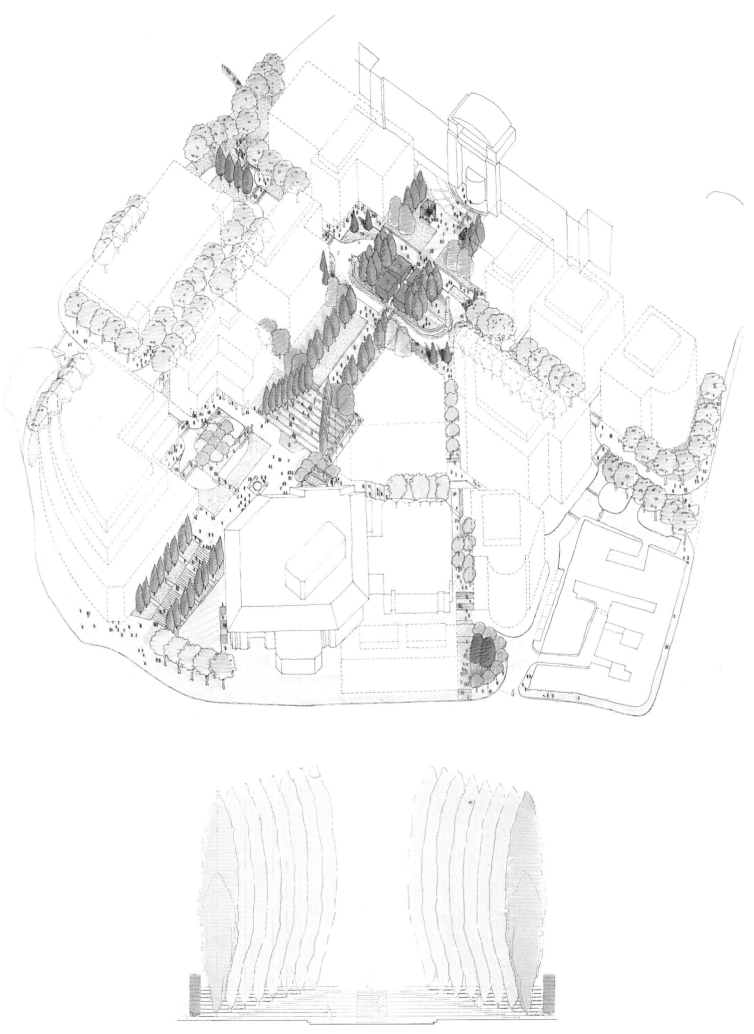

LANDSCAPE STUDIES

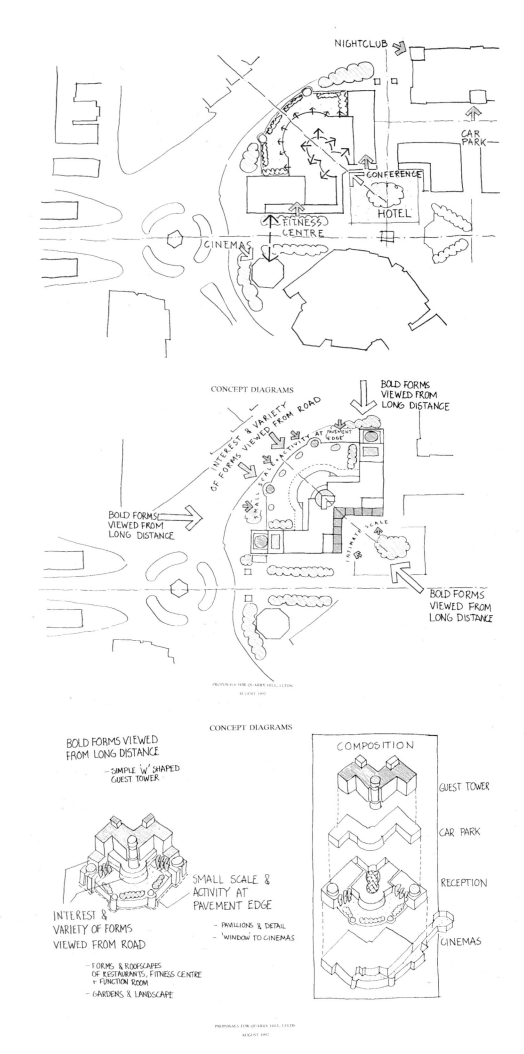

NIGHTCLUB

CAR
PARK

CONFERENCE

HOTEL

FITNESS
CENTRE

CINEMAS

CONCEPT DIAGRAMS

BOLD FORMS
VIEWED FROM
LONG DISTANCE

INTEREST & VARIETY
OF FORMS VIEWED FROM ROAD

SMALL SCALE ACTIVITY AT PAVEMENT EDGE

BOLD FORMS
VIEWED FROM
LONG DISTANCE

INTIMATE SCALE

BOLD FORMS
VIEWED FROM
LONG DISTANCE

PROPOSALS FOR QUARRY HILL, LEEDS
AUGUST 1992

CONCEPT DIAGRAMS

BOLD FORMS VIEWED
FROM LONG DISTANCE

- SIMPLE 'W' SHAPED
  GUEST TOWER

COMPOSITION

GUEST TOWER

CAR PARK

RECEPTION

CINEMAS

SMALL SCALE &
ACTIVITY AT
PAVEMENT EDGE

- PAVILLIONS & DETAIL
- 'WINDOW' TO CINEMAS

INTEREST &
VARIETY OF FORMS
VIEWED FROM ROAD

- FORMS & ROOFSCAPES
  OF RESTAURANTS, FITNESS CENTRE
  + FUNCTION ROOM
- GARDENS & LANDSCAPE

PROPOSALS FOR QUARRY HILL, LEEDS
AUGUST 1992

STUDIES FOR HOTEL AND LEISURE CORNER COMPLEX

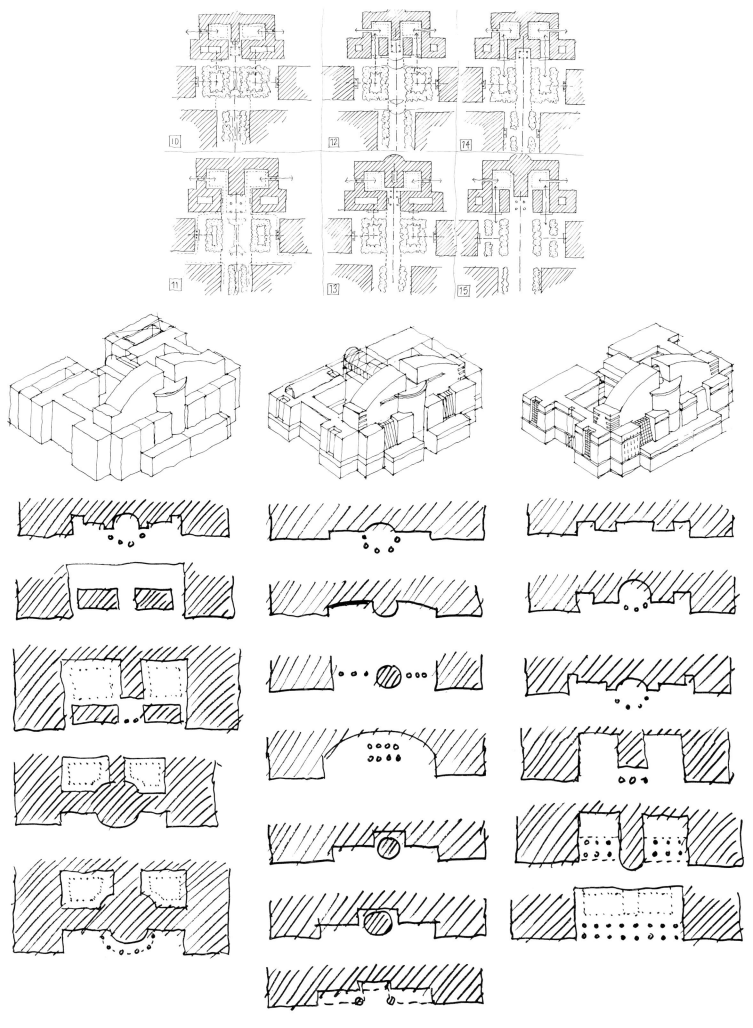

URBAN DESIGN GUIDELINES FOR GOVERNMENT HEADQUARTERS BUILDING

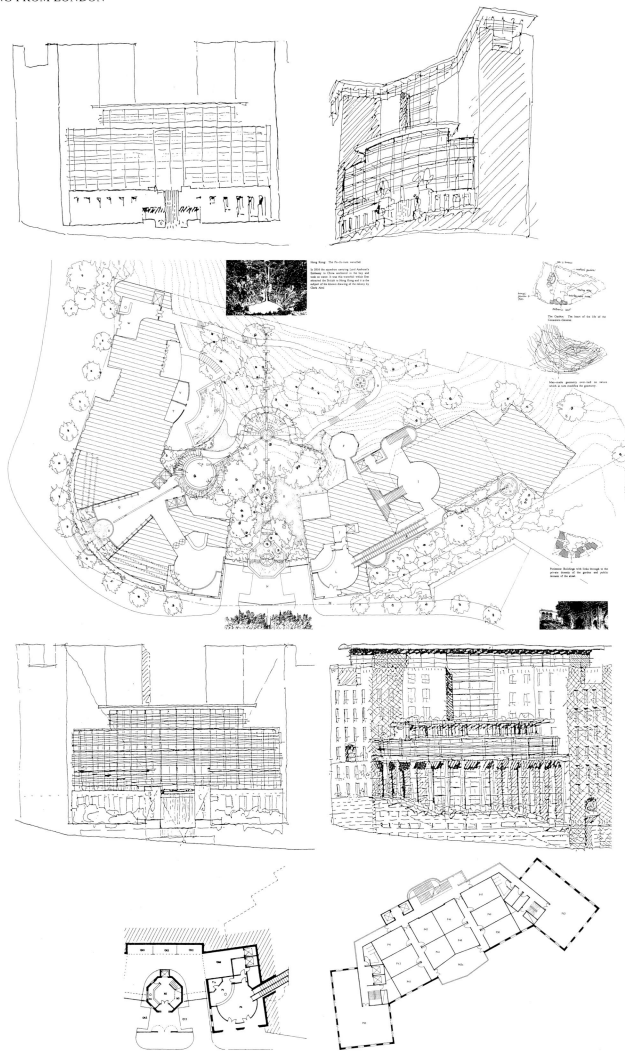

ELEVATION STUDIES, SITE PLAN AND BRITISH COUNCIL FLOOR PLANS

# CONSULATE AND BRITISH COUNCIL OFFICES
## HONG KONG 1992-

Hong Kong provided Farrell with the opportunity to work within a unique urban situation, where the city stands as a symbol of imperialism and capitalism on the edge of communist China and the recent physical expression of free enterprise has been the tower block. Just as the Roman city was a tool for control, the economic citadel of Hong Kong is a financial tool. Thus the city is based upon economic rules, rather than urban rules, where the pleasures of urbanity are rejected in favour of the power of urbanity. Another feature of Hong Kong is that the dominance of the car has yielded to the great intensity of people who instead rely totally upon major public transport systems. Farrell sees this rejection of the car in favour of the boat, train and bus as a model for 21st century urbanism.

Farrell's scheme for the Peak, as for an earlier project for Sunderland, was to design a symbol of identification for the city, just as the Eiffel Tower and Big Ben are symbols of their respective cities. Farrell drew upon the traditional precedent of the Chinese temple for the form of the building - the solid base, the open podium and upswept eaves - but also the unique physical presence the temple exerts upon its surroundings as a place for gathering and contemplation. The unique site for the building - on the Peak overlooking the city - provided the location for a building with these symbolic qualities that would exert a unique presence upon the city.

Until recently Hong Kong was distinguished by groups of dignified low-rise buildings, and for the Consulate project, Farrell designed a piece of street architecture. The main concept of the Consulate, as a linear horizontal building among the tower blocks, was to return to the principles of urban design rejected by the towers that contribute nothing to the concept of space positive in the city. The built elements of the scheme were placed around the perimeter of the site, enclosing a large private garden. As in the clubs or bank buildings of London, there was a sequence of space positive elements from the major public spaces outside to the entry gateways, which lead into the private realm.

Another project in Hong Kong was for a major railway interchange, Kowloon Station, that linked the city to the airport. Farrell used his work for British Rail, for new station complexes at Blackfriars and London Bridge, to understand the relationship between major transport systems and the city. The station was viewed as a machine with its own inherent disciplines, which functioned not as an independent object, but which had to integrate with the city and interface with traditional town planning logic. For Farrell the main task in the design of these monocultural elements was to view them as a mini-city and as such the normal rules of urban design - the need for amenities but also orientation, identification and symbolism - were relevant and essential to create an ordered and coherent piece of the city.

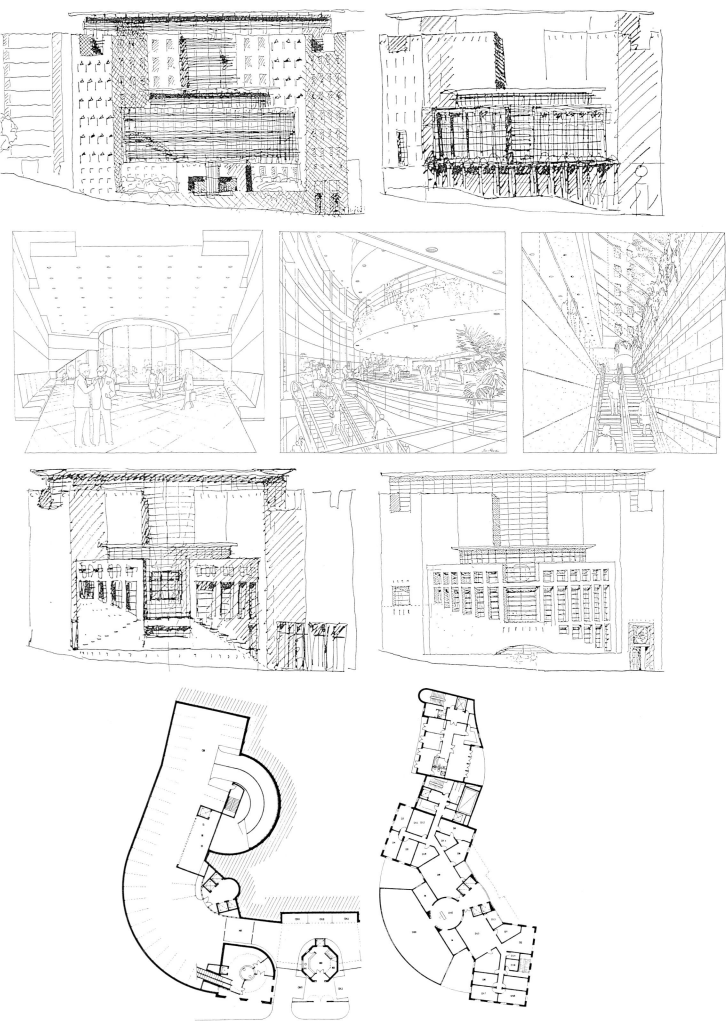

ELEVATION STUDIES, INTERIOR VIEWS AND CONSULATE FLOOR PLANS

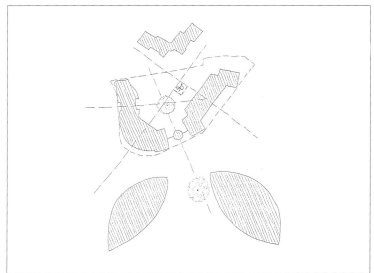

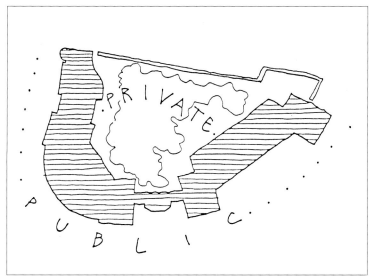

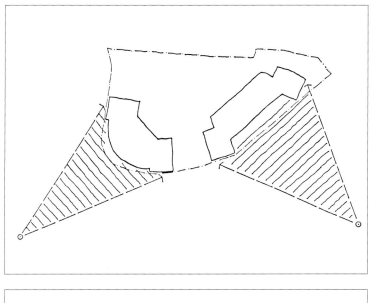

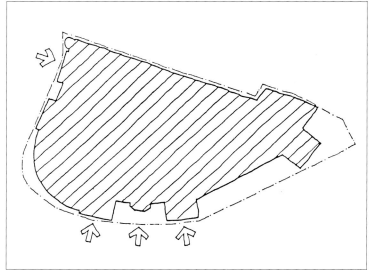

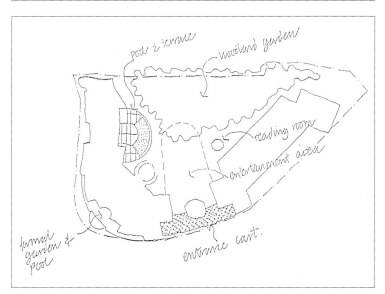

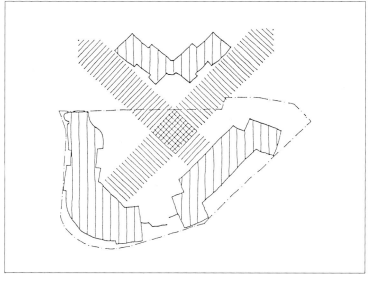

CONCEPT DIAGRAMS

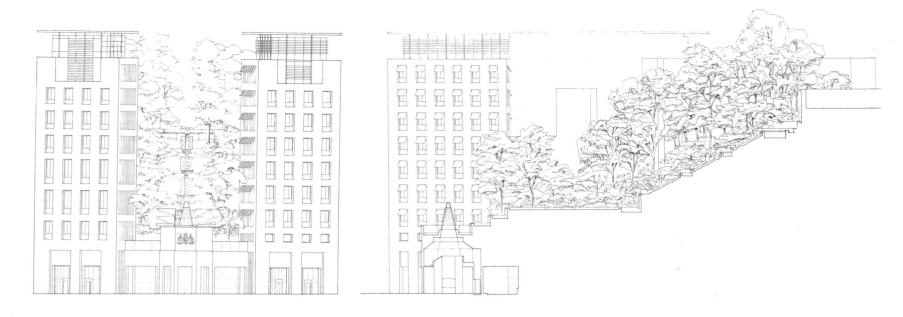

ELEVATIONS AND STUDY MODEL

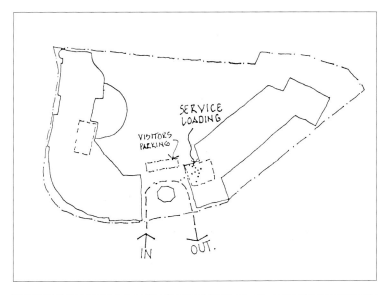

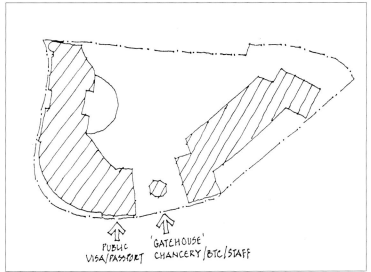

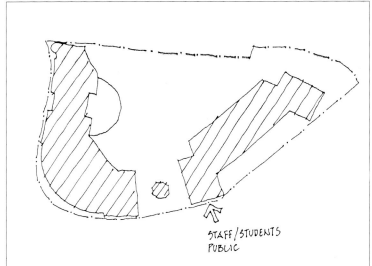

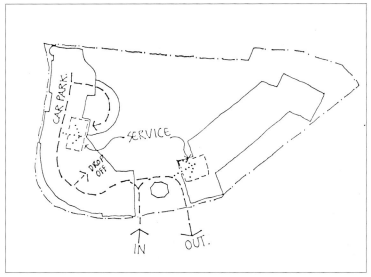

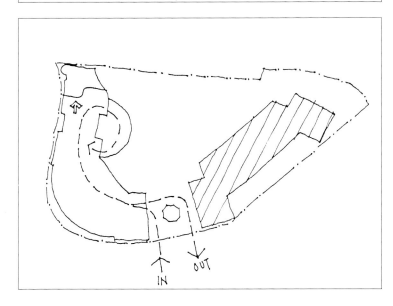

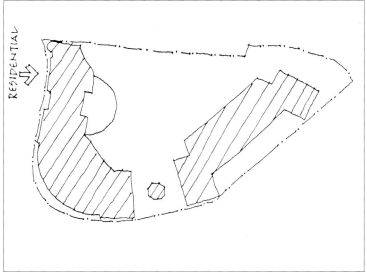

CONCEPT DIAGRAMS

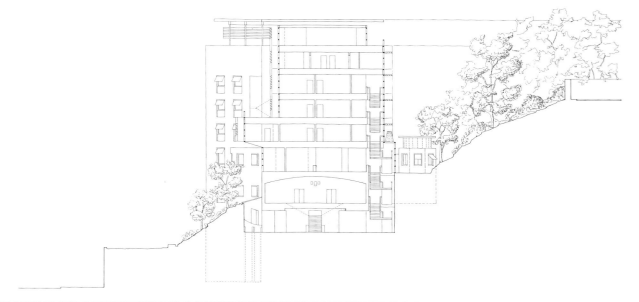

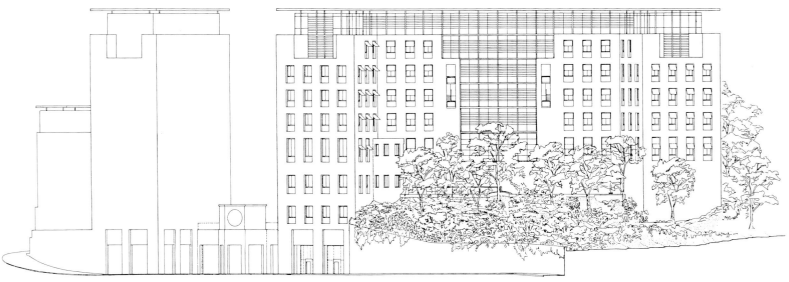

ELEVATIONS AND STUDY MODEL

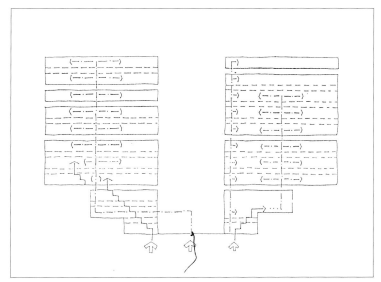

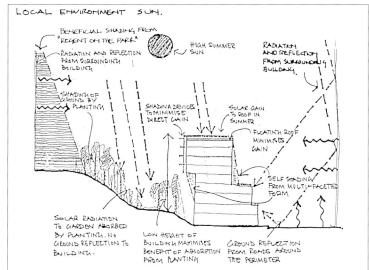

LOCAL ENVIRONMENT SUN.

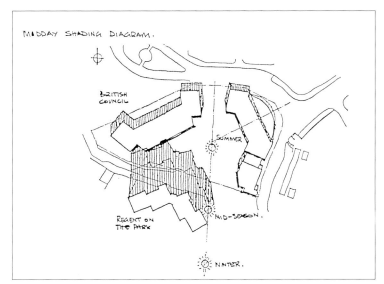

MIDDAY SHADING DIAGRAM.

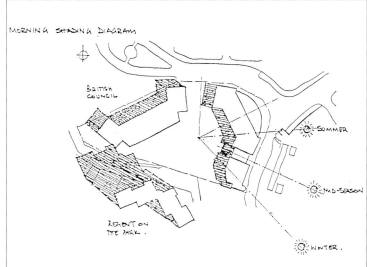

MORNING SHADING DIAGRAM

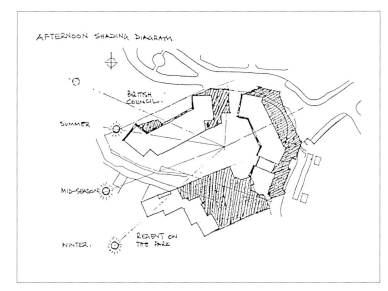

AFTERNOON SHADING DIAGRAM

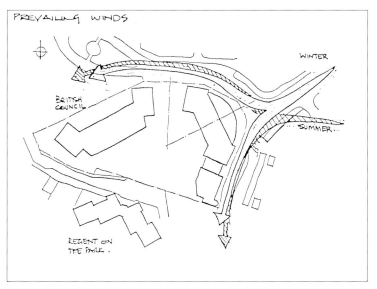

PREVAILING WINDS

CONCEPT DIAGRAMS

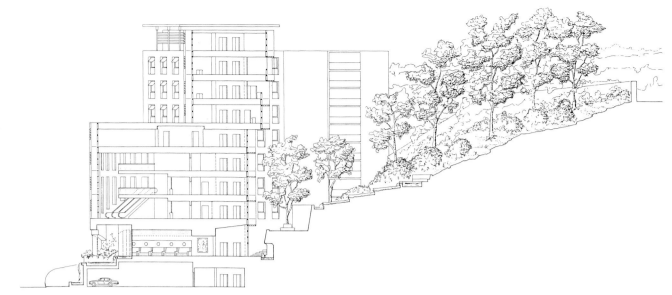

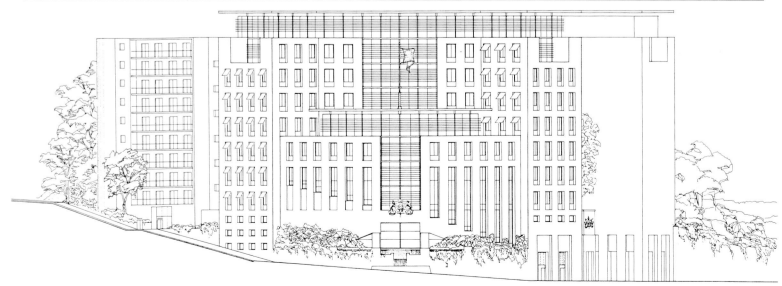

ELEVATIONS AND STUDY MODEL

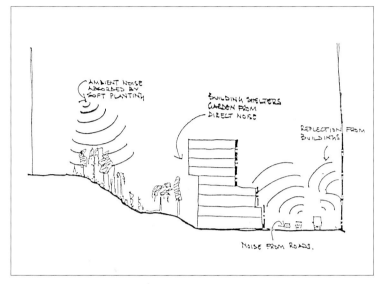

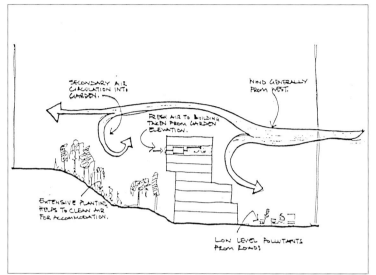

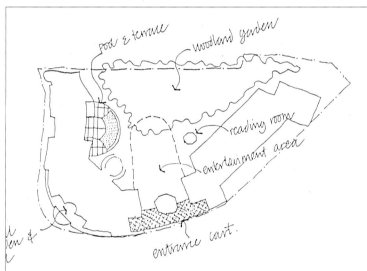

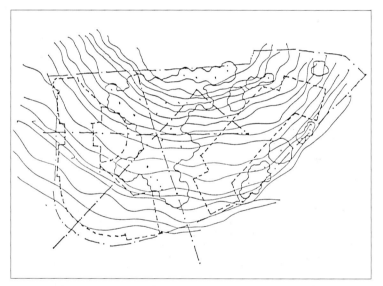

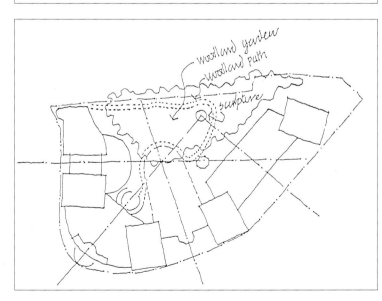

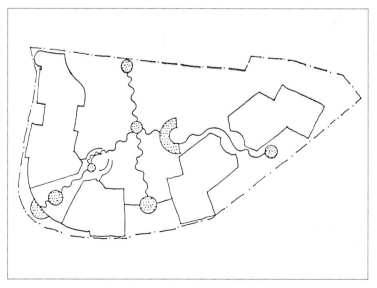

CONCEPT DIAGRAMS

# TERRY FARRELL & COMPANY
## *LIST OF BUILDINGS AND PROJECTS*

+ Schemes executed within Farrell/Grimshaw Partnership
* Unbuilt schemes

| | |
|---|---|
| 1968 | Hostel for Overseas Students+ |
| | Sussex Gardens, Paddington, London W2 |
| 1970 | Forty Co-owner Flats+ |
| | 125 Park Road, Marylebone, London NW8 |
| 1973 | Runnymede Warehouse+ |
| | Runnymede, Berkshire, England |
| 1975 | Rehabilitation Study of 1,000 older council-owned dwellings*+ |
| | City of Westminster, London |
| 1974-76 | The Colonnades Urban Redevelopment+ |
| | Bishops Bridge Road, London W2 |
| 1976 | Herman Miller Factory+ |
| | Bath, Avon, England |
| 1979 | BMW Distribution Centre+ |
| | Bracknell, Berkshire, England |
| 1972-80 | Maunsel Housing Society Schemes+ |
| 1979-80 | Clifton Nurseries Bayswater |
| | Bishops Bridge Road, London W2 |
| 1979-80 | Private House |
| | Lansdowne Walk, Holland Park, London W11 |
| 1979-81 | Digital Factory Conversion+ |
| | Reading, Berkshire, England |
| 1980-81 | Clifton Nurseries Covent Garden |
| | Covent Garden, London WC2 |
| 1974-81 | Warrington New Town |
| | Warrington, England |
| 1979-81 | Urban Infill Factories |
| | Wood Green, Haringey, London N22 |
| 1980-81 | Architects' Own Offices |
| | Paddington Street, Marylebone, London W1 |
| 1980-81 | Crafts Council Gallery |
| | Waterloo Place, London WC2 |
| 1980-81 | Alexandra Pavilion |
| | Alexandra Park, Haringey, London N22 |
| 1979-82 | Thames Water Authority |
| | Reading, Berkshire, England |
| 1981-82 | Private House |
| | St John's Wood, London |
| 1981-82 | TVam |
| | Hawley Crescent, Camden, London NW1 |
| 1982 | Festival Exhibition Building* |
| | Liverpool, England |
| 1982 | Vauxhall Cross National Competition* |
| | Vauxhall, London SE1 |
| 1982-83 | Radio Headquarters for the British Broadcasting Corporation* |
| | Langham Place, Portland Place, London W1 |
| 1982-83 | Limehouse Studios |
| | West India Docks, London E14 |
| 1980-84 | Royal Opera House* |
| | Covent Garden, London WC2 |
| 1982-84 | Graphex |
| | Roslin Road, South Acton, London W3 |
| 1984 | Hammersmith Island* |
| | Hammersmith Broadway, London W6 |
| 1978-85 | Comyn Ching Triangle |
| | Seven Dials, Covent Garden, London WC2 |
| 1982-85 | Allied Irish Bank, Queen Street |
| | Queen Street, The City of London, EC4 |
| 1983-85 | Henley Royal Regatta Headquarters |
| | Henley-on-Thames, Berkshire, England |

| | |
|---|---|
| 1983-86 | Midland Bank, Fenchurch Street |
| | Fenchurch Street, The City of London, EC3 |
| 1985-86 | Rules Restaurant |
| | Covent Garden, London WC2 |
| 1983-87 | East Putney Station |
| | Richmond Road, East Putney, London SW18 |
| 1986-87 | Savoy* |
| | The Savoy Hotel, The Strand, London WC2 |
| 1987 | King's Cross* |
| | King's Cross/St Pancras Stations, London |
| 1988 | Port Greenwich* |
| | East Greenwich, London SE10 |
| 1987-88 | Wimbledon Town Centre* |
| | Wimbledon, London SW19 |
| 1985-88 | Hatton Street |
| | 17 Hatton Street, London NW8 |
| 1989 | Frankfurt Flughafen* |
| | Frankfurt, Germany |
| 1990 | Garosud* |
| | Montpelier, France |
| 1985-90 | Tobacco Dock |
| | Pennington Street, Wapping, London E1 |
| 1987-90 | The Redevelopment of Charing Cross |
| | 1 Embankment Place, Villiers Street, London WC2 |
| 1988-91 | Temple Island |
| | Henley-on-Thames, Berkshire, England |
| 1989-91 | Tower Hill Wine Vaults |
| | Tower Hill, London EC3 |
| 1991 | Thames Study* |
| 1991 | Spitalfields* |
| 1991 | Report on The Development of Heathrow Airport* |
| | For the British Airports Authority |
| 1987-92 | Alban Gate |
| | Lee House, 125 London Wall, London EC2 |
| 1988-92 | Vauxhall Cross |
| | Albert Embankment, London SE1 |
| 1992 | Singapore Radio Tower |
| 1991- | Edinburgh International Conference and Finance Centre |
| | Edinburgh, Scotland |
| 1991- | The Peak, Hong Kong |
| 1992- | British Consulate, Hong Kong |

ONGOING SCHEMES AND PROJECTS
Bloomsbury Health Authority, London
Brindleyplace, Birmingham
Chiswick Park, London
The Commonwealth Trust
Hungerford Bridge, London
Lockmeadow, Maidstone
Lombard Street, London
Moor House, London
Newcastle, Grey Street
Newcastle, Quayside
Paternoster Square, London
Quarry Hill, London
South Bank Arts Centre, London
South Birmingham Medical Centre
York
No. 1 Waterloo Place, London
Westminster Hospital, Horseferry Road, London

*Opposite*: Alban Gate

# ACKNOWLEDGEMENTS

This book was organised in Terry Farrell's office by Jo Farrell, together with Susan Dawson (Project Director), Philip Smithies (Design Director), Louise Parker, Janet Male and Susan Farrell.

The text is by Alicia Pivaro based on Terry Farrell's notes.

The projects cover such an extended period of Terry Farrell's work that it is impossible to include here all those who have been involved. The office is organised on the basis that Terry Farrell is in charge of all design and overall direction of the work; Ashok Tendle is his Joint Managing Director and is in charge of the implementation of all projects. Project Directors take overall charge of each project and among these are the following who have been involved in the projects covered in this book: Susan Dawson, David Beynon, Nick Birchall, Kate Taylor, Mike Stowell, Derek Nolan, Toby Bridge. The Design Directors are Steve Smith and Doug Streeter who have been here for many years and worked on many of these projects; and in recent times Philip Smithies has joined the office and made an important contribution. Past Design Directors and past senior design staff include Clive Wilkinson, Simon Sturgis, Gary Young, Nigel Fitton and Andy Bow.

Within the office John Campbell is overall Technical Director for all projects, Drummond Robson is the Planning Director and Brian Chantler is the Company Secretary. Other key staff include John Letherland, Steven Brown, Martin Sagar, Tim Thompson, Martin Summersgill, Chris Wood, Eugene Uys, Jes Worre and Stuart Armstrong. All the names mentioned above are senior staff at Associate level and above. There are many more who have made important contributions but space does not allow inclusion of all their names. On a personal level, Maggie Jones is Terry Farrell's secretary and personal assistant and has made a most invaluable contribution for over 25 years.

There are also senior people no longer with us who made important contributions including John Chatwin, Colin Laine, Barry Stobbs, Rollin Schlicht, Neil Bennett, Alastair Barr, Alan Corrigan, Graham Fairley, Kevin Lewendon, Ian Macduff, Edward Rutherford, Jon Wallsgrove, John Fitzgerald, John Grant, Simon Wing, Robert James, Tryfon Kalyvides.

Mention whould also be made of Harvey van Sickle, who does all the historical research.

*NOTE ON PATERNOSTER SQUARE: Paternoster Associates, the present owners of the site, responded to a challenge of the Prince of Wales to develop the St Paul's area in sympathy with Wren's great cathedral. Using as a basis John Simpson's masterplan for the St Paul's area which featured in an exhibition in the cathedral in 1989, they commissioned John Simpson and Tom Beeby, with Terry Farrell co-ordinating, to develop a traditional masterplan for Paternoster Square. In addition to the masterplanners, a group of eminent classical architects was commissioned to design individual buildings These included Robert Adam, Paul Gibson, Allan Greenberg, Demetri Porphyrios and Quinlan Terry.*

## PHOTOGRAPHIC ACKNOWLEDGEMENTS

*Nigel Young: 2, 6, 11, 13, 37, 40, 54, 67, 120/121, 124/125, 165, 172, 222, 223, 224, 232, 245, 265, 274, 289, 292, 294, 296*
*Martin Charles: 8, 34, 43, 46, 47*
*Aerofilms: 27, 51, 77, 101, 127, 149, 161, 169, 197, 211, 215, 244, 257, 270, 279*
*Anthony Weller: 42, 44, 45, 47, 154, 298*
*Peter Cook: 43, 48, 163, 165, 167*
*Dennis Gilbert: 84, 89, 94, 95, 96, 98, 116, 119, 122, 162, 163, 207*
*Richard Bryant: 57, 166, 176, 178, 180, 181, 204*
*Jo Reid and John Peck: 64, 65, 66, 68, 69, 144, 146/147, 164, 174, 176, 205, 252, 253*
*Richard Turpin: 207, 254*
*Airfotos, Guildhall, Antiquaries, Guy Woodland, Museum of London, Tim Motion, Athos Lecce, National Monument Records.*